Communications in Computer and Information Science 446

Lorna Uden Jane Sinclair Yu-Hui Tao
Dario Liberona (Eds.)

Learning Technology for Education in Cloud

MOOC and Big Data

Third International Workshop, LTEC 2014
Santiago, Chile, September 2-5, 2014
Proceedings

Springer

Volume Editors

Lorna Uden
Staffordshire University, Stafford, UK
E-mail: l.uden@staffs.ac.uk

Jane Sinclair
University of Warwick, Coventry, UK
E-mail: j.e.sinclair@warwick.ac.uk

Yu-Hui Tao
National University of Kaohsiung, Taiwan
E-mail: ytao@nuk.edu.tw

Dario Liberona
Universidad Federico Santa Maria, Santiago, Chile
E-mail: jose.liberona@usm.cl

ISSN 1865-0929 e-ISSN 1865-0937
ISBN 978-3-319-10670-0 e-ISBN 978-3-319-10671-7
DOI 10.1007/978-3-319-10671-7
Springer Cham Heidelberg New York Dordrecht London

Library of Congress Control Number: 2014946415

Typesetting: Camera-ready by author, data conversion by Scientific Publishing Services, Chennai, India

Printed on acid-free paper

Springer is part of Springer Science+Business Media (www.springer.com)

Preface

The use of technology for learning has grown tremendously in the last decade. The need for continuous just-in-time training has made learning technology an indispensable part of life for workers. Today, we live in a world of increased mobility where proliferation of mobile technologies is creating a host of new anytime and anywhere contexts.

Technology is a key trend in imparting learning in a faster, simpler, and more effective way. The necessity to disseminate information to large masses in educational settings has led to an explosion of various technological innovations in education. Cloud computing is attractive for online education. It supports shared information repositories as well as the sharing of real-time and asynchronous interactions between teachers and learners. The promise of virtual universities in the cloud has been highlighted by the growing interest in MOOCs (massive open online courses) that are naturally hosted on clouds. However, the potential of big data collected from MOOCs has not been fully explored yet.

With the rise of more and more online education and the development of MOOCs, data take on a completely new meaning. Big data allow for very exciting changes in the educational field that will revolutionize the way students learn and teachers teach. Big data in the online learning space will give institutions the predictive tools they need to improve learning outcomes for individual students. Universities using big data in admissions, budgeting, and student services to ensure transparency, better distribution of resources, and identification of at-risk students. Data analytics can be used to figure out how to tailor teaching techniques to individual students, rather than using the "one size fits all" approach.

The International Workshop on Learning Technology for Education in the Cloud (LTEC) focuses on the exchange of relevant trends and research results in cloud computing for education, MOOCS, and big data for learning as well as the presentation of practical experiences gained while developing and testing these applications. It also explores the potential impact of learning analytics and big data for the future of learning and teaching. The workshop invites researchers, practitioners, and academics to present their research findings, work in progress, case studies, and conceptual advances in areas of work relating to cloud computing for education, MOOCs, and big data. It brings together researchers across all educational sectors - from primary years, to informal learning, to higher education - across a range of disciplines from humanities to computer science, media, and cultural studies with different perspectives, experiences, and knowledge in one location. It aims to help practitioners find ways of putting research into practice and to help researchers gain an understanding of real-world problems, needs, and aspirations.

These proceedings consist of 21 papers presented at LTEC 2014, held during September 2–5, 2014, in Santiago, Chile. They cover various aspects of technologies for learning including :

- MOOC for learning
- Learning technologies
- Learning in higher education
- Case studies in learning

The authors come from many different countries including Australia, Austria, Brazil, Canada, Chile, Colombia, Estonia, Finland, France, Germany, Guatemala, Malaysia, Mexico, New Zealand, Oman, Taiwan, and the UK.

We would like to thank our authors, reviewers, and Program Committee for their contributions and the Universidad Federico Santa Maria for hosting the conference. Special thanks to the authors and participants at the conference.

Without their efforts, there would be no conference or proceedings.

September 2014

Lorna Uden
Jane Sinclair
Yu-Hui Tao
Dario Liberona

Organization

General Conference Chair

Lorna Uden	Staffordshire University, UK

Program Chairs

Jane Sinclair	University of Warwick, UK
Yu-Hui Tao	National University Kaohsiung, Taiwan

Local Chair

Dario Liberona	Universidad Federico Santa Maria, Chile

Organization Committee

Darcy Fuenzalida	Universidad Federico Santa Maria, Chile
Dario Liberona	Universidad Federico Santa Maria, Chile
Jaime Rubin de Celis	Universidad Federico Santa Maria, Chile
Lionel Valenzuela	Universidad Federico Santa Maria, Chile
Pedro Fernandez	Universidad Federico Santa Maria, Chile
Pilar Garate	Universidad Federico Santa Maria, Chile
Teresita Arenas	Universidad Federico Santa Maria, Chile
Walter Fraser	Universidad Federico Santa Maria, Chile
Andrea Urrutia	Universidad Federico Santa Maria, Chile

Program Committee

Birgit Feldmann	FernUniversität in Hagen, Germany
Dario Liberona	Universidad Santa Maria, Chile
Elvira Popescu	University of Craiova, Romania
Georgina Cosma	Nottingham Trent University, UK
I. Chun Tsai	University of Akron, USA
Jane Sinclair	University of Warwick, UK
Jeremiah Sullins	University of Mobile, USA
Jonathan Kaplan	West Paris University, France
Kyparisia Papanikolaou	School of Pedagogical & Technological Education, Greece
Lorna Uden	Staffordshire University, UK

Lucia Giraffa	PUCRS, Brazil
Luciana A.M. Zaina	University of São Carlos, Brazil
Manuel Santos-Trigo	Center for Research and Advanced Studies, Cinvestav-IPN, Mexico
Michael Vallance	Future University Hakodate, Japan
Natasa Hoic-Bozic	University of Rijeka, Croatia
Richard Self	University of Derby, UK
Rocael Hernández	Universidad Galileo, Guatemala

Table of Contents

Mooc for Learning

Learning Technologies

Learning in Higher Education

Case Study in Learning

Connectivism and Interactionism Reloaded Knowledge Networks in the Cloud

A Theoretical Approach to a Shift in Learning through Connectivism and MOOCs

Sabine Siemsen and Rainer Jansen

Fernuniversität in Hagen, Hagen, Germany
{sabine.siemsen,rainer.jansen}@fernuni-hagen.de

Abstract. Knowledge is not 'a thing' and not a mere pool of data which can be managed. Knowledge is the process of learning. So what really matters is the question of how the process of learning changes in context with *Social Media* and Social Network Technologies. Gregory Bateson's definition of *Learning III*, the "*learning about how to learn to learn*" predicted very early what kind of learning culture is needed today to meet the requirements of a world which becomes more closely and quickly connected and dependent on networks in all aspects of work and private life. With their theory of *Connectivism* George Siemens and Stephen Downs offered not only a learning theory that fits those needs exactly, but also a tool: *MOOCs*. They surely are not the "digital Tsunami" many proclaim (and fear) but – consciously used - could open the door to a new culture of learning in the clouds.

Keywords: Bateson, Connectivism, MOOCs, Learning, Knowledge, Knowledge-Sharing, Knowledge-Creation, Learning, Networks, Learning Theory, Paradigm Shift.

1 Introduction

Recent discussions, dealing with learning in clouds, tend to speak about a new culture of learning. Regardless if they focus on pedagogical, methodological or technological aspects they have one thing in common: A new learning culture is shifting its focus from teaching to learning. The question is no longer how to teach as efficiently as possible but what learning is; how *to learn to learn*. Typical elements of this culture of learning are, according to Langer [1], *Peer-to-Peer-Learning, changed roles* (tutor, facilitator), the attribute '*open*' (to share and participate) and *situated learning*. The fact that communities of learners are becoming more and more heterogeneous due to the impact of a call for *lifelong learning* and fast-paced changes and innovations in technology is without controversy. And not only the community of learners is getting more and more heterogeneous, but also the group of those who take an active part in sharing and creating information presented in the cloud. Roles change and differentiations like teacher/learner, expert/layman or producer/user seem to vanish.

L. Uden et al. (Eds.): LTEC 2014, CCIS 446, pp. 1–12, 2014.

Big data cause the necessity of new kinds of *competencies*, like being able to deal with all this information critically.

This paper aims to show that the ability to *learn to learn* – Bateson's [2] *Learning II* or *Deutero Learning* is not sufficient to cope with a heterogeneity not only relating to different generations and new definitions of roles but to formations of learning communities which bring together learners and teachers speaking different languages and having different cultural and social backgrounds. *Learning II* implies a common appreciation of what learning is – which can no longer be postulated. But only if one is conscious about the fact that everyone has a different "*sense making*" [2] about what learning is, but that it still **it** remains learning, one can create a learning theory which is really different – in a way of a "*difference that makes a difference*" [2] which means to "*define something in terms of its relationships using contrast and context instead of isolating it with a name*" [3].

But not only does everyone have a different understanding of what learning is, definitions of learning within societies have also changed. A correlation between the definition of terms and social changes can be explained by means of the German expressions "*Ausbildung*" and "*Abschluss*", the first one meaning apprenticeship, the latter documenting the successful training qualification. The words "aus" (ended) and "Schluss" (end) both stand for having finished something finally, so "*Ausbildung*" and "*Abschluss*" stand for a comprehension of learning as a clear-cut period, and a static content of knowledge – in German "*Wissensbestand*" which literally says: a knowledge which endures and is sufficient for the whole professional life. There is no doubt that this definition of knowledge does not fit the needs of a society, defining itself as a *Knowledge Society*. There is no cut, no time when learning is finished and working starts. A vita in which learning is limited to a defined period in life or in which attending university follows subsequent to school attendance, is no longer standard and will become more an exception than a rule. Periods of leisure, work and learning will fuse and alternate and knowledge is no longer only *expert knowledge* that is collected and transferred, not a static thing but a dynamic process. *Lifelong learning* is not a political or social phrase but a prerequisite to social participation.

Of course there will still be information that constitutes a kind of basic knowledge, a background for understanding and reflecting historical and social development but „*more and more of our knowledge* [is] *rapidly changing, complex, connected, global, social* [and] *technologically mediated*" [6]. Concepts for knowledge-based learning will have to come up to both, the new definition of learning (*learning culture)* and the new definition and emergence of knowledge.

So prior to considerations about didactics, methods and contents there have to be ideas and concepts of how to enable and allow learning communities to recognize different premises about what learning is, and to set new, commonly found and shared *context markers* [2] as a pre-condition to reach a level of what Bateson defines as *Learning III*.

And before asking what knowledge is and how to manage it, we should ask how we know, how knowledge comes to be, how we acquire knowledge.

2 Learning and Knowledge

2.1 From "Knowledge-Transfer" to "Knowledge Generating"

"*Can we see a bigger picture; can we think about the way we think*?" [3]

Nora Bateson [3] says the moment you realize that you used to think about something in a special way but now start to think it could also be otherwise, that is the moment you have learned something.

In Cybernetics and system theory both, individuals and systems are regarded as being homeostatic thus self-regulating systems. „*Basically these systems are always **conservative** of something* [...] *changes occur to conserve the truth of some descriptive statement, some component of the **status quo***" [2]. On the other hand, enhancement is transformation and learning is nothing else than to enhance oneself. Thus, new theories, didactics and models are always confronted with the implied antagonism or, to speak in Bateson's words, with the *Double Bind* [2] of enabling transformation within systems being geared to Conservation. Conscious as well as unconscious acts are based upon (totally different) patterns and structures, that were imprinted in one's memory while enhancing oneself and used to be productive and helpful within specific individual and/or cultural contexts. From a global point of view they can reflect only a marginal and distorted part of reality. „*Culture and Religion filter and frame our perception*"[3]. So "*context of learning*" can be something totally different depending on the various and different frames and context markers.

The competency *to learn to learn* is demonstrated by the time learners are capable to transfer something that was learned within a specific context to another context. For example, within the context of school attendance, where there are clearly fixed guidelines as to what has to be learned when and where, someone can have made the experience that speaking about and explaining things to others makes it easier for him or her to remember things. Within the context of attending university, where it is expected to compile (given) workloads and module-contents in a self-managed and autonomous way, he or she will probably be open-minded about cooperative learning. Nevertheless, both contexts are based upon a common understanding of learning as *knowledge transfer* with the intent of being able to reproduce facts. It is exactly this aspect of internalized premises, where the definition of *Learning III* comes in. Whoever remains on a level of Learning *II* comes to an "***economy** of the thought processes*" [2], premises proved to be helpful will be retained, others, following a structure of trial and error, corrected, but never frankly be called into question per se, in principle. One could assert that *Learning II* enables a transfer of knowledge on a different context, to change behavior to adapt the means to the end, but the premises underlying these actions will not be reflected, doubted or changed. But that is what makes up Learning *III*; context in this regard means internal premises with respect to their emergence and rootedness.

Risku & Peschl [8] consider the premise, that knowledge is a thing that can be transferred from one person to another, to be the reason for being stuck halfway to becoming a knowledge society. Only if such premises as well as their emergence and their consequences to all fields of economy, technology and science become known, a new comprehension of knowledge and of generating knowledge can come into being. Not till then can new forms of cooperative learning lead to cooperatively generating knowledge [8]. To capture such a comprehension of learning through a theory, and to implement it into the praxis of learning-course-offerings, science and didactics too have to become aware of their internal premises. They have to get rid of limitations, to step back and stand beyond innate contexts, to include interdisciplinary findings and hence reach Bateson's Level of *Learning III*.

Volkmar Langer [9], professor and education manager, cites in his inaugural speech a weblog-article by Donald Clark [13], according to whom only 10 technological innovations caused more pedagogical changes in 10 years than ever took place during the last 1000 years. He listed *asynchronous learning, hyperlinks, search and rescue, crowd sourced knowledge, network, blogging, micro-learning, games, tools and open source*. Some of them I would not attribute to technology nor a time frame of 10 years, as for example approaches of learning through play, search and rescue, cooperative learning and the impact of being networked with peers can be found within the whole era of reform pedagogy which began approximately at the end of the 19th century [14]. Nevertheless, changes provoked through the potentials of the internet and hyperlinks and even more through what can be summarized as *Web 2.0* technologies, *social media* and "*Openness*" (OER, Open Courses, Open Licensing, Creative Commons and others more) have altered roles, requirements to and definitions of teaching and learning in formal and informal contexts fundamentally.

Speaking of reform pedagogy leads to another correlation with learning in the clouds. What makes reform pedagogy differ from previous theories is that it is child-oriented and allows children to play an active role instead of "being educated". This can be translated into a wider context as learner-oriented. A similar shift can be stated regarding the leap from *Web 1.0* to *Web 2.0*, centering on the user and turning users into producers – at least to give them the possibility to become active. Usability becomes a keyword. Both approaches challenge authorities and call the role of experts into question. Both call for a change of established roles. However, premises about the process of learning remain more or less unquestioned. But the most significant change and challenge is not the shift from teaching-orientation to learner-orientation but the fact that learning communities in both, informal and formal settings became more and more heterogeneous in many aspects, as described above.

The above mentioned impacts on learning like the call for *lifelong learning* and fast-paced changes and innovations in technology, as well in institutional as in workplace settings are only one of many reasons for a growing heterogeneity. Caused by altered and flexible roles (learner/teacher, expert/layman) and global and open access to many courses, not only the group of learners becomes more heterogeneous but also the group of those taking the most influential part in the Internet (which in turn has become the most important and most frequently used source for information) by producing and sharing information. This results in new *competencies* like being able to critically judge information and to get along with *big data*, and subsequently also widens heterogeneity by widening the digital divide. These facts have a heavy impact on what learning has to be or, to the point, what it cannot be any longer: Unreflected and unquestioned transfer of knowledge.

Buzz words like *knowledge society*, *network society* and their impact on and challenge to anyone producing and offering educational courses and learning-settings illustrate the importance of these changes to the whole educational system and to all sciences being engaged with learning and knowledge. Different approaches, not all of them new, try to meet and master these transformations, for example the method of *learning by teaching*[11, 12], the concept of the *flipped or inverted classroom* [10] and many innovations in the field of *eLearning* which meanwhile exceed former behavioristic learning scenarios and settings by far. On the other hand, they tend to produce another premise, on which many settings in the area of *eLearning* and learning environments in the cloud rely: That the efficiency of courses, methods and learning scenarios could be boosted (solely) through didactic designed implementation of new technology and tools.

Connectivism as "*A Learning Theory for the Digital Age*" [4] joins in at exactly this point, as it focusses on the *learning network* as a complex system of interrelationships and not on learners, teachers and technological tools as independent parts or ends of a relationship. George Siemens [6] answers to the question what Connectivism is, that it is "*the network itself*" which, "*in the form of technology and people, holds and filters knowledge and information.*" That fits to Gregory Bateson's words "*you cannot study one end of a relationship and make any sense. What you will make is disaster*" [3].

2.2 Connectivism: Generating Knowledge in and through Learning Networks

George Siemens' [6] idea of "*Rethinking Learning*" expresses exactly what was explained above about the shift from *Learning II* to *Learning III* and why the first does no longer fulfills today's requirements to learning in complex and heterogeneous communities and what the latter is about: "*Exponentially developing knowledge and complexification of society requires nonlinear models of learning (process) and knowing (state). We cannot sustain ourselves as learning/knowing beings in the current climate with our current approaches. Networked (social, technological) approaches scale in line with changes, but require a redesign of how we teach, learn (and see learning), and come to know.*" [6]

Downes [5] wrote that according to connectivistic paradigm knowledge can neither be transferred, nor produced or constructed. Knowledge is, what grows and enhances while individuals and societies enhance through and in networks. Eventually, this means nothing else than to recognize heterogeneity as a resource for enhancement. Being enabled to include different contexts in innate experiences and therefore to become aware of premises underlying one's own and others' actions, communication and expectations. This enables thinking on the level of *Learning III*. Defining *Learning III* and defining what kind of knowledge emerges from it consequently leads to the question: "What skills do our learners need today?" George Siemens' [6] answer to this question is: "*Pattern recognition, Network formation and evaluation, Critical/creative thinking, Acceptance of uncertainty/ambiguity, Contextualizing*" [6].

Peschl [7] gets down to a similar compilation of capacities. Necessary skills to generate knowledge are *observing, making abstractions and inductions/classifications, profound understanding, developing and creating new knowledge and reflecting to find solutions;* dimensions which „*cannot be seen as separated from each other, as they are mutually dependent on each other.*"

The proclamation of a rethinking not only of what learning is, but consequently about the needs of new "knowledge skills" [6] consequently is the next step, before thinking about design, technology, didactics or new learning settings. Fitting to Bateson's ideas, and taking into account today's level of technology, he assumes that "*from an epistemological and cognitive science perspective one has to shift the focus of attention from particular skills or competencies to the underlying cognitive operations*". I would go one step further and say, one has to shift the focus to the underlying patterns and premises of the cognitive operations, as those are responsible for the emergence of new (definitions of) *competencies* and enable us to see a need for them.

Once these steps (rethinking learning, rethinking knowledge and rethinking competencies/skills) have consciously been considered, one can start to think about learning settings, which – consequently – have to be "*performed in a collective setting*" [7]. Connectivism as „*A Learning Theory for the Digital Age*"[4] therefore developed the concept of MOOCs – a model to generate knowledge in and through network.

3 MOOCs

3.1 Revolution or Evolution

In 2010 Siemens [16] described MOOCs as "*An online phenomenon gathering momentum over the past two years or so* [… integrating] *the connectivity of social networking, the facilitation of an acknowledged expert in a field of study, and a collection of freely accessible online resources* [… that] *builds on the active engagement of several hundred to several thousand 'students' who self-organize their participation according to learning goals, prior knowledge and skills, and common interests.*"

Since MOOCs emerged from the OER movement in 2008, they have become more and more popular, not only in academic discourses between learning theoreticians but meanwhile also to the general public, and especially to providers of learning environments and learning settings in the cloud. The New York Times proclaimed the year 2012 as *The Year of the MOOC* [15].

Siemens' above description contains many aspects of what was described in chapter two as being crucial factors for a new learning culture that enables the generation of knowledge through *Learning III*. And it is obvious that questioning premises and rethinking learning provokes fear and offense, and meets with criticism in traditional settings and long-established institutions.

A commonly used point of criticism is the immense rate of "*drop outs*" and small rate (especially in comparison to the number of participants and the claim of being a *massive* course) of participants who complete the course. But acting on the assumption of a new learning culture, as described above, consequently brings about a challenge to traditional definitions of educational objectives and learning outcomes. Success can no longer be reduced to "finishing" a course within a fixed time by passing through a determined content. A course won't end with a group of learners having gained or reached the same knowledge. It will have been successful if new knowledge has been generated, if each participant has enhanced his individual knowledge and shared it within the community. Heterogeneity of a learning community implies different criteria for success. Success is when knowledge has been shared and created and premises have become conscious and have been changed, when one succeeded in *learning how to learn to learn*. The point in time and the correlation to specific modules will be as heterogeneous as the learning community is.

3.2 MOOCs, POOCs and the Needlessness of Prefixes

Another highly controversial issue is the form and shape of MOOCs, expressed through prefixes or alteration of the acronym. Proponents of *xMOOCs* and *cMOOCs* both claim to have found the one and only MOOC-Modell, the former often accused of not being something new at all and just traversing conventional or even outmoded concepts into the clouds to save money; the latter accused of lacking didactics, being chaotic, unstructured and therefore overwhelming students instead of being conducive to learning processes. Others get to the conclusion that open online courses should not focus on being "*massive*" and instead try to become "*personalized*": *POOCs* instead of *MOOCs*. They state that the great potential of digitalization remains unused as long as everyone is expected to learn the same thing in a uniform manner while having totally different preconditions and ambitions [17]. Even though this conclusion meets the arguments about a new learning culture presented in this paper, I am convinced that "*massive*" does not inevitably exclude *personalization* just as cooperative learning does not exclude individual learning.

To judge or evaluate MOOCs with regard to the question of whether they (per se) are "something really new" or just "old wine in new skins" is therefore pointless as there is neither *the* MOOC nor does a label like *c* or *m* or *POOC* instead of *MOOC* guarantee finding the same or even similar didactics and methods within the course. On the other hand, it is quite easy to answer the question as to what will be needed to define what would turn an open online course into a course that meets the requirements of the above described learning culture and the level of *Learning III* and therefore would be "something really new"; or as to what would clearly hinder this.

As worked out before, the main focus of a new learning culture (in which heterogeneity is regarded to be the source and potential to generate new knowledge) layers on a comprehension of learning as a process that enables becoming aware of previous premises and to create cooperatively new *context markers* as a basis for learning and generating new knowledge in networks. As this implies that traditional roles seem to merge, everyone in a learning setting can be regarded as a learner, as a part of the learning community. This has to be of greatest importance for the design of learning settings and it consequently eliminates at this point all courses, which just transfer traditional lectures from the auditorium into the cloud. For the same reasons, courses that separate the (learning) participants from the (teaching/performing) lectures and exclude communication between those from the very beginning can evidently not lead to this comprehension of learning and creating knowledge.

Another fact that was accentuated above is the dynamic of learning and knowledge creation, the definition as something that never ends, and that needs and constitutes at once permanent change and permanent discussion, reflection and calling of premises into question. A course that takes this demand seriously cannot "close its doors" after a limited time and cut off the conversations, the newly and commonly created knowledge and the environment where it took place and where networks arose. It must enable the development of a life of its own, that is not bound to and dependent on the initiator or institute that offered the course. This is possible and was demonstrated in one of the first MOOCs in 2008, the CCK08 about which Siemens [16] wrote: "*We found quickly that the course took a life of its own as participants created Second Life meeting areas, Google groups to discuss certain topic areas, study groups for people in similar locations, Facebook groups, and so on. Additionally, the course syllabus was translated into at least five different languages as participants from dozens of countries around the world joined.*"

3.3 What a MOOC Can Be But Not Necessarily Is: Experiences in the Field

"*Participation in a MOOC is emergent, fragmented, diffuse, and diverse. It can be frustrating. It's not unlike life.*" [16]

This chapter neither intends to present new results of empirical field investigation nor to analyze the different former level of education of MOOC-participants or the relation between registered participants and participants staying till the end of the course or going for badges. There is already plenty of evaluation and data available. What it will do is putting the above mentioned aspects, about what defines a MOOC as a tool enabling *Learning III*, into praxis context. This is done by setting in context the example of two MOOCs and the above worked out theoretical frame in order to analyze:

- What can be said about the role allocation within the course?
- Did the course offer the possibility to communicate with the lecturers? Did lectures engage in forum discussions?
- Did the course offer and encourage communication about expectations, about the understanding of learning and knowledge, before starting to deal with content?
- What about the syllabus – did it aim to generate new knowledge?
- What happened with "the interaction" and the content after the end of the course?
- What could be pointed out as something "really new"?

Canvas network [20] invites "*let's transform learning together*" and defines itself as a platform that "*gives teachers, learners and institutions alike the place* [...] *to define the world of open online learning in a way that makes sense for everyone*" and learning "*a pretty great thing* [that] *when the people who provide and participate in it can interact in new, imaginative ways* [.] *gets even better*". This attitude matches the above statements and requests a closer look to some courses offered.

The Canvas MOOC "College Foundations: Reading, Writing and Math." [18]
This MOOC aimed to provide "*prospective college students with a primer in college level reading, writing, and mathematics*". It therefore offered standardized pretests and "*self-paced learning modules*" and stressed not to forget "*the importance of human touch*" and therefore to "*oversee*" the course and to be "*available to assist and encourage students along their journey to college readiness*".

The course forum was divided into an "introduction" forum and forums to discuss topics of the course-contents. Reading through the introduction forum shows that the instructor read and answered some of them, pointing out interesting aspects of the vita or asking for feedback. This communicates openness for not only teaching but also being curious to learn about and from others' experiences. The question what learning and knowledge meant to the participants was not discussed or encouraged.

The syllabus itself was very traditional. It focused on conventional methods and aspects to "*college foundations*". Putting them into question or generating new knowledge was not in demand.

The interaction took place within the canvas platform. One has access to it as long as one is enrolled (at Canvas Network). In case the provider would close its doors it would be lost. Discussion or learning groups via social networks were not encouraged and the communication, offered through the instructors was limited to asynchronous communication.

Apart from rudimentary changes in role-(self)definitions, it could not be worked out that there had been something "really new" offered through this MOOC.

The Canvas MOOC "Learning Beyond Letter Grades." [19]
Already the course's name makes explicit that it did not aim to transfer contents but to put conventional methods about measuring and evaluating learning outcomes into question. The instructor introduced himself as a *tour guide* who is "*learning alongside*" the participants. Those were encouraged and invited to network; using different *social media*, such as a *Google+* group established for this purpose and *Twitter* discussions as "*opportunities to have ongoing and informal sharing and connections around the course topics.*" Within the *Google+* Group very soon different discussion groups and an intense network started to stay informed about and learn from each other's professional and informal experiences around the topics. Also the instructor took an active part here and shared and asked for experiences and ideas. At the end of the official course he encouraged to "*feel free to use this as a place to share your ongoing thoughts and efforts related to Learning Beyond Letter Grades.*"

The course provided various sources for information and discourses, supplemented by weekly live events. Those were not only presentations, followed up by an offer to pose questions, but were real discourses in which participants were actively integrated and encouraged to influence the event with ideas, questions and feedback. The live events took place as *Google+ Hangouts* where they remain accessible. The conception of the live-sessions differed from "conventional ones" as it was not divided in separate parts of "presentation" followed by discussions or different ways to ask questions. It was more like a discourse where participants could join in at any time with questions but also with hints and own experiences which influenced the ongoing event as well as the conception and planning of further events.

So really new about this MOOC was the active part and importance of communication which not only dealt with content but aimed to create new knowledge and to arrange for a sustainable and ongoing network process in addition to the MOOC. This met nearly all aspects described above as crucial for a MOOC that aims to fulfill the above discussed and highlighted aspects.

4 Conclusion

When Gregory Bateson [2] wrote in 1964 that Learning III is "*difficult and rare even in human beings*" he was surely right. Since then, many aspects influencing learning have changed and many theories and concepts have been developed, to meet these changes. But as described above they remained predominantly on a level of *learning II*. As long as learning settings and learning communities were situated in relatively narrow national, social and cultural contexts, this seemed to work more or less. But as soon as technologies and *Web 2.0* opened new frontiers and learning was expected to become "global", they no longer fit the needs and requirements of a global knowledge society any more.

Connectivism, as a learning theory, is based on conclusions very similar to those Bateson found when defining the level of *learning III*. But at the time this learning theory emerged, at least the *external* preconditions for learning III had become "*less difficult and rare*" as *Web 2.0*, *social media* and networks, connecting learners from all over the world (or at least having the potential to do so), provide tools and technologies that may facilitate transferring theoretical descriptions into praxis.

Nevertheless todays' "global society" is still far away from global networking and realizing and transforming the potential of digitalization into praxis or even equal chances to education for everyone. Most approaches still remain on specific national or cultural levels and those, becoming open to a globally heterogeneous community of learners, rarely integrate or ask for cultural diversity in regard to previous learning contexts and underlying premises.

Recent discourses and statements about connectivism, being a "really new" learning theory or not, and MOOCs being a "really new" learning concept or not, cover the whole range from euphoria to degradation. Neither one does justice to the changes in society and the resulting changes in needs and demands of learners in this dynamic and fast-paced process of innovations. To argue that connectivism does not meet one or several demands to be a theory or to bring about a paradigm shift, or MOOCs, to be nothing more than recorded videos of a traditional lecture where support is limited to multiple-choice-questions and quizzes, is as indifferent and useless as to glorify MOOCs as a miracle cure to all current challenges universities are confronted with. Neither a new theory nor MOOCs are magic bullets, but probably forerunners of future scenery of academic learning where conventional methods no longer meet the needs.

> *"We can't see the way out yet because we are thinking within the existing structure. That's why we are still having discussions about constructivism vs connectivism (or some such model). Connectivism is entirely different – not fixated on the learning model of 'in head with aid of socialization'. Knowledge – and the affiliated concepts of learning and understanding – is a function of 'the network'"* [6]

References

1. Langer, V.: Antrittsvorlesung. Slideshow (2013), http://de.slideshare.net/volkmarl?utm_campaign=profiletracking&utm_medium=sssite&utm_source=ssslideview
2. Bateson, G.: Steps to an ecology of mind; Collected essays in anthropology, psychiatry, evolution, and epistemology. Chandler Pub. Co., San Francisco (1972)
3. Bateson, N.: An Ecology of Mind. A Daughter's Portrait of Gregory Bateson. Remember the Future. Nora Bateson (Regie). DVD: Carl-Auer Verlag, DGSF, mindjazz, Alive (2010)
4. Siemens, G.: Connectivism: A Learning Theory for the Digital Age (2005), Online verfügbar unter, http://www.ingedewaard.net/papers/connectivism/2005_siemens_ALearningTheoryForTheDigitalAge.pdf, (zuletzt aktualisiert am October 11, 2011, zuletzt geprüft am February 9, 2014)
5. Downes, S.: Connectivism and Connective Knowledge (2012), Online verfügbar unter, http://www.downes.ca/files/books/Connective_Knowledge-19May2012.pdf (zuletzt aktualisiert am May 19, 2012, zuletzt geprüft am April 19, 2013)
6. Siemens, G.: Connectivism. Learning conceptualized through the lens of today's world (2007), Online verfügbar unter, http://www.elearnspace.org/presentations/connectivism_online_OCC2007.ppt (zuletzt geprüft am February 9, 2014)
7. Peschl, M.F.: Knowledge constructing and knowledge creation as key factors in educational an innovation processes. In: Risku, H. (Hg.) Kognition und Technologie im kooperativen Lernen. Vom Wissenstransfer zur Knowledge Creation, pp. S.16–S.31. V & R Unipress, Vienna Univ. Press, Aufl. Göttingen (2010)
8. Risku, H., Peschl, M.: Einführung: Lernen als kooperative Wissensgenerierung. In: Risku, H. (Hg.) Kognition und Technologie im kooperativen Lernen. Vom Wissenstransfer zur Knowledge Creation. pp. S.7–S.11. V & R Unipress, Vienna Univ. Press, Aufl. Göttingen (2010)
9. Langer, V.: Social Learning: Internet-gestütztes soziales Lernen als neuer Trend. Auswirkungen auf die Zukunft des Lernens (2013), Online verfügbar unter, http://de.slideshare.net/volkmarl?utm_campaign=profiletracking&utm_medium=sssite&utm_source=ssslideview (zuletzt geprüft am February 9, 2014)

10. EDUCAUSE Learning Initiative: 7 Things You Should Know About Flipped Classrooms (2012), Online verfügbar unter, http://net.educause.edu/ir/library/pdf/eli7081.pdf (zuletzt aktualisiert am February 7, 2012, zuletzt geprüft am February 10, 2014)
11. Martin, J.-P., Kelchner, R.: Lernen durch Lehren. In: Timm, J.-P. (ed.) Englisch lernen und lehren - Didaktik des Englischunterrichts, pp. S.211–S.219. Cornelsen, Berlin (1998), Online verfügbar unter, http://www.lernen-durch-lehren.de/Material/Publikationen/timm.pdf (zuletzt geprüft am February 2, 2014)
12. Chinese University of Hong Kong - Department of Physics Learning Through Teaching (2009), Online verfügbar unter, http://www.phy.cuhk.edu.hk/tdg/ (zuletzt aktualisiert am January 1, 2012, zuletzt geprüft am February 10, 2014)
13. Clark, D.: Plan B (2011), http://donaldclarkplanb.blogspot.de/
14. Eichelberger, H. (n. d.): The Importance of Reform Pedagogy., http://www.blikk.it/angebote/reformpaedagogik/downloads/rp_englisch.pdf
15. Pappano, L.: The Year of the MOOC. In: The New York Times. Education (2012), http://www.nytimes.com/2012/11/04/education/edlife/massive-open-online-courses-are-multiplying-at-a-rapid-pace.html?pagewanted=all&_r=0
16. McAuley, A., Stewart, B., Siemens, G.: The MOOC Model for Digital Practice (2013), https://oerknowledgecloud.org/sites/oerknowledgecloud.org/files/MOOC_Final_0.pdf
17. Bertelsmann Stiftung, Jedem seine eigene Vorlesung (2013), http://www.bertelsmann-stiftung.de/cps/rde/xchg/SID-2317932C-29901F94/bst/hs.xsl/nachrichten_119201.htm
18. Canvas NETWORK, College Foundations: Reading, Writing, and Math. (2013), https://www.canvas.net/courses/college-foundations-spring-2014-reading-writing-and-math
19. Canvas NETWORK, Learning Beyond Letter Grades (2013), https://learn.canvas.net/courses/76
20. Canvas NETWOKR (2013) About us, https://www.canvas.net/about-us

MOOC User Persistence

Lessons from French Educational Policy Adoption and Deployment of a Pilot Course

Jean Heutte[1], Jonathan Kaplan[2], Fabien Fenouillet[2], Pierre-André Caron[1], and Marilyne Rosselle[3]

[1] CIREL –*Centre Interuniversitaire de Recherche en Education de Lille*– Research Centre (EA 4354), Université Lille 1, France
{jean.heutte,pierre-andre.caron}@univ-lille1.fr
[2] CHArt-UPON –*Cognitions Humaine et Artificielle*– lab (EA 4004)
Department of Psychology
West Paris University (Université Paris 10), France
kaplan@kaplan-consultants.org, fabienfenouillet@yahoo.fr
[3] MIS –*Modélisation Information Système*– Lab (EA 4290)
Université de Picardie Jules Verne (UPJV), France
marilyne.rosselle@u-picardie.fr

Abstract. This research explores user persistence in a massive open online course (MOOC) that was set up as an experiment before the French Ministry of Higher Education and Research launched in October 2013 the French Digital University initiative–a French platform for MOOCs. Persistence was looked into from the perspective of emotions. Digital trail data, demographic data and data from six scales were analysed. The scales were Positive Affect and Negative Affect Scales (PANAS) plus the Flow in Education scales (EduFlow). Results show that many registrants logged on, participated in activities and accessed resources seldom, while a few persisted and were active. Correlations between persistence and residence in Europe or Africa were found as well as patterns relating to negative affect and to well-being, again linked to geographic variables.

Keywords: Massive open online course, MOOC, Persistence, Well-being, Affect, Flow.

1 Introduction

Massive open online courses (MOOCs) have become the trend in university education and have "taken universities in North America and elsewhere by storm" [12]. This trend is spreading to France too where central policy is pushing universities to endorse this form of e-learning. The French government adopted a road map for its digital development [7] that led to the launch of a plan for digital deployment in higher education, revealed on October 2, 2013, that includes a French Digital University (FDU). The FDU online courses are referred

L. Uden et al. (Eds.): LTEC 2014, CCIS 446, pp. 13–24, 2014.

to as MOOCs which are delivered off a central platform by the French Ministry of Higher Education and Research (MHER). The first phase in deployment was a course on digital literacy, named MOOC iNum, that can be used to prepare level 1 of a national certificate, the *Certificat informatique et internet* (C2i). Accreditation for the certificate itself needs to be sought separately, by applying for it at a certifying institution.

A team of researchers took on the task of assessing the pilot course for the MHER. The report [5], which is a description of the project and its deployment, including statistical data, was mostly used by the MHER as a step to validate the FDU setup before its formal launch. The data collected on the application running the MOOC was supplemented by data collected through several questionnaires from scales to measure dimensions related to motivation, emotions and self-efficacy beliefs. Digital trail data, demographic data and the data collected through the questionnaires were later analysed in search of patterns to better understand persistence of usage or lack thereof. This paper reports the findings of these analyses.

2 Background

MOOC implementation, in terms of the learning paradigm that underpins the way services are organised for the learners and the associated instructional activities, have been classified under two general categories: "Connectivist" MOOCs (c-MOOCs) in which learning is the outcome of knowledge collectively constructed by peers, and more "traditional" MOOCs (x-MOOCs) in which the dominating paradigm is one of knowledge transmitted from instructor to student [3,12,16]. When a platform for MOOCs is set up, the learning paradigm adhered to should in principal lead to choosing a Learning Management System (LMS), to be served through the Web with its e-services (modules), that would support activities in accordance with the underpinning learning theory. An instructor who may be able to make certain services available to learners would then fine-tune the course design. For instance, a MOOCs LMS set up with a c-MOOC approach in mind would have at its core, services and end-user ergonomics that revolve around enabling learners to communicate among themselves, support each other, exchange ideas and co-create knowledge. This would not be the core of a system set up with an x-MOOC approach in mind. In the latter, static information that cannot be remodelled, such as videos of lectures, would likely be at the fore.

When an LMS in set up with a social constructivist epistemology and an open education initiative guiding choices, it is most likely that a c-MOOC implementation would be sought. Participating as a learner through the use of such a platform requires of learners in addition to engaging in the activity individually, to be active in contributing to online discussions, creating the learning material as they go along and construct knowledge through peer supported and peer supporting activities. Participants need to be self-directed learners who interact in an open environment [16]. For peers to actively contribute to each other's knowledge formation, motivational and volitional characteristics of learners' engagement and persistence need to be enabled by environmental conditions that are favourable to agency. Research in these areas is needed to elucidate features and learner characteristics that could lead to improving the learning experience. Little empirical research to conceptualise and measure participation in open learning platforms has been done despite its importance [1].

Implementation of the iNum course followed a c-MOOC approach, at least in intention, referred to as following the principles of a "self-telic" [4] functioning system in which the driving force is produced by the interactions taking place, primarily through learners' contributions. Registrants in the pilot course were asked to respond to questions from scales to measure various learner characteristics in order to explore participation on the FDU platform. Limited participation in the iNum course led to picking out data regarding three scales and to analyse their correlations with digital trail data and demographic data. These scales are:

1. Positive Affect and Negative Affect Scales (PANAS) [18], transposed to French by Bouffard and Lapierre [2]. Positive and negative affect are two decisive dimensions of mood.
2. EduFlow [9] which bears on the state of flow in educational contexts. It is measured through four dimensions that constitute a sub-set of Csikszentmihalyi's [6] nine dimensions, refined for the purpose [9,8]. The four dimensions are cognitive absorption i.e., feeling in control of the activity one is in as a result of knowing that the activity is doable and that one's skills are adequate, producing no anxiety nor boredom (D1); an altered perception of time i.e., feeling of timeliness which is the result of being intensely focused on one's present activity (D2); loss of self-consciousness i.e., not being concerned with oneself (D3); well-being i.e., being outside of daily reality to a degree that one feels ecstatic (D4). Flow is a subjective state of engagement in activity. It is a state of strong absorption in the activity that results from intrinsic motivation to engage in it for the pleasure that the activity affords. With such motivation, it is the state itself that is the reward for the activity.

2.1 iNum, the Pilot MOOC

Sakai (version CLE 2.9) was the platform used to manage the course. The course, named Digital Identity (*Identité Numérique*, abbreviated to iNum), lasted from may 6 to july 18, 2013. Activities in iNum revolved around four core tasks:

1. Creating one's digital identity
2. Starting one's e-portfolio
3. Creating an object through collaboration and setting out to communicate it
4. Writing a guide to using an online social network

According to the MOOC's designers, these activities are guided by a learning-by-doing approach. A fortnight separated each task deadline. In between, it was expected that learners would engage in developing their skills needed for successful completion of the task. Learning could involve individual activities which could last beyond the deadline for each task, but other activities were expected to be done collectively before the due date. Instant messaging, forums and document sharing areas served for discussion and sharing to accomplish these. Developing each competence involved three or four focused activities and a multiple-choice test for self-assessment. Students were encouraged to write up a summary of their activities in relation to the skills they were to develop. Documenting their learning would be helpful if they intended to seek certification once the course was completed.

Launching the iNum course was preceded by an information campaign. Information on MHER's website was relayed through Twitter and Facebook, the network of C2i contacts of French universities, the eLearning Africa network, French overseas embassies, the *Agence Universitaire de la Francophonie* (AUF), etc.

The campaign was effective to the degree that the FDU team decided to close enrolment sooner than planned, out of fear of being overwhelmed. Registration was open from April 10 to 24, 2013. Closing the course to further enrolments is somewhat paradoxical for a MOOC. Though this should not be of much concern under the circumstances of a pilot experiment, it nevertheless had its consequences. The population breakdown (see further along) may be a reflection of where the campaign to promote MOOC iNum hit first or strongest.

2.2 Linking Affect, Flow and User Persistence

Engaging in a MOOC is the result of a decision made by individual learners for whom motives are not the focus of this article. Persistence of learners in a MOOC however, which is central to this article, could be a concern. Accounting for both would help to better grasp reasons for dropping online course activities. Research has shown that large numbers of users drop out of MOOCs, sometimes very early after having registered. The numbers of those who persist and complete their course has sometimes been pointed to as a weakness. In a study conducted on HarvardX and MITx courses hosted on the edX platform [10], the authors insist on the fact that percentages are not numbers. Although 5% of typical registrants completed courses, the numbers of certified participants is high. 43,196 registrants were certified during the 2012–2013 academic year. The debate seems to miss the point. It is not a question of how many people access courses or end up with a certificate or credits for it; rather, the concern should be how adequate the MOOC environment is in satisfying participants' goals and conditions for learning. This is where improvement can take place.

Remaining an active participant in a course i.e., moving through stages of engagement until the point of course completion, is a matter of the adequateness of the learning environment combined with the learner's dispositions. Both the learning environment, which includes media used, content, quality of interaction and so on, and learner dispositions, are interdependent. They are mutually forming. The environment will affect learner motivation and volition; in turn, these will affect learner participation and interaction. Interactions, as part of the environment, will in turn affect the dispositions of other participants which again will interact and contribute to reshaping the environment, and so on. A c-MOOC in principal should be more susceptible to changes and malleable as its design follows from the idea of participants co-creating through their interactions.

Our research strives to bring awareness to the need to explore facets of learners' dispositions as this could contribute to MOOC course designs that are favourable to the learning experience. The exploration of affect and flow can inform about the learning experience to help elucidate reasons for which registrants leave a course. Pekrun et al. [14,13,15] link emotions and cognition in learning contexts. PANAS in combination with EduFlow enable measuring the main components of well-being, those of affect and flow. The hypothesis for this research was that a relation exists between the emotional experiences of learners and their persistence in participating in the MOOC they enrolled in.

3 Methodology

Participants received an e-mail with a request to take part in a survey just before the end of the course. A link in each e-mail pointed to a webpage with the survey questions. Each link contained a unique token associated with that person's e-mail address. This enabled sending reminder requests only to registrants who had not yet responded. Commitment to confidentiality was given in the e-mail inviting participants to take part in the survey as well as on the LMS.

3.1 Analysis Procedures

Analyses were accomplished using SPSS (version 22). Analyses of data describing the population included: age, gender, country, student or professional status (ICT related profession, education related profession, retirement, leave for training, part-time), level of formal education, time the registrant expected to spend in the MOOC, and reasons for dropping the course. Digital trail data such as the number of visits to course areas, activity in each course area and content access were analysed as well as their relations to the demographic variables. These analyses were followed by the verification of internal consistency of responses to the PANAS and EduFlow scales. Analyses of correlations between data from the scales and digital trail data as well as with demographic data were followed up with an analysis of variance.

4 Findings

During the period open to registration (April 10–24, 2013), 1,189 persons registered out of whom 326 accepted to respond to the questionnaires. An analysis of frequencies enabled to determine a typical registrant profile. The typical registrant is a male (66.7%) who is not enrolled in a formal education programme (62.6%) nor any other course (77.0%), who owns a master's degree (42.5%) and who is between 31 and 39 years old. This profile fits 29 cases, representing 8.9% of respondents. This points to the variety of users and to the limited significance of a description of a typical user in iNum.

The country of residence of registrants was France for 17.9% and a similar percentage resided in Senegal. Following were Morocco (14.4%), Cameroon (13.3%) and Burkina Faso (12.3%). Apart for those registrants from France (a negligible number from Belgium, Canada and Switzerland; four in total), all others were residing in African countries. This may have been the result of the networks in Africa being quick in relaying the information about the opening of the course. Relaying networks in other parts of the world may have disseminated information later. By the time they did, registration may have no longer been possible (cf. Sect. 2.1).

Analysis of digital trail data reveals that of the 1,198 registrations, 272 never returned to the platform. There was less dropping out of registrants over 40 when testing for differences between age groups ($\chi^2(2) = 8.6, p < .05$). There was no effect of gender on the number of times users logged on to the platform ($\chi^2(3) = 2.16, ns$) or renounced participating in the course ($\chi^2(1) = 0.19, ns$). Of the 917 registrants who did return, 885 accessed the main course area (some had directly accessed task areas without passing through the main course area), 706 persons engaged in activities and 677 consulted resources in the main course area.

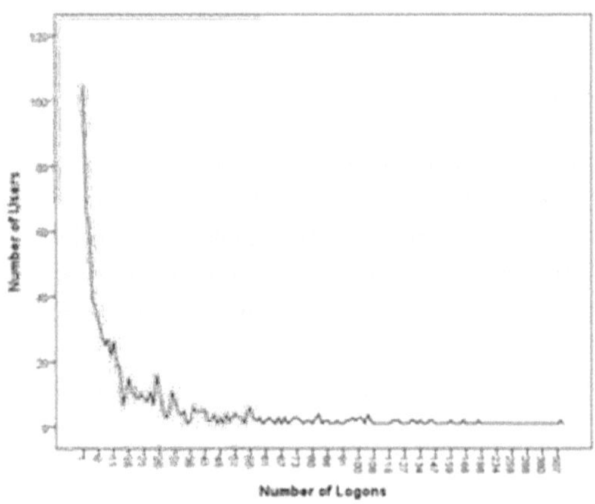

Fig. 1. Frequency of Users in Relation to the Number of Times They Logged On

The frequency of users in relation to the frequency of times they logged on; in relation to the frequency of activities they engaged in; and in relation to the frequency of resources they consulted, are all similarly distributed. Many users logged on, engaged in activities and accessed resources a few times, while a few users who logged on, engaged in activities and accessed resources many times. 25.4% of registrants logged on 3 times or less while only 27.4% logged on more

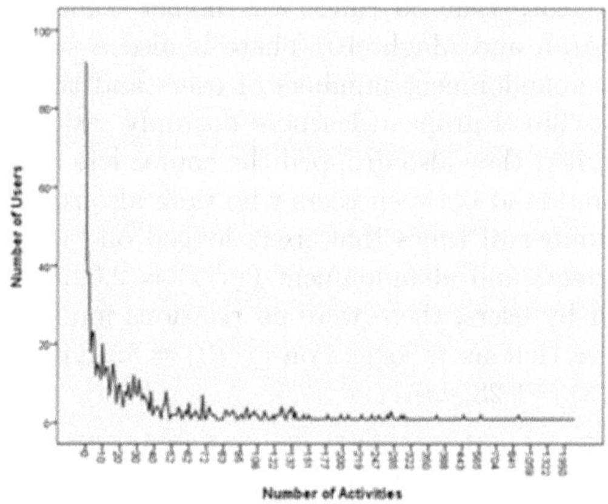

Fig. 2. Frequency of Users in Relation to the Number of Activities They Engaged In

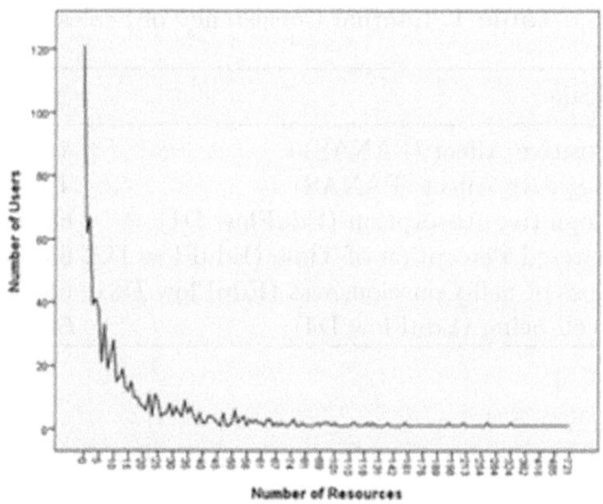

Fig. 3. Frequency of Users in Relation to the Number of Resources They Consulted

than 30 times (see Fig. 1). This same pattern is noted in Fig. 2 and Fig. 3, pointing to a general tendency in usage of the MOOC.

Analyses point to differences between the number of times registrants logged on and geographical variables. To explore these variables, three geographical zones were defined: one including the countries in sub-Saharan Africa, one including countries in the Maghreb, and one for those in Europe. The division into these zones was based on what could be considered as roughly corresponding to cultural differences related to the history of French colonialism in these zones. Results point to statistically significant differences between the number of times registrants logged on to the MOOC and the geographical zones ($\chi^2(6) = 19.32, p < .01$). The frequency of European residents who logged on to the MOOC more that 30 times was higher than that of the African residents (sub-Saharan and Maghreb). There is also a statistically significant difference between abandonment numbers of users and the geographical zones ($\chi^2(2) = 6.95, p < .05$). European learners not only visited the MOOC more often as we saw earlier, they also dropped the course less often.

No relations were found between users who were also students in other institutions and the number of times that users logged on ($\chi^2(3) = 4.01, ns$), nor between these students and abandonment ($\chi^2(1) = 2.62, ns$). Concerning academic degrees held by users, there were no relations found between these and the number of times that users logged on ($\chi^2(9) = 8.41, ns$), nor in relation to abandonment ($\chi^2(3) = 1.28, ns$).

4.1 Analyses of Affect, Flow and User Persistence

Internal consistencies of the PANAS and EduFlow scales were verified, they are presented in Table 1.

Table 1. Internal Consistency of Scales

Scale	n	α
Positive Affect (PANAS)	47	.86
Negative Affect (PANAS)	43	.90
Cognitive Absorption (EduFlow D1)	63	.71
Altered Perception of Time (EduFlow D2)	63	.79
Loss of Self-Consciousness (EduFlow D3)	65	.88
Well-being (EduFlow D4)	64	.88

Descriptive statistics for scores obtained on the PANAS and EduFlow scales are presented in Table 2.

Table 2. Descriptive Statistics for Scale Scores

Scale	Min	Max	M	SD
Positive Affect (PANAS)	1.00	5.00	3.64	0.86
Negative Affect (PANAS)	1.00	5.00	2.07	0.97
Cognitive Absorption (EduFlow D1)	1.50	7.00	4.47	1.29
Altered Perception of Time (EduFlow D2)	1.00	7.00	4.51	1.50
Loss of Self-Consciousness (EduFlow D3)	1.00	7.00	4.12	1.67
Well-being (EduFlow D4)	1.00	7.00	4.46	1.52

Before testing for correlation, logarithmic transformation was used to normalise the digital trail data after skewness and kurtosis were checked. A correlation exists between the number of times users logged on and the altered perception of time dimension (D2) of flow. Users who had an altered perception of time also logged on to the MOOC more often ($r = .25, p < .05$). Activity on the MOOC and the number of consulted resources are negatively correlated with loss of self-consciousness (D3 in EduFlow). This could perhaps be explained by the fact that the LMS design and setup were inadequate in providing a 'connected' experience. Users may have been more self-conscious, assessing how they appear to others as they sought ways to be seen and recognised as worthy interlocutors in an environment that was deficient in providing for connectedness [5]. The lack of possibilities to share and communicate among peers, qualifies the platform as an x-MOOC type [17], contrary to the declared intention of its planners.

Differences in patterns concerning the number of times users logged on and persistence, while accounting for users' residence, was the next step in the exploration of correlations. Correlations were sought between the sub-groups of users residing in Europe and African regions with affect and flow dimensions. Differences were noted and confirmed through analyses of variance (ANOVA). A statistically significant difference in emotions exists between European and African residents ($F[2,61] = 3.55, p < .05$). European users had less negative affect when learning in the MOOC than Africans from the Maghreb and sub-Saharan Africa. While the African residents had more negative feelings, they also experienced enthusiasm, comfort and wanting to share feelings (see Table 3). As the ANOVA confirmed, this well-being dimension of flow (D4 in EduFlow) was stronger than that felt by their European counterparts ($F[2,64] = 5.74, p < .01$).

Table 3. Means and Standard Deviations for Emotional Dimensions Differentiated According to User Residence

Scale	User Residence	*M*	SD
Negative Affect (PANAS)			
	Europe	1.68	.76
	Northern Africa (Maghreb)	2.62	1.13
	Sub-Saharan Africa	2.16	.98
Well-being (EduFlow D4)			
	Europe	3.57	1.42
	Northern Africa (Maghreb)	5.00	1.63
	Sub-Saharan Africa	4.81	1.38

5 Discussion

It may seem contradictory to have negative feelings while experiencing well-being. Taking a closer look at what is being explored in these dimensions, negative affect is conceived as stress, fluster, guilt, threat, hostility, irritation, shame and anxiety that may have been felt by the user, in this case when using iNum

MOOC. Well-being in EduFlow is conceived as enthusiasm, comfort and wanting to share one's feelings with others, experienced while learning. It is plausible that users may have had momentarily felt negatively while still experiencing enthusiasm, comfort and eagerness to share the experience of learning in the MOOC. The Negative Affect scale in PANAS accounts for sporadic feelings, while EduFlow measures a continuous state. The eagerness felt by the residents in African regions may be understood as a feeling of being part of something innovative and exciting, to the extent that it links the user with an activity that has aura and value, perhaps even through connotations to prestigious institutions in countries looked up to. But this will require further exploration. Well-being could have been specked with frustration due to the absence of support to provide for connectedness [5]. This explanation also corroborates with the absence of loss of self-consciousness mentioned earlier.

While well-being was experienced by the African residents, it appears not to have been sufficient to sustain activity and to encourage persistence. African residents logged on less often and were more prone to drop out of the course. This may point to the inability for the learning environment, through its design, to provide for the needs of participants with different cultural references. As MOOCs are products of wealthy institutions in so-called Western countries, they are an expression of conceptualisations that are typical of them. People living in other cultural environments may not feel 'at home' in unfamiliar environments, even if they may be enthusiastic about being able to experience them, like one may feel when traveling to discover a new country for the first time.

It is also worth noting that as the MOOC was an experiment with a limited number of users, users were probably not representative of future course enrolees on FDU; not in terms of regional distribution nor in terms of numbers, as registration was closed earlier than expected, two weeks after registration was opened (cf. Sect. 2.1).

6 Conclusions

This research attempts to provide insight into learners' emotional experiences and the relation that such experiences have with persistence within an open online course. Though the experimental course was not massive in terms of the number of participants, it did offer an opportunity to explore facets of learners' experiences in an emerging e-learning environment and their relation to hanging in or dropping out of the course. Furthermore, linking emotions to cognitive activity is a step towards understanding the effects of opening up e-learning to massive enrolment and the reasons that enrolees leave a course before it ends. There is a subtle difference between registering for a course and enrolling in it that can be made by distinguishing between those who just register and those who actually explore available resources and further move to become active learners plus interact with others in the process. This research highlights this subtle distinction by providing insight to the patterns of engagement with the online course. Few users engage in frequent access, activities and resources, while many engage only scarcely. To further understand user persistence, future research could explore well-being in conjunction with interest, motivation and strategies used to regulate one's learning [11], as these are crucial to active engagement and persistence, and to the effectiveness of the process.

References

1. Ahn, J., Butler, B.S., Alam, A., Webster, S.A.: Learner participation and engagement in open online courses: Insights from the peer 2 peer university. MERLOT Journal of Online Learning and Teaching 9(2), 160–171 (2013)
2. Bouffard, L., Lapierre, S.: La mesure du bonheur / the measurement of happiness. Revue Québécoise de Psychologie 18(2), 271–310 (1997)
3. Boyatt, R., Joy, M., Rocks, C., Sinclair, J.: What (use) is a MOOC? In: Uden, L., Tao, Y.H., Yang, H.C., Ting, I.H. (eds.) The 2nd International Workshop on Learning Technology for Education in Cloud, pp. 133–145. Springer, Dordrecht (2014)
4. Caron, P.A., Heutte, J.: MOOC et gamification: vers une ingénierie de formation autotélique? In: 6e Conférence Environnements Informatiques pour l'Apprentissage Humain (EIAH 2013), Toulouse (2013)
5. Caron, P.A., Heutte, J., Rosselle, M.: Rapport d'expertise et accompagnement par la recherche du dispositif expérimental MOOC iNum, p. 78 (2014)
6. Csikszentmihalyi, M.: Flow: The Psychology of Optimal Experience. Harper & Row, New York (1990)
7. French Government: Feuille de route pour le numérique (2013)
8. Heutte, J., Fenouillet, F.: Propositions pour une mesure de l'expérience optimale (état de flow) en contexte éducatif. [proposals for measuring optimal experience (state of flow) in educational contexts]. In: 26e Congrès International d'Actualité de la Recherche en Éducation et en Formation (AREF), Université de Genève, Geneva (2010)
9. Heutte, J., Fenouillet, F., Boniwell, I., Martin-Krumm, C., Csikszentmihalyi, M.: Eduflow: Proposal for a new measure of flow in education (forthcoming)
10. Ho, A.D., Reich, J., Nesterko, S.O., Seaton, D.T., Mullaney, T., Waldo, J., Chuang, I.: HarvardX and MITx: The first year of open online courses, fall 2012-summer 2013 (harvardX and MITx working paper no. 1). SSRN Journal (2014)
11. Kaplan, J.: Co-regulation in technology enhanced learning environments. In: Uden, L., et al. (eds.) The 3rd International Workshop on Learning Technology for Education in Cloud, pp. 72–81. Springer, Dordrecht (2014)
12. Karsenti, T.: The MOOC - what the research says. International Journal of Technologies in Higher Education 10(2), 23–37 (2013)
13. Pekrun, R., Goetz, T., Perry, R.P., Kramer, K., Hochstadt, M., Molfenter, S.: Beyond test anxiety: Development and validation of the test emotions questionnaire (TEQ). Anxiety, Stress & Coping 17(3), 287–316 (2004)
14. Pekrun, R., Goetz, T., Titz, W., Perry, R.P.: Academic emotions in students' self-regulated learning and achievement: A program of qualitative and quantitative research. Educational Psychologist 37(2), 91–105 (2002)
15. Pekrun, R., Goetz, T., Titz, W., Perry, R.P.: Positive emotions in education. In: Frydenberg, E. (ed.) Beyond Coping: Meeting Goals, Visions, and Challenges, pp. 149–174. Elsevier, Oxford (2002)

16. Rodriguez, O.: The concept of openness behind c and x-MOOCs (massive open online courses). Open Praxis 5(1), 67–73 (2013)
17. Rosselle, M., Caron, P.A., Heutte, J.: A typology and dimensions of a description framework for MOOCs. In: The 2nd MOOC European Stakeholders Summit - EMOOCs, Lausanne, February 10-12 (2014)
18. Watson, D., Clark, L.A., Tellegen, A.: Development and validation of brief measures of positive and negative affect: The PANAS scales. Journal of Personality and Social Psychology 54(6), 1063–1070 (1988)

Cloud Learning Activities Orchestration for MOOC Environments

Rocael Hernández[1,*], Christian Gütl[2,3], and Hector R. Amado-Salvatierra[1]

[1] GES Department, Galileo University, Guatemala, Guatemala
{roc,hr_amado}@galileo.edu
[2] IICM, Graz University of Technology, Graz, Austria
[3] SIS, Curtin University, Perth, Western Australia
christian.guetl@iicm.tugraz.at

Abstract. In this paper we focus on an approach to using cloud-based (Web 2.0) tools for MOOCs applying a new version of an innovative architecture for 'cloud learning activities orchestration' (CLAO). This works presents the CLAO, and examine its effectiveness for the use of learning activities in the cloud for MOOC experiences, presenting results and findings. Having performed learning analytics to examine the actual behavior of learners using the CLAO, we present results describing how learners evolved, after doing several learning activities, to a more elaborated and meaningful use of the cloud-based tools. These results contribute to a better understanding of the use of a cloud education environment in three MOOC courses with different topics (Medical Urgencies, Introduction to E-Learning and Cloud Tool for Learning Activities), and will enable further discussion and insights to improve methodological and orchestration strategies, and the use of innovative cloud-based tools in future MOOCs.

Keywords: Cloud Education Environment, MOOC, E-Learning, Learning Analytics, Learning Orchestration, VLE, Cloud-based tools, Web 2.0.

1 Introduction

Over the last years, massive open online courses (MOOCs) have become increasingly interesting for students, educators, educational institutions, and researchers. Recent results from Coursera and other initiatives are very encouraging but have also raised various issues in terms of a sustainable business model and of the very high dropout rates during the course of the MOOC or even people who have registered but never participated [9].

Latin America has shown great interest in MOOCs, so Galileo University has launched an initiative called 'Telescope' to host multidisciplinary MOOCs. Description of the initiative and first experiences can be found elsewhere, in [9], [11], [14]. The proposed initiative became increasingly popular, and many professors and learners were attracted from over 20 Iberoamerican countries.

L. Uden et al. (Eds.): LTEC 2014, CCIS 446, pp. 25–36, 2014.

This work presents the latest version of our architecture [2] to deploy and orchestrate innovative learning activities (LA) using cloud-based tools (CBT). We present its use within 3 MOOC experiences, and the results of orchestrating learning activities that use CBT. More specifically, we have performed learning analytics of the users' behavior while they have done the aforementioned learning activities. We have analyzed the learners use the proposed cloud tools, and by some measures have identified how elaborate and complex is the work the learner has done with the tools. Finally we present the lessons learned, the improvements that we have made through the tests, and the pending improvements.

Results are from three MOOC experiences in the Telescope project at Galileo University, Guatemala. Galileo University is a technological university with the region's largest tradition in computer science. The Telescope project is an initiative carried out by the Galileo Educational System (GES) Department, which does educational technology research and development (R&D) at the university.

The remainder of the paper is structured as follows: Section 2 outlines a proposed cloud learning activities orchestration (CLAO) architecture; Section 3 briefly describes three MOOCs courses and their learning activities; Section 4 presents results from CLAO test results, explaining user's identified usage patterns and lessons learned; finally, Section 5 presents conclusions and future work with CLAO architecture.

2 Cloud Learning Activities Orchestration (CLAO)

Learning Orchestration (LO) is defined in [3] as the process in charge of productively coordinating interventions from learners across multiple learning activities (LA) [15]. The process of LO is based on teacher's functions, such as defining activities and evaluation rubrics, monitoring individual or group activities, and adapting deadlines and workload. In order to manage the orchestration of LA based on Web 2.0 tools (CBT) creating a truly cloud learning environment (CEE) [1,2], an infrastructure was created which we call *cloud learning activities orchestration* (CLAO). CLAO is designed to handle all the logic of communication, authentication, and integration with services and tools on the cloud and to provide a friendly user interface through a unified workspace environment. It enables teachers and students to interact with CBT used for LA. With this architecture implemented, CLAO manages the bureaucratic and complex work of orchestration in a distributed environment. The teacher can then devote her attention to the students and activities as mentioned in [3]. As presented in Figure 1, the architecture built for the CLAO consists of the following main layers: learning activities orchestrator (LAO); cloud interoperability system (CIS), and learning environment connector (LEC).

Learning Activities Orchestrator (LAO): This component constitutes the user interaction layer of the CLAO architecture (interface and interaction). It presents the "one-stop shop" for students with a description of the LA and an entry point to the CBT (e.g. Mindmister, Google Drive). Once the user is identified in the system, she can begin exploring the assigned LA in each course. Each LA presented to the student has a description, assessment rubric, examples, and entry point to the assigned learning CBT. LAO user interface creates a visual interface that is connected to the cloud tool, including features allowed by tool public API (e.g. in Google Drive, the online document editor embedded into the LAO and main controls such as 'create a document'). Tools and activities are configured by a professor who is also capable of creating students groups within a course. Assignments completed in such a tool can be sent to the LMS. Once students have finished their assignments with a tool, they can send them to the LMS for the professor to assess them. Figure 2 presents the LAO user interface. The process is organized as follows: it begins with the learning activity description, and then is given a list of CBT to be used for the LA. When the learner wants to use a CBT, a resizable window within the LAO will come up to operate with tool, allowing easy return to LAO's main UI. It is even possible to maintain more than one tools open in a multi-window presentation, although provider restrictions restrict user to just one window per tool. Having multiple windows helps students to go back and forth easily from tools while working in LA that require the use of multiple tools.

Learning Environment Connector (LEC): This component is used for integrate the CLAO architecture and the monolithic learning management system, providing a single user authentication. Examples of interaction between systems are user authentication (single sign-on), session management and assignments.

Cloud Interoperability System (CIS): This framework is the core component of the architecture [2], is named for the ability to integrate, reuse and personalize each of the CBT or services that will be added to CLAO. It achieves this interoperability through a semantic definition of services and definition and through definition of a common language of communication. The CIS component is divided into four layers: (a) the communication layer; (b) the authentication layer; (c) the analytic layer; and (d) the business layer. The CIS is based on Symfony2, a Web development framework (PHP); CLAO extends Symfony2 by implementing a custom bundle. The communication layer (a) in CIS identifies each CBT that can be used for learning, and for each of these tools prepares a custom integrated service communication bundle. Within this layer, tracking data are sent to be stored and used by the analytics layer. This layer performs all the API requests between the CIS and the CBT public API. The CLAO architecture has an authentication layer (b) that handles the required tokens exchange for application authentication, as well as the correspondent learner authentication towards the CBT. The analytics layer (c) records user behavior and interaction data from the CBT, and sends these data to cloud-based storage (Google Fusion Tables) for further analytics processing.

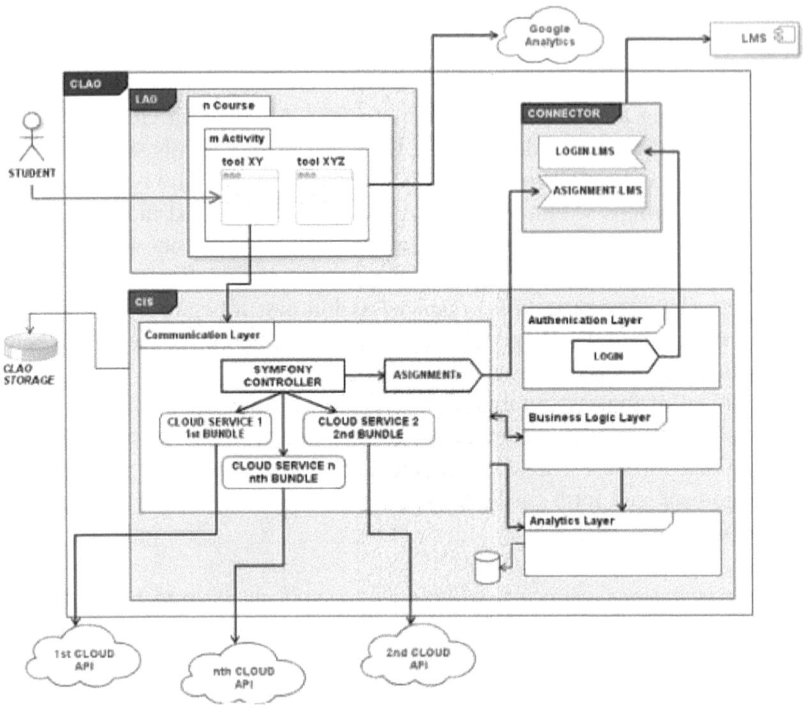

Fig. 1. Cloud Learning Activities Orchestration (CLAO) Architecture

User sessions and activities within CLAO are also recorded by the services provided by Google Analytics (GA), by feeding of customized data related to the LA and learner. Each time a user enters into the CLAO, a session is recorded in GA (according to GA, a session currently stands for uninterrupted activity for no longer than 30 minutes [16]). Additionally, we have added a recording script at LAO, which sends LA per tool, by tracking user window focus in a given tool. The recorded data provide useful information about usage analysis, collaboration level, and behavioral patterns in the cloud tools. All actions that the cloud service makes available are retrieved via this layer. The customized data feed we have made enables GA to provide time spent per session per tool; the limitations are that GA can give back user information only in an hour frame (i.e. from 12:00 to 13:00 hours), and that GA time cannot yield a more granular style. The business logic layer (d) creates interaction between the cloud tool interface and the LAO interface presented to the user. This layer identifies the business logic of each cloud tool; this business logic is then used by the communication layer—for instance, it is possible to add an *idea* to a mindmap through the CBT public API when a UI is presented at the LAO to do so. The business logic layer also handles the CLAO storage, for management of assignments, tools and user relationships. A complete description is presented in [2]. Finally, is relevant to note that CLAO architecture runs over a cloud infrastructure of Amazon's Elastic Compute Cloud (EC2) [10].

CIS services modules: The single components of CLAO are the CIS service modules. These modules are prepared for each one of the identified cloud tools used for learning activities. Each module is a bundle prepared with the Symfony2 framework, implementing the functionality of CBT's interfaces. A CIS service module is prepared with the elements described by the public API of the CBT (e.g. Dipity, SoundCloud, Cacoo, MindMeister). A CIS service module adopts the functionality provided by the API to enable professors to define the various activities in their own learning environment.

Each CIS service module uses each of the layers provided—communication, business, authentication, and analytics—and communicates with the service tool independently. Authentication is prepared according to the service method (e.g. OAuth, URL Tokenized). The business layer plays every CRUD operation upon the activity type (e.g. creation of a document). Figure 3 shows the representation of each cloud service represented by a bundle, describing interaction.

3 MOOCs Implementation: Description of Courses

The Telescope's MOOCs' 2013 experiences presented in this paper cover the following courses: (a) Cloud-based (Web 2.0) Tools for Education; (b) Introduction to E-Learning, and (c) Medical Urgencies. These courses had more than 6,000 enrolled students and drew learners from more than 15 countries, including Spain, Mexico, Guatemala, Colombia, and Peru.

Participants were equally distributed in gender, with an age average of 30 years (SD = 10.63) for courses a, b and c. Participants who visited the contents of the course at least once represented 60% of the total enrolled users; on average across the three courses, less than 10% of those active participants completed and approved the course. Interestingly, more than 70% of all the participants that this was their first MOOC experience.

The three courses take an xMOOC pedagogical approach (cognitive-behavioral teaching model): the MOOC courses have been prepared with a peer assessment type of evaluation and include a collaboration approach of question and answer (Q/A) forums with a support of four tutors. The courses have been designed with four learning units (one week per learning unit); each unit includes an introduction describing the main objectives and learning activities, presentations displaying the content, and short videos representing the main resources of the learning content. Each of the learning units has between two to four activities that are part of an evaluation rubric divided between peer assessment and tutor review of the work. Table 1, summarizes the three MOOCs' experiences, including the final product that students are expected to achieve.

Learning activities presented in MOOC courses are detailed in Table 2. This table presents the instructional objective, the activity, and the cloud-based tools (Google Drive document editor GD, MindMeister mind maps editor: MM) used within the proposed CLAO architecture to complete the activity.

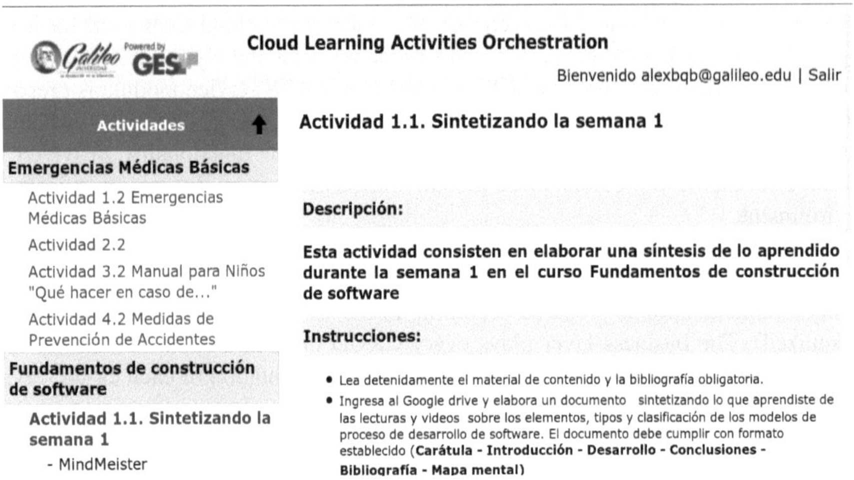

Fig. 2. LAO Interface for students linking with Learning Activities

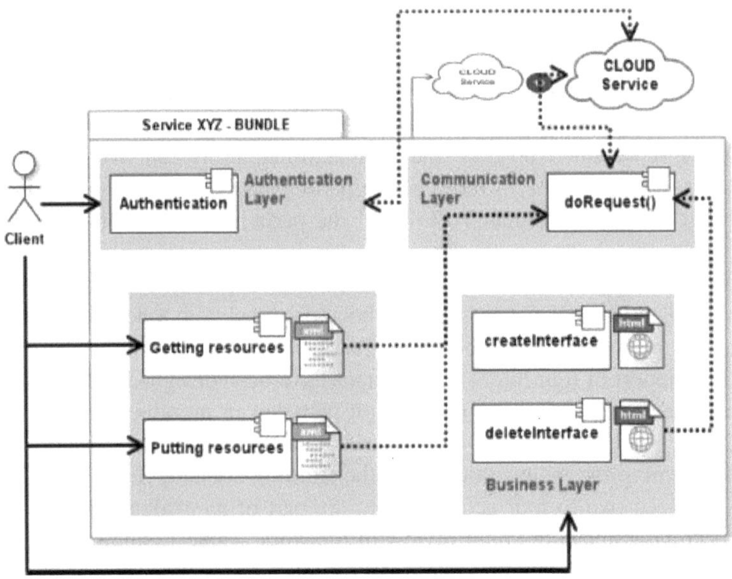

Fig 3.CIS Service Modules. Each cloud service represented by a bundle.

Table 1. Description of MOOC experiences

Learning Experience	(a) Cloud-based Tools for Education	(b) Introduction to e-Learning	(c) Medical Urgencies
Learning and instructional objectives	Understand how to include innovative learning activities using Web 2.0 tools and apply this knowledge in an online course	Understand the e-learning fundamentals, the related concepts and tools; apply knowledge by designing an online course	Understand basic skills in first aid techniques and apply knowledge to design a basic handbook for kids
Final product	Define learning activities using CBT for online courses	Create an Online Course	Production of a short tutorial for kids
Course offered	September 2013	October 2013	November 2013

Table 2. Instructional activities and selected cloud-based tools

Instructional Objective	Learning Activity Title (Google Drive (GD) or MindMeister (MM)) (Total Student Assignments)
Demonstrate an understanding of unit contents	(a.1) Benefits of learning in the cloud (GD) (219)
Acquire content	(a.2) Presenting a project with three innovative tools (MM) (111)
Demonstrate an understanding of unit contents	(b.1) Preparing a presentation on basic LMS functionality (GD) (161)
Learn-by-doing activity: create, produce the course based on content templates; design and build an introductory unit including a welcome video-message.	(b.2) Producing my first virtual course (GD) (72)
Structure for knowledge representation	(c.1) Creating my first mental map about medical emergencies (GD, MM) (83,71)
Structure for knowledge representation	(c.2) Accident prevention measures (GD,MM) (43,47)
Learn-by-doing activity	(c.3) Handbook for kids: "What to do in an emergency"(GD,MM) (56,58)

4 CLAO Test Results, Patterns Identified and Lessons Learned

The overall goal of the experience was to gain insights in how learners used the CBT enabled in CLAO for the 3 MOOCs, identifying usage and failure patterns in the learning activity and how effectively these tools were used. This identification will lead us to further improvement of the CLAO architecture. In LMS, the modified version of the .LRN LMS [17] was used and integrated using the LEC. Learning analytics is moving forward outside closed learning management systems [7], towards such environments as CLAO. The CIS analytics layer (described in section 2) was used to explore data about the user experience, based on previous conclusions in [4], [5]. In terms of learning analytics, the authors in [6] describe the four stages involved in the analysis: awareness, reflection, sense-making, and impact. In this sense, experiences prepared with the CIS analytics layer focus on the reflection stage, and our aim is to provide teachers and researchers with valuable information on how students interact with CBT when performing a learning activity, and examine at the same time the effectiveness of the proposed cloud-based tool for learning and the CLAO unified workspace environment. This experience is also intended to provide experiences with MOOC extending the work in [8].

The procedure conducted for this study was: following the basic enrollment and introduction steps presented in similar experiences [9], seven innovative learning activities (see Table 2) using two CBT (Google Drive editor GD and the mind-mapping tool MindMeister MM) were prepared in the CLAO architecture. Information presented was extracted from the CIS analytics layer dashboard. The three courses, described in Table 1, were executed in sequential order, providing feedback to the next course, thus improving the learner experience and data gathering (each group has a different group of learners).

For online document editor (GD), data generated from the CIS analytics layer is presented in Table 3. Some of the relevant identified variables for analysis are: number of words; number of paragraphs; revisions (number of editions in document); change rate between revisions; time used to complete the activity; number of sessions (NS) in the CLAO, and average time per session in minutes (TPS) where a session stands for use of GD in the CLAO with inactivity less than 30 minutes. The most important results from data generated, according to number of words, revisions, and TPS are the following: In MOOC activity (a.1) it was identified that students were not using the cloud-based tool directly, and the ones who used it through CLAO presented a small number of revisions, indicating possibly that they basically copied their final work from an offline document editor, and did not at all use the GD/CLAO interaction layers. For MOOC activity (b.1) results from Table 3 present a slightly better use of the CLAO, with an increased TPS. In (b.2), CLAO usage is improved in all observed variables. Interestingly, the same pattern is identified for MOOC (c), beginning with learners with fewer revisions in (c.1), for (c.2), with the use of GD increased significantly in (c.3); the results are in Table 3. These first results reflect a behavior in which the learners, as they grow more “used to” the CLAO and cloud-based tool, make a more enhanced and meaningful use of the tools.

Table 3. Results for Google Drive–based activities generated by CIS analytics layer

Activity	Revisions	Total words	TPS
a.1	M=1.08 (SD 0.37)	M=525 (SD 648)	M=5.44 (SD 3.56)
b.1	M=2.51 (SD 1.58)	M=736 (SD 599)	M=25.27 (SD 47.53)
b.2	M=3.60 (SD 3.17)	M=2237 (SD 1505)	M=66.09 (SD 170.66)
c.1	M=1.94 (SD 1.25)	M=916 (SD 1011)	M=41.39 (SD 57.22)
c.2	M=1.33 (SD 0.71)	M=547 (SD 249)	M=58.66 (SD 67.20)
c.3	M= 3.2 (SD 1.58)	M=1438 (SD 542)	M=54.76 (SD 72.71)

For the online mind map editor tool (MM) the following metrics were evaluated: total number of changes; number of first ideas (NFI); number of ideas in further depth level, (NFD; from 2nd level and further levels); time used to complete the activity; number of sessions (NS) in the CLAO, and average time per session in minutes (TPS). An exploratory activity with mind maps was prepared in activity (a.2), in which students were using the tool but the final work was not linked with the CLAO; results in number of ideas were (M = 16.73, SD = 13.81). In MOOC (c), a new implementation was made, activating the learning resource (mind map) directly in the CLAO; students started the mind map in the CLAO, and all related information was stored by the CLAO analytics layer. Activities are presented in Table 4, where (c.2) and (c.3) show an interesting increase in mind maps metrics, exposing how students learned to use the tool via LAO's UI. Once learners have an experience with MMs, they use it to create more elaborate work.

Table 4. Results for mind-map-based activities generated by CIS analytics layer

Act.	No. ideas	NFI	NFD	TPS
c.1	M=15.77 (SD 21.32)	M=8.72 (SD 2.46)	M=9.97 (SD 19.89)	M=55.30 (SD 69.78)
c.2	M=67.57 (SD 70.18)	M=5.07 (SD 0.88)	M=61.62 (SD 70.87)	M=40.07 (SD 63.98)
c.3	M=65.71 (SD 40.03)	M= 5.44 (SD 1.89)	M=59.27 (SD 38.90)	M=50.18 (SD 59.20)

The CIS analytics layer made clear how students used the CLAO and related tools, identifying failure/success patterns. A general pattern is evident: as time passes in the course, and learners grow used to the CLAO and related cloud-based tools, the assignments the learners present using these tools become more relevant, more detailed (with more complex structures in the case of MM), and more extensive.

Related to assignment submission, in the first two MOOCs (a) and part of (b), it was identified that students had the opportunity to send the assignment through the LMS, consisting in a static link of the work they had prepared in MM or GD as a standalone tool; but this approach gave rise to several problems.

First, students used the tools GD/MM and avoided using the proposed interface in the CLAO (reflected in results in MOOC (a)). Interestingly, a correction was introduced in MOOC (b) which clearly emerged in results presented in the learning activity (b.2) increasing CLAO usage.

Second, the MM or GD resource belonged to the learner, revealing the following issues: (1) a learner could modify an assignment even after submitting it, (2) a learner could erase the resource and all its history and so keep it from further analysis, and (3) a learner had to *manually share resource editing rights* with the CLAO in order for allow it to be able to perform automatic analytics.

The solution to these issues was twofold: first, to include an automatic process to send the assignment via the LAO user interface (this was the only way to send the assignment); and second, to have the GD or MM resources created automatically by the CLAO, and then shared to the learner, thus requiring the learner to work in an specific MM or GD instance and keeping the resource ownership with the CLAO. This also had the advantage of closing editing rights to the learner once he or she had submitted the assignment, making it impossible for learners to improve their assignments after the deadline. The final experience, MOOC (c), provided the best experience, as clearly shown in the data collection and CLAO usage. One factor that was key to improving overall data gathering was to clearly tell learners that they had to use the shared MM or GD at all times, and that they should not work in other MM or GD and then copy and paste to the final resource, because that would not keep the history of use within the tool, something we said the course would assess.

We could not model in detail the browsing behavior patterns when a learner was in CLAO. For example, a learner is in MM, then goes to the LMS, then goes back to GD, then to MM, then changes to another activity, and so on. The reason we cannot model such behavior in detail is that GA does not provide granular data for that kind of analysis; it keeps those data within itself and shows the data through a UI of *browsing pattern*, which can be used to identify browsing behavior patterns. We, however, registered to GA all requests under the same URL request, and used GET-method variables to further identify what each user was doing; but, for GA, all was under the same URL request, making it impossible to create a browsing pattern for it. We will improve this by having RESTFUL-style URL requests in the next experiences, making it possible to create browsing patterns within GA. Another problem that we faced was tracking sessions and time spent when learner decided to use GD or MM standalone, using the same resource that was shared through the CLAO but—instead of using it through the CLAO—entering and using the resource through the cloud-based tool website. In response, we are working on workarounds such as embedding scripts into the shared resource.

5 Conclusions and Future Work

In this paper we have presented both an innovative architecture for cloud learning activities orchestration (CLAO) and results from three MOOC courses and their learning activities using cloud-bases (Web 2.0) tools. CLAO architecture has proved to be a robust environment for deploying cloud-based learning activities.

We conclude the following from the experiences in terms of effectiveness:

When using cloud-based tools, the user needs to be conducted and guided by the system with the corresponding instructions on the usage of the tool. If a tool is somewhat detached from the learning environment, even if its use is required, expect that it will not be used as expected, or even at all.

Although previous studies has shown [11, 12, 13] that learners are willing and enjoy using cloud-based tools, some sort of summative evaluations and grades have to be embedded into the learning activity to ensure full exploitation of the learning experience as it was conceived by the teacher.

If a learning activity uses more than one cloud-based tool, the system must require the use of all of them: if not, the learner will tend to use just the tool presented for the final work.

This is a first analytics experience of learning activities' learner behavior using cloud-based tools and a unified workspace environment; we shall further analyze quality of content according to peer-review process, assessment metrics, and final grades. In learning activities using mind maps, we also need to analyze ideas and content richness (the inclusion of images, links, etc.).

Collaborative work has not yet been experimented within CLAO, and accessibility in LAO's interface should be considered for future work.

Future publications on this experience shall include both cognitive and metacognitive results, as well as dropout analysis.

Future work shall include the creation of a statistical-prediction dashboard to intervene during the learning process, rather than just summarizing behavior after course completion.

Acknowledgments. To the excellent software developers and instructional designers of GES at Galileo University involved in this experience. This work is partially supported by European Union through the project ALFA III – ESVI-AL ((DCI-ALA/19.09.01/11/21526/279-146/ALFA 111(2011)-11 www.esvial.org).

References

1. Mikroyannidis, A.: A semantic framework for cloud learning environments. In: Chao, L. (ed.) Cloud Computing for Teaching and Learning: Strategies for Design and Implementation, pp. 17–31. IGI Global, Hershey (2012)
2. Rizzardini, R.H., Linares, B.H., Mikroyannidis, A., Schmitz, H.C.: Cloud services, interoperability and analytics within a ROLE-enabled personal learning environment. Journal of Universal Computer Science 19(14), 2054–2074 (2013)

3. Dillenbourg, P., Järvelä, S., Fischer, F.: The evolution of research on computer-supported collaborative learning. In: Technology-Enhanced Learning, pp. 3–19. Springer Netherlands (2009)
4. Chatti, M.A., Dyckhoff, A.L., Schroeder, U., Thüs, H.: A reference model for learning analytics. International Journal of Technology Enhanced Learning 4(5), 318–331 (2012)
5. Daniel, J.: Making Sense of MOOCs: Musing in a Maze of Myth, Paradox and Possibility. Journal of Interactive Media in Education (2012)
6. Verbat, K., Duval, E., Klerkx, J., Govaerts, S., Santos, J.L.: Learning analytics dashboard applications. Americal Behavioral Scientist 57(10), 1500–1509 (2013)
7. Pardo, A., Kloos, C.D.: Stepping out of the box: towards analytics outside the learning management system. In: Proceedings of the 1st International Conference on Learning Analytics and Knowledge, pp. 163–167. ACM, New York (2011)
8. Clow, D.: MOOCs and the funnel of participation. In: Third Conference on Learning Analytics and Knowledge, pp. 185–189. ACM, New York (2013)
9. Rizzardini, R.H., Gütl, C., Chang, V., Morales, M.: MOOC in Latin America: Implementation and Lessons Learned. In: 2nd International Workshop on Learning Technology for Education in Cloud, pp. 147–158. Springer Netherlands (2014)
10. Juve, G., Deelman, E., Vahi, K., Mehta, G., Berriman, B., Berman, B.P., Maechling, P.: Scientific workflow applications on Amazon EC2. In: IEEE International Conference on E-Science, pp. 59–66. IEEE (2009)
11. Hernández, R., Amado-Salvatierra, H.R., Guetl, C.: Cloud-based Learning Environments: Investigating learning activities experiences from Motivation, Usability and Emotional Perspective. In: CSEDU 2013 Proceedings. SciTePress (2013)
12. Ko, C.-C., Young, S.S.-C.: Explore the next generation of cloud-based e-learning environment. In: Chang, M., Hwang, W.-Y., Chen, M.-P., Müller, W. (eds.) Edutainment 2011. LNCS, vol. 6872, pp. 107–114. Springer, Heidelberg (2011)
13. Conole, G., Alevizou, P.: A literature review of the use of Web 2.0 tools in Higher Education. A report commissioned by the Higher Education Academy (2010)
14. Rizzardini, R.H., Chang, V., Gütl, C., Amado-Salvatierra, H.: An Open Online Course with Accessibility Features. In: Herrington, J., et al. (eds.) Proceedings of World Conference on Educational Multimedia, Hypermedia and Telecommunications, pp. 635–643. AACE, Chesapeake (2013)
15. Beetham, H., Sharpe, R. (eds.): Rethinking pedagogy for a digital age: Designing for 21st century learning. Routledge (2013)
16. Claiborne, T.: Update to Sessions in Google Analytics. Google Analytics (2011), http://analytics.blogspot.com/2011/08/update-to-sessions-in-google-analytics.html
17. Hernandez, R., Pardo, A., Delgado, C.: Creating and Deploying Effective eLearning Experiences Using. LRN. IEEE Trans. on Education 50(4), 345–351 (2007)

Attrition in MOOC: Lessons Learned from Drop-Out Students

Christian Gütl[1,4], Rocael Hernández Rizzardini[1,2], Vanessa Chang[3,4], and Miguel Morales[2]

[1] IICM, Graz University of Technology, Graz, Austria
Christian.Guetl@iicm.tugraz.at
[2] GES Department, Galileo University, Guatemala
{roc,amorales}@galileo.edu
[3] Curtin Teaching and Learning, Curtin University, Perth, Western Australia
vanessa.chang@curtin.edu.au
[4] School of Information Systems, Curtin University, Perth, Western Australia

Abstract. Despite the popularity of Massive Open Online Course (MOOC), recent studies have found that completion rates are low with some reported to be significantly lower than 10%. The low retention and completion rates are major concerns for educators and institutions. This paper investigates motivations for enrolling in a MOOC on the topic of 'e-learning' and discusses reasons for the attrition rates during the course. A survey of 134 students who had not completed the MOOC reveals that only 22% of the students had intended to complete the MOOC but was unable to due to various factors including academic and personal reasons. A big majority of the students indicated that changes in their job, insufficient time, difficulty with the subject matter and unchallenging activities are some of the reasons for the drop-out.

Keywords: Massive Open Online Course, Retention Rate, Attrition Rate, Completion Rate.

1 Introduction

Over the last decades the concept of 'openness' had made significant impact in educational settings, from open source (learning tools and platforms) to open content (open learning and training content) to open online learning experience (open online courses). Free online courses have been available since mid-2000s. One of the earlier open online courses entitled 'Connectivism and Connective Knowledge' by G. Siemens and S. Downes recorded large enrolments. MOOCs have raised a lot of attention and a great number of such online courses have been offered and numerous MOOC platforms have also come on the market [9], [17]. So far two different MOOCs are described in the literature: *cMOOCs* which are based on 'connectivism and networking', and *xMOOCs* which are based on the 'behaviorist' approach [15].

The MOOC approach is popular in that it can reach a wide community of learners. Because of its openness it can bring a diverse group of learners together regardless of

L. Uden et al. (Eds.): LTEC 2014, CCIS 446, pp. 37–48, 2014.

their social and cultural background. It enables geographically dispersed groups to collaborate and learn autonomously. On the flip side, in a MOOC offering, students face issues of isolation and disconnect, similar to those experienced in distance learning environments [6]. It is also reported that students fail to self-organize in that they are not prepared to control their own learning and faces problems in using the learning tools and completing the learning activities. These issues might also lead to a large drop-out rate, with only a small proportion of about 10% who would complete the MOOCs successfully [5], [7], [14]. The high drop-out rate is a major concern especially to those who have invested time and effort and did not complete. In this instance, teachers and tutors would have also spent time supporting the learning group, assessing assignment and providing feedback. Multiple reasons may have caused the attrition rates and this would require a deeper investigation of the root cause of such high drop-out rates. Some strategies are required to curtail the attrition rate which includes ensuring that students are well supported. From an Information Communications and Technology (ICT) perspective, universities must provide stable and reliable learning platforms and network infrastructure that are able to cope with hundreds and thousands of students. Students, on the other hand, must also ensure a reciprocal technical arrangement to access the learning tools, materials and activities.

Given the concerns, we have started a collaborative research on drop-out issues on MOOCs between Galileo University in Guatemala, Graz University of Technology in Austria and Curtin University in Australia. A study focused on students who had finished a MOOC on e-learning was reported elsewhere [9]. This research has now been extended to include an investigation specifically targeting students who had not finished the MOOC. In this paper we report the findings of the drop-out aspects both from the literature and the study. A comparison of the groups' perceptions on MOOC characteristics, emotional and motivational aspects will also be discussed. The structure of the paper is organized as follows: Section 2 outlines drop-out and retention findings from the literature. Section 3 gives on overview on the study design and findings from the study. Section 4 concludes the papers and emphasizes directions for further research.

2 Attrition and Retention in Online Learning

The terms 'attrition' and 'retention' vary greatly in the literature. The opinions may be different depending on the types of learning settings. In this work retention is defined according to Berge and Huang [3] where students participate in a course with the intention to complete the learning event. Attrition is defined as decline in the number of students from the beginning to the end of the event.

Research on retention and attrition is an active research spanning across 8 decades. This includes traditional physical presence learning settings to distance education and e-learning settings. Drop-out rates in the physical presence of higher education settings is reported to be between 40 and 50% and online learning drop-out rates may be between 10 to 20% higher. Research in e-learning settings revealed that drop-out experiences may lead to frustration and lower confidence in learning. Models to understand and describe the effects of attritions have been developed since the beginning of education. An early model in 1975 from Tinto, the Student Integration Model (SIM), takes the individual's motivation and academic ability into account. Bean and Metzner [2] developed the Student Attrition Model that included aspects of student's beliefs and attitudes. Rovai [16] introduced a blend of both models, the Composite Persistence Model [3], [12], [19].

The findings from a large body of research on attrition and retention were summarized and categorized by Berge & Huang [3]. The three categories were (1) *Personal variables* subsuming demographic aspects (such as age, ethnicity, economic status), individual aspects (such as academic skills and abilities, motivation) and prior education experiences (such as academic achievements). (2) *Circumstantial variables* distinguishing institutional interaction (such as academic and social interaction) and external interaction (such as life and work circumstances). (3) *Institutional variables* comprising social aspects (mechanism for social integration), academic aspects (structural and normative system) and bureaucratic aspects (such as mission and policy and institutional funding).

Compared to other forms e-learning, MOOC settings have a very low retention rate reported to be usually between 3 to 8%, but it can be as low as 0.4% [13]. Despite this, not much research was devoted to find the reasons of the high drop-out rate. Kizilcec, Piech, and Schneider [11] investigated patterns of engagement and disengagement and found groups characterized as completing, auditing, disengaging and sampling learners. Yang, Sinha, Adamson, and Rose [20] emphasize other aspects as students having *"substantially more freedom to determine what, when, where, and how they will learn"*. Also the barrier with starting a MOOC is low and drop-out has no penalties. Adamopoulos [1] used the Grounded Theory Method (GTM) to analyze real-world data set with user-generated online reviews to determine the influential factors for retention. The findings suggest that other characteristics of students, platform, university/organization, course, and student course evaluation must be strongly considered.

3 Experimentation and Lessons Learned

3.1 Experimentation Setup and Methodology

The MOOC is focused on the topic of 'e-learning' and it is organized into four parts to be completed within four consecutive weeks: (1) Introduction to e-learning, (2) Technological platforms for e-Learning, (3) How to create a fascinating e-learning course, and (4) Developing an e-Learning course. A detailed description can be found elsewhere [9].

The overall goal of this research was to uncover motivation for enrolling in the MOOC, the reasons for leaving the MOOC and how students organized (when and where) to work on the MOOC. A comparison between these groups, those who had finished and those who left the MOOC mid-way is presented. This study will also determine insights on motivational, emotional and usability issues. In this paper, we highlighted some of the important and interesting findings.

The experimentation procedure for both groups included the following steps (see also [9]): (1) students enroll in the MOOC, (2) students complete a pre-questionnaire to gather demographic details, (3) students undertake an orientation week to familiarize themselves in the MOOC environment, (4) students access four weeks of learning activities, participate in online collaboration and complete assessments. Finally, (5) students who had completed the MOOC were asked to fill in a post-questionnaire to evaluate their own performance and the overall MOOC experience. To complement the initial research as reported in [9], an additional questionnaire focusing on the drop-out aspects were developed for this study. This questionnaire was sent to the group of students who did not complete the MOOC. In this regard, two questionnaires were made available to cater for step 5, one specifically for 'completers' and the other for 'non-completers'.

The instrument included the MOOC tools, content, the cloud-based tools, the surveys, user behavior and user collaborative contributions over online forums, data entries from the peer assessment process, views and experiences from the instructors/professors, and interviews with the tutors and students.

The pre-questionnaire contained questions on demographics and learning preferences. The post-questionnaire for the group who had finished the MOOC contained the standard measurements listed above. Open-ended questions captured the learners' opinions about cloud-based tools and the overall MOOC experience. For the group who left the MOOC, questions on drop-out aspects were adapted from Willging and Johnson [19]. For both groups the following standard measurement instruments were used: Computer Emotions Scale (CES) by Kay and Loverock [10], Intrinsic Motivations Measure (IMM) by Tseng and Tsai [18], and the System Usability Scale (SUS) by Brooke [4] were used. For CES and IMM, a four point Likert scale was used and a five point Likert scale for SUS.

3.2 Experimentation Results and Discussion

Detailed information about the MOOC and analysis of the students who had completed the course were reported in [9]. Important facts from the previous study will be included here in order to provide an overall picture. The MOOC is a four-week course and it was offered in October 2012, with 1680 enrolled learners from 30 countries. As the MOOC organizers are located in Guatemala, the majority of the participants were based in Guatemala (76.60%), followed by Spain (5.11%), U.S.A (3.63%), Honduras (3.09%), México (2.20%) and others (9.04%).

In line with findings from other MOOC experiments, the drop-out rate is very high, with only 143 participants or 8.50% of the enrolled users completed the course. Interestingly, all (100%) of the participants have also responded to the post-questionnaire. Forty-four percent of the participants were female and 56% were male participants. The average age for this group is M=39 (σ=11), and 67% of the participants hold a degree qualification. Statistics on the active involvement of enrolled users shed some light toward the final high drop-out rate.

In the first week of the MOOC only 21.60% of the learners completed the learning tasks, while 33.01% actively participated in the forums. In the second week, there was a further attrition with 13.80% of learners completing the learning tasks. Although the attrition had increased, 26.02% had actively participated in the forums. Similar behavior occurred in the third week, with decreased participation to 10.24% learners who had completed the task while 18.05% participated in the forums. Finally only 8.50% of learners had completed the MOOC.

A total of 1537 (91.50%) of the enrolled users did not finish the course. All users were contacted by email and asked to participate in an online survey focusing on drop-out aspects. Four hundred and thirty seven (437) participants (28.43%) responded. Three hundred and three (303), which accounted to 69.34% of users, responded to the questionnaire, but fail to complete the survey; and 134 (30.66%) completed and returned the questionnaire. The response and completion rate of 30.66% is very high for quantitative measures and statistical confidence.

The findings are based on data collected from the 134 students who had not completed the course but answered the questionnaire of the follow-up study. The participants were almost equally distributed, with 69 (51.49%) male and 56 (48.51%) female. Guatemala had a response of 76.12%, 4.47% from the USA, and 2.24% from Spain and Mexico. In average they were M=39.95 (σ=11.32) years old, with the age ranging from 17 to 63 years. Fifty users (or 37%) had MOOC experiences, 84 (63%) have never been exposed to this experience.

Not surprisingly but interestingly, the given reasons for enrolling and starting the MOOCs were diverse (see also Figure 1). The majority of users - 45 (33.58%) - indicated the reason to enrol in a MOOC was to experience MOOC or to 'get a feeling about MOOCs', followed by 30 (22.39%) to 'complete the course', 24 (17.92%) to 'take a 'sneak preview' into the topic'. Twelve (or 8.96%) indicated the desire to 'learning without formally completing the course', and 5 participants (or 3.73%) who were interested with the content (i.e. 'access to content I am interested without finishing the course'). Eighteen (or 13.43%) participants had given 'other reason' which included 'having a quick view of the subject', 'deepening knowledge on a subject', 'contributes to my job activities', 'refresh and update the knowledge in a subject', and 'learn about the methodology'.

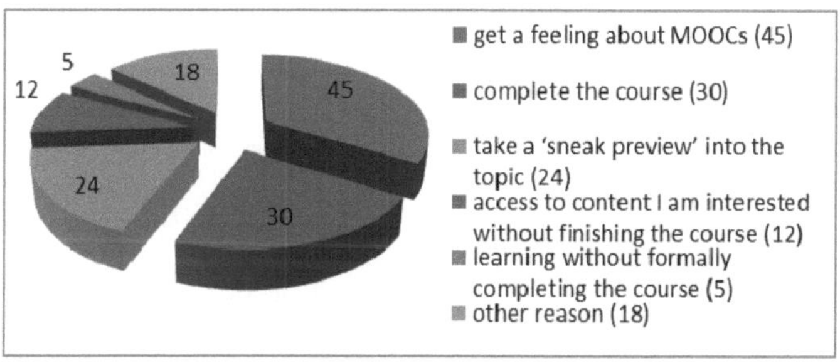

Fig. 1. Reasons why users enrol and start the MOOC

To get a better understanding of the reasons why the participants did not finish the MOOC, they were asked about personal, academic, support and learning environment reasons. Among the personal issues (see Figure 2), 92 participants (or 69.40%) indicated the main reason was a change in job responsibilities during the course. This was followed by 20 (14.93%) indicating 'personal health problems', 18 (13.43%) found the program did not meet their expectations, 11 (8.21%) stated 'family problems', 10 (7.46%) raised 'financial difficulties', and 4 (2.99%) said the 'company did not support MOOC participation'. In terms of academic reasons for leaving the MOOC (see Figure 3), 94 participants (or 70.15%) indicated it was difficult to work and study at the same time. Twenty participants (or 14.93%) indicated they were 'not technically prepared for this program', 12 (8.96%) stated the program was too difficult, and in contrast 10 (7.46%) emphasized that the 'program was not challenging'. Nine respondents (or 6.72%) indicated that 'classes were poorly taught' and 5 (3.73%) said the course was poorly designed, and finally 4 (2.99%) found they were 'not academically prepared for this program'.

In terms of help and support reasons (see Figure 4), 47 participants (35.82%) indicated the main issue was that they did 'not get enough encouragement/support to continue from colleagues, family or employer'. This is followed by poor feedback (i.e. 'have not received useful feedback on assignments and tests') by 43 participants (or 32.09%). Thirty participants (22.39%) indicated they 'have not received the necessary training to use the technologies required in the course' and 'not enough support from the technical staff' was raised by 24 participants (17.91%). The learning environment aspect (see Figure 5) revealed a number of reasons. The most selected category by 44 (32.84%) participants was 'other' which included issues such as 'slow internet connection', 'too many forums which caused confusion' and 'lengthy and boring videos'. This was followed by 38 (28.36%) participants with issue that they had little interaction with other students, 33 (24.63%) perceived 'too little interaction with the instructors', 22 (17.16%) found their 'typing skills were not sufficient enough to interact with the class', and 20 (14.93%) emphasized that the 'learning environment was not personalized'.

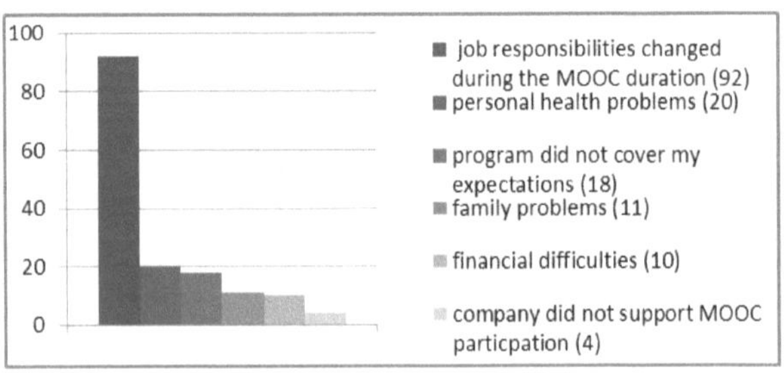

Fig. 2. Personal reasons for leaving the MOOC (multiple answers possible)

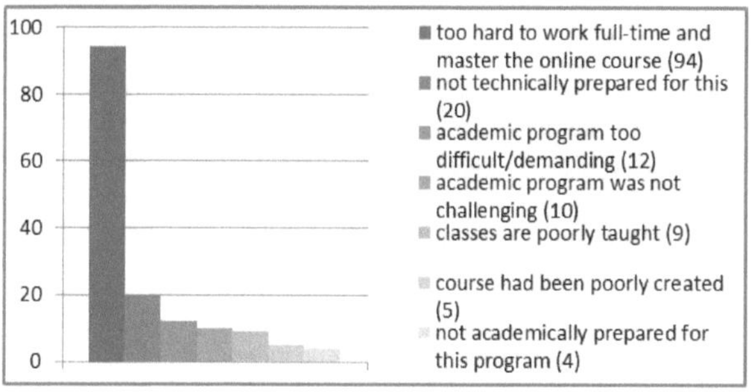

Fig. 3. Academic reasons for leaving the MOOC (multiple answers possible)

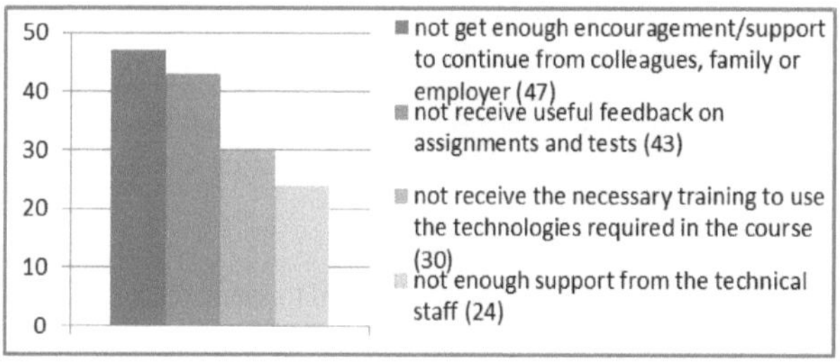

Fig. 4. Insufficient support reasons for leaving the MOOC (multiple answers possible)

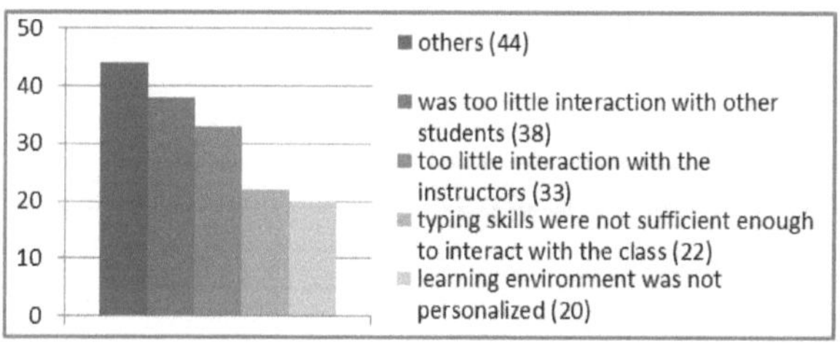

Fig. 5. Learning environment reasons for leaving the MOOC (multiple answers possible)

To learn more about how the students had participated in the MOOC, they were asked when they had set time to work on the course (see Figure 6). Sixty eight (or 50.75%) participants had indicated 'at home after work', followed by 20 (14.93%) who spent the 'weekends' going over the learning tasks. Fifteen (or 11.19%) worked on the course 'during lunch time' and 14 (10.45%) allocated time 'at work'. Seventeen (or 12.69%) gave 'other' reasons which included 'at work and home', 'at night' or 'did not have time'. The allocated 'time' to work on the course was also quite low (see Figure 7). Sixty one participants which accounted to almost half of the respondents (or 45.52%), did not allocate more than 1 to 2 hours and only 15 respondents (11.19%) spent 5 hours or more studying the course each week. Twenty four (17.9%) did not specify their effort.

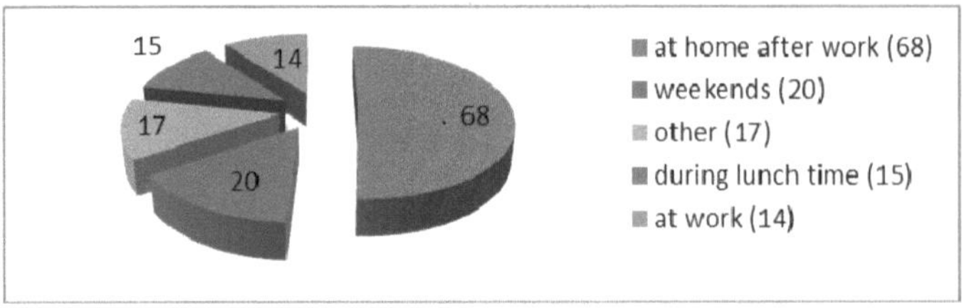

Fig. 6. When students set time aside to work on the course

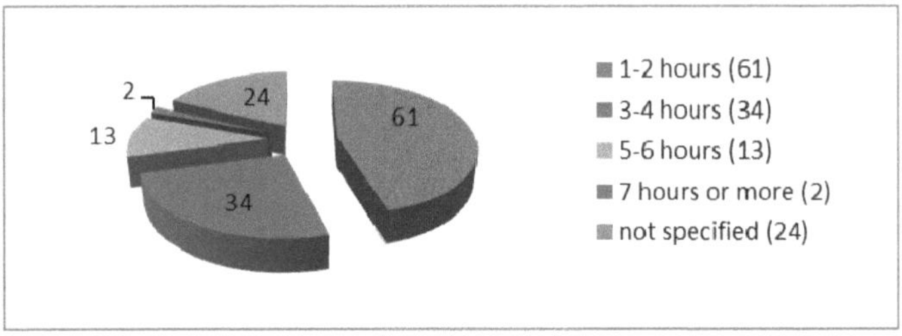

Fig. 7. Average hours per week allocated to spend on the MOOC

A set of questions using a 5 point Likert scale (from *totally dislike* to *totally like*) was used to determine the overall perception of the MOOC on the content course features. Table 1 gives the details. Among all subjects there was neither a clear preference for specific media nor dislike of the media.

Table 1. MOOC core feature student's perception

	M	σ
Text content	3.85	1.07
Multimedia and animated content	3.73	1.17
Graphical information	3.81	1.08
Concept and content videos taught by instructor	3.61	1.22
Video Tutorial	3.67	1.17
Online forums and discussion	3.34	1.06
Earn Karma point through course participation	3.26	0.97
Peer assessment	3.19	1.11

In order to uncover differences between the groups of users who had and had not finished, a comparison on students' perception on learning activities, emotional and motivational aspects were conducted. Results for the group of students who had completed the MOOC are also reported in [9].

A 5 point Likert scale (from *totally disagree* to *totally agree*) was used to determine the overall perception of the MOOC experience between those who had and had not finished the MOOC (see Table 2). The perception on the various aspects of the group who had finished is notable better than from the other group.

Table 2. MOOC Learning Activities student's perception

	finished		drop-out	
Students ...	M	σ	M	σ
I didn't have any problems with planning the learning activities.	4.06	1.15	3.30	1.06
It was difficult for me solving the learning activities.	2.41	1.34	3.06	1.07
I would have needed more information to solve the learning activities	2.59	1.30	3.11	1.14
It was fun doing the learning activities.	4.37	0.99	3.49	0.98
I liked the idea of doing these learning activities to represent knowledge acquisition.	4.67	0.74	3.76	1.05
The time I spent in the learning activities was appropriate for my learning progress.	4.01	1.12	3.09	1.10

Focusing on the emotional aspects, the Computer Emotional Scale (CES) from Kay and Loverock [10] were applied. Four different emotions - happiness, sadness, anxiety, and anger – are described by 12 items. The item on "helpless" (on the "anxiety" dimension) has not been included in the analysis because of inconsistences with the data. Table 3 shows the results for both groups. The findings revealed that MOOC participants perceived low anger and sadness as well as significantly higher happiness while performing learning activities. The difference between both groups is marginal and is slightly better for the group who had completed the MOOC (reverse calculated for negative emotions).

Table 3. MOOC Computer Emotions Scale with 4-point Likert scale from 0 to 3 after (Kay & Loverock [10])

Students		finished		drop-out	
Emotion	Explanation "When I used the tool, I felt ..."	Value	σ	Value	σ
Happiness	... satisfied/excited/curious?	2.27	0.79	2.09	0.98
Sadness	... disheartened/dispirited?	0.52	0.66	0.64	0.80
Anxiety	... anxious/insecure/helpless*/nervous?	0.83	0.77	0.90	0.88
Anger	... felt irritable/frustrated/angry?	0.36	0.60	0.49	0.76

* The item "helpless" was not been included in the analysis because of inconsistences in the database.

For the motivational aspects, the intrinsic motivation measures according to Tseng and Tsai [18] were applied to assess the learners' perception of the MOOC learning experience [8]. More specifically, Table 4 shows the motivational attitude with learning a new set of tools, utilizing the tools to finish the learning tasks and reflecting the knowledge gained from completing the learning activities. The findings reveal for both groups a remarkable high intrinsic motivation to learn with and learn about the tools, although the dropout group had a less motivated response in learning to use new tools.

Table 4. Intrinsic Motivations Measure of cloud-based tools after Tseng &Tsai [18]

Intrinsic Motivation	Completing learning activities (using cloud-based tools)		Learning to use new tools (which are cloud-based)		Reflecting knowledge (using the cloud-based tools)	
Students	finished	drop-out	finished	drop-out	finished	drop-out
Absolutely Unmotivated	0.70%	1.03%	0.00%	3.09%	0.00%	2.06%
Unmotivated	2.10%	5.15%	0.00%	3.09%	3.50%	3.09%
Motivated	29.37%	23.71%	18.18%	34.02%	25.87%	28.87%
Very Motivated	67.83%	70.10%	81.82%	59.79%	70.63%	65.98%

With respect to the usability aspects, the System Usability Scale (SUS) after Brooke [4] showed a good results with M=77.46 (σ=16.28) for students who had finished the course and M=59.94 (σ=16.51) for students who had dropped out. The perceived usability is significantly lower for the group of students who had not finished the MOOC compared with the other group.

Focusing on overall aspects of the MOOC, the 134 students belonging to the group who had not finished the MOOC were asked to answer open ended questions. Responses on the question to what they 'did the most like' confirmed the findings above but also revealed advantages of 'flexible schedule', 'methodology' and 'easy access to new knowledge'. Answers to the questions what they 'did not like at all' emphasized issues on 'the length of the videos', 'the lack of monitoring and feedback from tutors', 'participation in forums' and the 'effort to master activities'. Suggestions on the organization could improve to support the MOOC experience included 'more time and flexibility for finishing assignments', 'less content and assignments per week', and 'monitoring and feedback by tutors'. In the open-ended section, the participants indicated that they needed to improve their overall effort to succeed. Comments such as 'discipline', 'focus', 'time management and planning', 'developing digital abilities', 'active communication' were some of the initiatives required to complete the MOOC.

Interestingly, despite the fact that all 134 students who had not finished the MOOC, 131 (97.76%) consider MOOC as a useful way to study online courses, and 132 (98.51%) would also consider taking a MOOC in the future. An illustrative selection of reasons included 'setting is flexible', 'eliminates distances and optimizes time', 'learning methodology is effective and innovative', and 'it enables to acquire new knowledge' were some of the intrinsic desires.

4 Summary and Future Work

The issue of high attrition, low retention and low completion of students studying MOOCs is the main discussion among academics and students. This paper is an extension of an earlier study [9]. One main motivating factor that many seek to enroll in a MOOC was to find out what MOOC was and to encounter the MOOC experience. This study, however investigated the motivations of students who had enrolled in a MOOC and whose initial desire was complete the course but were non-completers due to a variety of reasons. A majority of students who had not completed noted personal reasons such as changes in their job, lack of employer's support or health reasons. In terms of academic reasons, some of the main problems which hinder the completion were difficulty in juggling work and study, technical inability, poor course design, and high demand in learning workload.

Interestingly, 98% of those who had not completed the MOOC consider MOOC as a useful way to study and would undertake a MOOC in the future. Many of these participants view the MOOC as providing a flexible alternative that eliminates geographical barriers in terms of time and distance. It also allows for another way to acquire new skills and knowledge.

The study revealed that there was no significant difference with the Computer Emotion Scale of happiness, sadness, anxiety, and anger, between the two groups of students. In terms of the System Usability Scale it is not surprising that the perceived usability is lower for the non-completers. For the Intrinsic Motivations Measure, the findings revealed a high motivation for both groups to learn, although the drop-out students were less motivated to learn to use new tools.

The next steps for future work are to include dynamic learning activities to capture the motivation and volition of the students to retain the students and the students' interests. This may include the use of serious games or gamification in the learning activities and ability to provide automatic feedback where relevant.

Acknowledgements. This paper is part of research collaboration resulting from visiting academic activities of Professor Christian Gütl at the School of Information Systems, Curtin University. The visits were supported and sponsored by School of Information Systems and Curtin Business School, Curtin University, and Institute for Information Systems and Computer Media (IICM) at Graz University of Technology.

References

1. Adamopoulos, A.: What Makes a Great MOOC? An Interdisciplinary Analysis of Student Retention in Online Courses. In: Proceedings of the 34th International Conference on Information Systems (ICIS), Milan, Italy (2013)
2. Bean, J., Metzner, B.S.: A Conceptual Model of Nontraditional Undergraduate Student Attrition. Review of Educational Research 55, 485–540 (1985)
3. Berge, Z.L., Huang, Y.P.: A Model for Sustainable Student Retention: A Holistic Perspective on the Student Dropout Problem with Special Attention to e-Learning. DEOSNEWS 13(5) (May 2004)
4. Brooke, J.: SUS: A 'quick and dirty' usability scale. Usability Evaluation in Industry. Taylor & Francis, London (1996)
5. Chamberlin, L., Parish, T.: MOOCs: Massive open online courses or massive and often obtuse courses? eLearn 8 (2011), `http://doi.acm.org/10.1145/2016016.2016017`, doi:10.1145/2016016.2016017
6. Croft, N., Dalton, A., Grant, M.: Overcoming Isolation in Distance Learning: Building a Learning Community through Time and Space. Journal for Education in the Built Environment 5(1) (July 2010)

7. Daniel, J.: Making sense of MOOCs: Musings in a maze of myth, paradox and possibility. Journal of Interactive Media in Education, 18 (2012), http://jime.open.ac.uk/2012/18 (accessed February 26, 2013)
8. Hernández Rizzardini, R., Amado-Salvatierra, H., Gütl, C.: Cloud-based Learning Environments: Investigating learning activities experiences from Motivation, Usability and Emotional Perspective. In: Proceedings of the 5th International Conference on Computer Supported Education, Aachen, Germany (May 2013)
9. Hernández Rizzardini, R., Gütl, C., Chang, V., Morales, M.: MOOC in Latin America: Implementation and Lessons Learned. In: 2nd International Workshop on Learning Technology for Education in Cloud (LTEC), Knowledge Management in Organizations, pp. 147–158. Springer Netherlands (2013)
10. Kay, R.H., Loverock, S.: Assessing emotions related to learning new software: The computer emotion scale. Computers in Human Behavior 24, 1605–1623 (2008)
11. Kizilcec, R.F., Piech, C., Schneider, E.: Deconstructing Disengagement: Analyzing Learner Subpopulations in Massive Open Online Courses. In: Proceedings of 3rd International Conference on Learning Analytics and Knowledge, Leuven, Belgium (2013), http://www.stanford.edu/~cpiech/bio/papers/deconstructingDisengagement.pdf. (accessed April 22, 2013)
12. Lee, Y., Choi, J., Kim, T.: Discriminating factors between completers of and dropouts from online learning courses. British Journal of Educational Technology 44(2), 328–337 (2013)
13. Liu, M., Kang, J., Cao, M., Lim, M., Ko, Y., Schmitz Weiss, A.: Understanding MOOCs as an Emerging Online Learning Tool: Perspectives from the Students. In: Proceedings of E-Learn (2013)
14. McAuley, A., Stewart, B., Siemens, G., Cormier, D.: The MOOC model for digital practice (2010), http://www.elearnspace.org/Articles/MOOC_Final.pdf (accessed February 2, 2013)
15. Rodriguez, O.: The concept of openness behind c and x-MOOCs (Massive Open Online Courses). Open Praxis 5(1), 67–73 (2013)
16. Rovai, A.P.: In search of higher persistence rates in distance education online programs. The Internet and Higher Education 6, 1–16 (2003), http://cmapspublic2.ihmc.us/rid%3D1150160110784_1923299501_2758/rovai%25202003%2520persistenace%2520in%2520de%2520and%2520online%2520ed-%2520theory.pdf (accessed February 2, 2014)
17. Siemens, G.: MOOCs are really a platform. Elearnspace (2012), http://www.elearnspace.org/blog/2012/07/25/moocs-are-really-a-platform/ (last edited July 25, 2012) (accessed 15 February 2013)
18. Tseng, S.C., Tsai, C.C.: Taiwan college students' self-efficacy and motivation of learning in online peer-assessment environments. Internet and Higher Education 13, 164–169 (2010)
19. Willging, P.A., Johnson, S.D.: Factors that Influence Students' Decision to Dropout of Online Courses. Journal of Asynchronous Learning Networks, 8(4) (December 2004)
20. Yang, D., Sinha, T., Adamson, D., Rose, C.P.: Turn on, Tune in, Drop out: Anticipating student dropouts in Massive Open Online Courses. In: NIPS Data-Driven Education Workshop (2013), http://lytics.stanford.edu/datadriveneducation/papers/yangetal.pdf (accessed February 2, 2014)

A Tale of Two Modes: Initial Reflections on an Innovative MOOC

Jane Sinclair, Russell Boyatt, Jonathan Foss, and Claire Rocks

Department of Computer Science, University of Warwick, Coventry, CV4 7AL, UK
{J.E.Sinclair,Russell.Boyatt,J.Foss,C.L.Rocks}@warwick.ac.uk

Abstract. Massive Open Online Courses (MOOCs) are offered by many universities, with hundreds thousands of people worldwide having registered for one or more of the many available courses. Despite the potential that has been claimed for these courses to transform education, in practice the majority are deeply conservative in maintaining the educational status quo. Lacking innovative pedagogic foundation and with the need for approaches that scale, many courses rely heavily on very traditional methods such as mini-lectures and quizzes. In particular, learner support is proving to be insufficient for many participants. This paper reports initial results and experience from developing and presenting a MOOC which provides both "traditional" and supported modes. We present the motivation and objectives for the course, discuss initial results and reflect on lessons learned in the process.

1 Introduction

Massive Open Online Courses (MOOCs) have recently shot to prominence with top universities competing to provide free online courses for all via platforms such as Coursera [8] and edX [11]. The term "MOOC" was originally coined to describe a connectivist approach to learning in which each participant sets their own learning goals and works, through social interaction and the development of digital artefacts, to generate knowledge in a network [24,7]. The term is now used more broadly, encompassing widely differing perspectives on learning theory, pedagogy, support and even the meaning of the basic terms "massive", "open" and "course" [4]. The predominant model has become the Coursera/edX type course (or xMOOC) [27,9] with these and similar platforms signing up rapidly increasing numbers of university partners [23,8] and now offering hundreds of courses free of charge to anyone who wishes to sign up. Many universities have invested substantially in providing this type of MOOC [34] despite a lack of evidence as to their effectiveness (and for what purposes) and dearth of knowledge on suitable pedagogy [4].

The rapid rise of the MOOC has been driven by high expectations of what they can achieve. It has been suggested that these courses will greatly reduce tuition costs by reducing teaching staff levels [34]; that they can democratise education by making high class tuition freely available for all [22]; that they can solve educational needs for developing countries by removing monetary and geographical limitations [19]; that they represent a disruptive educational technology which can challenge and reshape

L. Uden et al. (Eds.): LTEC 2014, CCIS 446, pp. 49–60, 2014.

existing norms [35] and that they "challenge universities' conventional societal role as purveyors of knowledge and credentials" [30].

Despite the envisaged potential for disruption and transformation of higher education, the majority of courses at the moment follow a fairly typical xMOOC model. Although there are differences between platforms, these large courses generally feature pre-recorded video lectures or mini presentations from subject experts, with quizzes (or other automated assessment), forum discussions and (sometimes) peer assessment. Material is often derived from courses taught in the university, as in, for example, the Software Engineering MOOC from Berkeley [13]. At one level, this is seen as a major benefit (since anyone, anywhere can now access modules similar to those studied by students enrolled at the university). However, such modules offer little flexibility to anyone who is not fully fluent in the digital literacies and independent learning skills required or who simply finds themself unable to cope with the pace and lack of support. This dissemination of pre-packaged, standardised fare is referred to by Lane and Kinser as the "MacDonaldization of Higher Education" [21]. Students who do succeed in their course are likely to find their reward is a MOOC certificate rather than an award of university level credits [3].

In recognition of the limitations, initiatives are emerging to address aspects of pedagogy and adaptivity. The "E-learning and Digital Cultures" MOOC from the University of Edinburgh was delivered on the Coursera platform but is noted for its tutor presence through live video conferencing [18]. Other work has attempted to account for different learning styles [16]. A more recent platform, NovoED [26] aims to support online courses with greater interaction. Supported by a number of major universities such as Stanford, NovoED incorporates real time feedback from learning analytics and aims to provide a social and collaborative experience.

Learning analytics provides a powerful predictive tool which can accurately identify students in danger of dropping out [1]. However, the question still remains as to what, in practice, can be done to assist students in danger and to support them in continuing with the course. This is an area of active research, the challenge being to find effective pedagogy and technical support which allows the limited staff effort combined with some model of peer support to be harnessed for maximum impact.

The issue of student support is a crucial one for the success of the MOOC enterprise. It represents a major difference between merely pushing out packaged learning materials and being able to offer a real educational service to individual learners. Within standard xMOOCs, there is evidence that existing models are insufficient to deliver this support. As a participant of Harvard's CS50X Computer Programming course put it: "Too few helpful students, and the questions of the confused majority will not be answered quickly enough, and the faculty are too outnumbered by the 100,000 students to keep up" [17]. The completion rate was 0.9%. Although many people who register for a MOOC generally do not even start the course, high drop-out rates may well be related to the fact that there are not enough participants who feel confident with the course material to answer questions in peer support forums.

Lack of support is frustrating to students in courses taken as spare time activities for those with interest and self-motivated learning skills. It becomes critical when the role of a MOOC is taken beyond that of the "take it or leave it" learning resource.

For example, a program introduced by San Jose State University and Udacity to run remedial courses in popular subjects ended in a failure rate of up to 71% [10]. Yet there is an indication that introductory and remedial classes with large enrolments are being perceived as particularly suitable for MOOC treatment [12]. In reality, students with remedial needs or those who just beginning their independent learning journey may not be equipped with the skills necessary to thrive in a MOOC.

There have been a number of initiatives to provide a more learner-focussed model of support. Vihavainen et al. [32] report on a programming MOOC in which a high level of support was provided by on-campus degree students. In a framework the authors call "Extreme Apprentice", the students providing tutor support were given credits towards their own degree for the work on the MOOC. Over 16% of students who registered completed at least 90% of the course tasks.

MOOCs can also be used as part of a more traditional tutored class such as a "flipped classroom" where students learn the basics from online presentations and use the face-to-face sessions to provide instructor input for problem solving and discussion [5,28]. This model of MOOC is about using staff time more beneficially rather than trying to provide education with one instructor per 50,000 students [34].

Whatever method of support is chosen it needs to be scalable and sustainable. Most universities have a great resource in terms of their PhD students who are often very experienced in helping out with on-campus undergraduate teaching. The "Extreme Apprentice" model of tuition-for-credit is appealing but does not transfer to PhD students who do not have credit-based assessment.

This paper reports on a computing MOOC offered in two separate, simultaneous modes. The first mode follows a "standard" approach, with all materials freely accessible and support provided via forums (mainly peer supported). The second approach adds support via regular real-time tutorial sessions and a tutor-monitored forum. For the second mode a (modest) payment was required. Engagement and achievements of students on each mode can thus be directly compared.

The MOOC is still in its first delivery, so full results for a run are not yet available. In this paper we describe the context for the MOOC and how it was set up. Some indicative preliminary results are presented together with reflection on the providers' perspective and lessons learned. We feel that the experience of staff developing such online courses is an important aspect of the MOOC narrative. While there have been some development-focussed reports and estimates of costs (for example by Belanger et al. [2] and Kolowick [20]) there has been only limited discussion of the necessary skills and the amount of input required from a staff perspective.

2 The Computing for Teachers MOOC: Context

In September 2014 a new computing curriculum is being introduced in UK schools. Computing will be a required subject for all children both in primary and secondary schools. Previously, many schools taught IT skills only. Despite the changes, there has been no formal, central initiative to train the teachers who will be required to teach the new curriculum. The University of Warwick (as part of the Network of Excellence organised by the UK's Computing at Schools organisation [6]) runs face to face activities and continuing professional development (CPD) sessions for teachers. This reaches a limited number of participants and is geographically restrictive. Supported in part by an award from Google's Computer Science for High Schools program a MOOC was developed for the needs of UK teachers. In practice, registration was open to all so there is a small number of non-teacher and non-UK participants. The course is aimed at teachers with no previous computing experience and provides preparation for teaching at a UK KS4 level (ages 14 to 16). Course content was based on the UK Teaching Agency's requirements for trainee computer science teachers [31]. There are three basic concerns for teachers approaching the subject.

- **Computing concepts** Areas of knowledge needed, covered at appropriate level.
- **Programming** Text based language suitable for KS4 assignments.
- **Teaching issues** Addressing issues of how to teach computing in the classroom.

The MOOC was designed to incorporate three strands relating to these aspects. The "Concepts" strand covered material relating to the Teaching Agency document; the "Programming" strand introduced practical programming in Python with lots of practical exercises and hands-on tasks; the "Teaching" strand made use of teachers' expertise to create resources on pedagogy and lesson planning.

The MOOC started in October 2013 and was presented as an initial introductory session followed by 8 main sessions spaced 2 weeks apart with an additional break over Christmas. The introduction helped participants find their way in the online learning environment and ensured everyone had a suitable programming environment to work with before the main work of the course began. Fortnightly release of materials allowed enough time for busy teachers to engage with the materials and attempt the exercises without leaving it too long and risking loss of momentum.

The CfT MOOC is different to many in that it is aimed at a specific group of learners and targeted towards CPD for a particular purpose. Teachers might be supposed to be a group who are highly effective independent learners and thus are able to manage their learning in the context of a MOOC. Given that the participants would soon be expected to teach computing, it also seemed reasonable to suppose that they would have a reasonable level of digital skills (although not necessarily be familiar with the specific technologies used in the course). Further, since many of the participants needed to develop the knowledge and skills in order to start teaching the topics themselves, it might also be supposed that their motivation to complete the course would be high. It might also be the case that an identified community with similar professional interests would find it easier to form learning communities and to become active in peer support through the peer support forums.

3 The Computing for Teachers MOOC: Development

This section outlines some of the design and development issues faced.

3.1 Platform and Programming Language

Choice of platform influences what is provided and so, to some degree, the pedagogy and approach adopted. The University of Warwick is a partner in the Future Learn initiative (developed by the UK's Open University) [14]. However, at the time the CfT

MOOC was being developed Future Learn was still at an early stage. It was therefore decided to use the learning environment, Moodle [25] as a framework for organising materials. Moodle is a VLE rather than a MOOC platform but local expertise was available to help create an environment adapted to our needs.

Although it would be possible to host videos locally, it was decided to use a hosting service to take of this. Vimeo [33] was chosen as a straight-forward and low cost hosting solution. For the real-time programming labs, Google Hangouts [15] were used, providing support for voice, video, text and screen communication.

The language taught was Python, chosen as an accessible but powerful text-based programming language. Introductory videos clearly explained how to install Python on different operating systems. Information on different development environments was also provided. However, in order to make the barrier to getting started as low as possible we provided a web-based environment using Skulpt [29] which provides immediate type-and-run functionality without the need for installation of any kind.

3.2 Different Modes

The MOOC was offered in two different modes.

Traditional. All materials were made freely available to participants. Peer support was provided through forums, with some intervention from tutors. Progress was assessed using quizzes (for both programming and computing concepts). Participants will receive a certificate with a record of their achievement at the end of the course.

Supported. Payment of £100 was required for this mode. In addition to the above, participants had access to small group hangouts where they could receive immediate help from experienced PhD/post-doctoral tutors. An additional forum was provided with guaranteed tutor response. Students on this mode will be also undertake a programming task which will be marked by course staff and for which feedback will be provided. A separate certificate will be awarded. Finally, a post-course workshop will be held. As well as providing more support for those who require it, the two modes allow direct comparison and evaluation of students on each.

3.3 Resources Provided

The following were made available for each main teaching session.

- **Computing concepts** video, slides, quiz.
- **Programming** video, slides, quiz, lab sessions and solutions.
- **Teaching issues** video or audio recording from teachers or support organisation.

Additional exercise and solutions were made available where appropriate. Forums and links to further resources were also provided. We had not originally planned to provide transcripts of videos but, following a request from a hearing-impaired student the process of transcription was begun (although this remains to be completed).

4 Initial Results

The course is still in its first delivery. The results given here provide a preliminary perspective based on evaluation of the first two sessions. Data is being collected both through Moodle's own logging system and via our own evaluation forms completed by participants at the start of the course and after every session.

Registration
Registration was allowed up to the launch of session 2. From this point, further requests to join were turned down. We were prepared to accept up to 100 registration on the supported mode, but, as shown in Figure 1, only 30 participants signed up.

	Registrations	Never logged in
Traditional	618	73
Supported	30	0
Total	648	73

Fig. 1. Registrations on the two different modes of the MOOC

Participants' Background
Over 90% of participants were UK-based teachers. Figure 2 shows other participant information taken from the pre-course survey. Nearly a quarter of the participants thought they had good knowledge of computing already. Over three quarters were confident about teaching. About two thirds were familiar with online learning.

Participation
Figure 3 shows the number of accesses logged by Moodle for resources from main teaching sessions 1 to 4. This will include individuals making repeated accesses but gives an indication of which resources participants are making greatest use of. Students could access each quiz as many times as they wished (perhaps completing part of it and returning later) but they could submit each quiz only once. Figures for transcripts in later sessions are not available (n/a) as these are currently still being produced. Also, numbers of quiz attempts in Session 3 are missing as there was a problem in recording these figures. As would be expected there is a steady drop-off in successive weeks. Many more accesses are observed to the "active" parts of the course (quizzes and labs) than the "passive" learning materials. For some, this may be because they are using these elements to check that their existing knowledge is sufficient without engaging with all elements of the course. Participants appear to be putting the greatest amount of their time into tackling the programming labs and it is interesting to see that the majority of people who access Lab A each session also progress to looking at the (more challenging) part C. Transcripts of videos were not initially planned and the effort to produce them

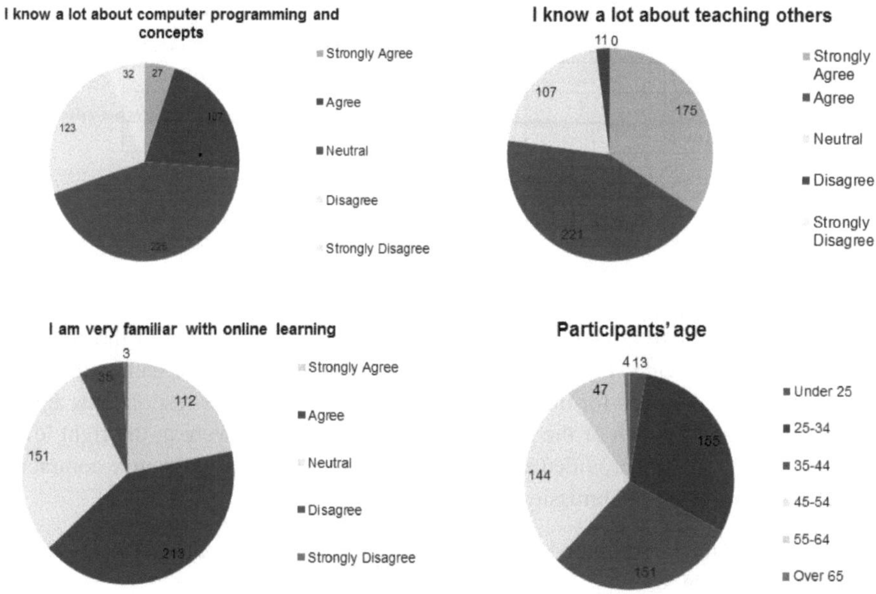

Fig. 2. Indicative background information from the pre-course survey

	Header	Concepts			Programming			Labs		
	Transcript	Slides	Transcript	Quiz	Slides	Transcript	Quiz	Lab A	Lab B	Lab C
Session 1	146	260	173	597	266	70	448	547	371	322
Session 2	71	179	124	458	173	94	383	376	236	220
Session 3	64	74	n/a	n/a	67	n/a	n/a	297	210	200
Session 4	63	90	n/a	278	91	n/a	133	146	121	122

Fig. 3. Preliminary participation figures for the first four sessions

began only after the start of the course. However, these have proved surprisingly popular and we have received a number of comments on how useful they are.

Scores

Figure 4 shows the results obtained in each quiz. Each participant is allowed only one submission for each quiz. As this is the first run of the course, and the first time we have set quizzes at this level, the scores may be assessing our success in question setting as much as the participants' ability to answer. However, the figures suggest that participants who submit quiz solutions are generally taking the task seriously and obtaining good results. Although numbers decrease from one session to the next, it is interesting to note that some participants are still working on the earlier material and quiz submissions continue to be received. There is no cut off date for this (until the very end of the course) and some participants are obviously still making progress although they are now many weeks behind the release of materials.

	Concepts		Programming	
	No. submitted	Ave. score/10	No. submitted	Ave. score/10
Session 1	142	7.74	126	7.86
Session 2	119	9.04	105	7.61
Session 4	78	7.64	41	8.93

Fig. 4. Quiz scores from sessions 1 to 4

Qualitative Feedback

A full analysis of qualitative feedback will be conducted once the run of the course is ended. Here we provide some indicative extracts from the feedback gathered via the end of session evaluations for the first three sessions. Over 98% of respondents agreed or strongly agreed to each of the statements that the materials were at the right level, were well produced and provided a good introduction to the topics. Positive comments common to a number of submissions include:

- gentle introduction (not too intimidating) but non-patronising and with enough material to challenge;
- good use of simple examples and avoidance of jargon;
- the programming practicals and quizzes;
- good to see the "faces" behind the course.

There are also some very useful observations on areas for improvement including:

- shorter videos (the longest is 24 minutes) and snappier presentations;
- increased volume on audio recordings;
- provision of handy look-up guide/index to topics covered and where;
- use most recent version of Python used.

All of these will be helpful for future runs of the course. The last one is particularly interesting. The initial plan was to use Python version 3. However, choosing the Skulpt environment meant using Python 2.7. In fact, the situation is even worse in that Skulpt has certain features relating to the print statement which are neither fully 2.7 nor 3. A mapping of all the topics to be covered and a guide of where to find them plus an easy syntax guide were also commonly requested, showing learners' need to gain a high level view and to quickly reference things they need.

5 Reflections

Although we have so far gathered preliminary results only, some useful insights have already been gained.

Effectiveness of Supported Mode

The limited interest in the supported mode (only 30 registrations) was surprising. The cost was very low (for the additional services offered) and it had been thought that many schools would be keen to sponsor teachers to learn the necessary skills for the teaching they will soon be expected to do. Teachers would have the added benefit of a certificate attesting to their programming skills as evidenced by the assignment.

Hangout sessions were set up with 5 participants to 1 tutor. However, the take-up has been low and in practice 1 or 2 dedicated participants join their tutor for each hangout. We will be exploring the reasons for this in the end of course survey, however, factors suggested so far include difficulty with the timings (teachers often have to attend evening events), lack of progress with the work and a dislike (or disinclination to get started with) the hangout technology.

Environment Choices Made

Moodle provides a good learning environment which is familiar to many teachers. "Doing it yourself" also provides a lot of flexibility and control. However, it does mean that the MOOC development team is not just responsible for developing learning materials but also takes on many other decisions and responsibilities, from video hosting to dealing with user registration. When time is short this can be an onerous task. The use of an external video hosting site proved to be a good decision, relieving the team of one aspect of management.

Although Skulpt is very useful as an initial web-based environment for getting started with no installation required, it has proved to be limiting. The problem of the version of Python supported was mentioned above. Also, there are issues with supporting certain aspects such as file handling which mean that moving on to running "real" Python becomes necessary. With hindsight, it may be better simply to do this at the start of the course.

Costs

Producing a MOOC is no small undertaking. Effort is obviously required to develop teaching and learning materials, but time and personnel are also needed to record, edit, transcribe and build the sessions. Administration is needed both for the system and for tasks such as participant registration. Ongoing input is needed to support the hangouts and monitor course queries and forum questions. The team also met weekly for management meetings and MOOC troubleshooting. Obviously, it is hoped that most of the materials will be reusable and subsequent runs of the course will be much less effort-intensive, however, the amount of time needed initially should not be underestimated.

We were grateful for support from a university film crew to help produce a good quality introductory video for each session. However, the time they could offer was limited and all of the teaching videos were produced and edited by members of the MOOC team themselves using standard capture and editing software. Resources needed included: equipment and software for video and audio recording, lecture capture and editing; server; video hosting facility; Moodle platform; programming environment; resource email account.

A rough estimate of costs incurred in developing and running this relatively small MOOC is £22,000. This is a conservative figure based on estimates of time spent and does not include the overheads that would normally be charged to a project.

Lessons Learned

Although the CfT team members are experienced in teaching computer science, producing and delivering this MOOC has required development of new skills. The different audience, level and mode of delivery have necessitated the development of completely new teaching materials, rather than simply reworking a course delivered to undergraduates. We have experimented with the use of a number of different technologies and platforms and gained experience in lecture capture, audio recording and innovative use of graphics tablets. These are all very useful skills to bring back in to the university context and to incorporate in undergraduate and postgraduate teaching.

There is also a lot to learn about MOOC teaching. Good pace, very short chunks of teaching materials and practical activities are proving important for participants. In addition, we have been surprised by the popularity of transcripts. Conversely, the lack of take-up for the supported mode and low attendance at hangouts indicate that this has not been a particularly effective means of support.

Members of the CfT team have not been given remission from other duties so all work on the MOOC has been fitted in around existing commitments. This has proved to be very difficult to sustain at times and on occasion, the delivery of materials for a MOOC session has continued to the last moment. Further, development of a MOOC is very different to the individual face-to-face courses we are used to presenting. It requires project management and forward planning to a degree we perhaps underestimated at the outset.

Learners' Progress

The initial expectation was that the more homogeneous learning community of teachers would make our task easier in that participants would have similar objectives and commonality of background. They might be assumed to be good independent learners and many have a high extrinsic motivation in the need to teach this material very soon. However, teachers are also extremely busy and, even with fortnightly sessions, many have fallen behind. It is interesting to note that many started to engage very late into the course but have since been making good progress. Unlike many courses where it seems that, once behind, participants generally drop out, many of our teachers are coming back to the course and moving at their own pace as and when they can. Thus the usual learning analytics predictors of drop out may not be entirely applicable in this case. It may be that the temporal structure usually associate with a MOOC may not be helpful in all cases.

Because of the shortage of time, for many of our participants the overriding need is to have material to deliver in the classroom. Developing their own wider understanding of the topic is seen as a luxury for which there may not be time. While learning the fundamental concepts of computing and the basics of programming should be achievable for all, it still requires time to become familiar with ideas and practice the practical aspects. Schools expecting teachers to learn these new skills must recognise the need to allow the necessary time. Otherwise there is a real risk of the topic being badly taught by teachers who have not had time to gain confidence in a new area.

6 Conclusions

Overall, the CfT MOOC is proving successful, but there are a number of aspects which require reconsidering for a future run. The supported version has not proved popular and, although a full evaluation will be conducted when this run of the course is over, it is likely that we would not repeat this part. Any additional resources may be better-placed in supporting all participants with active monitoring a responses to the programming forum and additional "community building" activities such as weekly topical discussion threads to encourage active engagement .

The British Computer Society is currently piloting a scheme to offer accreditation for teachers moving into computing and a we hope that in future it will be possible to gain automatic accreditation for successful participants in our course.

We are also considering further ways to best support teachers, for example with a "mini MOOC" with reduced content to be offered in a short time period, for example during a week in the summer holidays, or with a MOOC directed at school students.

References

1. Barber, R., Sharkey, M.: Course correction: using analytics to predict course success. In: Proceedings of the 2nd International Conference on Learning Analytics and Knowledge, pp. 259–262. ACM (2012)
2. Belanger, Y., Thornton, J.: Bioelectricity: A quantitative approach. duke university's first mooc. Technical report, Duke University (2013) (accessed March 19, 2013)
3. Billington, P.J., Fronmueller, M.P.: Moocs and the future of higher education. Journal of Higher Education Theory & Practice 13 (2013)
4. Boyatt, R., Joy, M., Rocks, C., Sinclair, J.: What (use) is a mooc? In: The 2nd International Workshop on Learning Technology for Education in Cloud, pp. 133–145. Springer (2014)
5. Bruff, D.O., Fisher, D.H., McEwen, K.E., Smith, B.E.: Wrapping a mooc: Student perceptions of an experiment in blended learning. Journal of Online Learning & Teaching 9(2) (2013)
6. Computing at School, `http://www.computingatschool.org.uk/` (accessed March 10, 2014)
7. Cormier, D., Siemens, G.: The open course: Through the open door–open courses as research, learning, and engagement. Educause Review 45(4), 30–32 (2010)
8. Coursera, `https://www.coursera.org/` (accessed March 19, 2013)
9. Daniel, J.: Making sense of moocs: Musings in a maze of myth, paradox and possibility. Journal of Interactive Media in Education 3 (2012)
10. Devlin, K.: MOOC Mania Meets the Sober Reality of Education. Huffington Post (August 19, 2013)
11. edX, `https://www.edx.org/` (accessed March 19, 2013)
12. Fain, P., Rivard, R.: Outsourcing public higher ed. Inside Higher Ed. (March 13, 2013)
13. Fox, A.: What was it like to teach a mooc (2013), `http://www.armandofox.com/2013/01/14/what-was-it-like-to-teach-a-mooc/` (accessed March 10, 2014)
14. Futurelearn, `http://futurelearn.com/` (accessed March 19, 2013)
15. Google Hangout, `http://www.google.com/+/learnmore/hangouts/` (accessed march 10, 2014)
16. Grünewald, F., Meinel, C., Totschnig, M., Willems, C.: Designing moocs for the support of multiple learning styles. In: Hernández-Leo, D., Ley, T., Klamma, R., Harrer, A. (eds.) EC-TEL 2013. LNCS, vol. 8095, pp. 371–382. Springer, Heidelberg (2013)
17. Kern, J.: Learning from harvard: Mooc story, `http://elearningindustry.com/subjects/concepts/item/450-learning-from-harvard-mooc-story-pt4` (accessed March 19, 2013)

18. Knox, J.K.: The Forum, the Sardine Can and the Fake: contesting, adapting and practicing the Massive Open Online Course. Selected Papers of Internet Research 3 (2013)
19. Koller, D.: What we're learning from online education. In: TED Talk (June 2012), http://www.youtube.com/watch
20. Kolowich, S.: The professors who make the MOOCs. In: The Chronicle of Higher Education (March 25, 2013)
21. Lane, J., Kinser, K.: MOOCs and the McDonaldization of Global Higher Education. Education 30536, 1 (2012)
22. Lewin, T.: Instruction for masses knocks down campus walls. New York Times, Newspaper article (2012)
23. Lewin, T.: Universities abroad join partnerships on the web. The New York Times (February 21, 2013)
24. McAuley, A., Stewart, B., Siemens, G., Cormier, D.: Massive Open Online Courses. Digital ways of knowing and learning. The Mooc Model For Digital Practice (2010)
25. Moodle, https://moodle.org/ (accessed March 10, 2014)
26. NovoED, https://novoed.com/ (accessed March 10, 2014)
27. Rodriguez, C.O.: MOOCs and the AI-Stanford like courses: Two successful and distinct course formats for massive open online courses. In: Learning (2012)
28. Sandeen, C.: Integrating MOOCS into Traditional Higher Education: The Emerging MOOC 3.0 Era. Change: The Magazine of Higher Learning 45(6), 34–39 (2013)
29. Skulpt, http://www.skulpt.org (accessed March 10, 2014)
30. Stewart, B.: Massiveness + openness = new literacies of participation? Journal of Online Learning & Teaching 9(2) (2013)
31. Teaching Agency, UK Department for Education. Subject knowledge requirements for entry into computer science teacher training, http://www.education.gov.uk/ (accessed March 10, 2014)
32. Vihavainen, A., Luukkainen, M., Kurhila, J.: Multi-faceted support for mooc in programming. In: SIGITE 2012 (2012)
33. Vimeo, http://www.vimeo.com (accessed March 10, 2014)
34. Young, J.R.: Inside the coursera contract: How an upstart company might profit from free courses. The Chronicle of Higher Education (July 19, 2012)
35. Yuan, L., Powell, S.: Moocs and open education: Implications for higher education. Cetis White Paper (2013)

The Coordinated Use of Digital Technologies in Learning Environments

Manuel Santos-Trigo and Isaid Reyes-Martínez

Centre for Research and Advanced Studies, Cinvestav-IPN, Mexico
{msantos,ireyes}@cinvestav.mx

Abstract. The purpose of this paper is to outline a framework to reflect on the extent to which the coordinated use of several digital technologies offers learners diverse opportunities to construct mathematical knowledge. An example is used to argue that different technologies could provide distinct affordances for learners to represent, explore, and solve mathematical tasks. Thus, YouTube videos are used to foster problem formulation and communication, the use of GeoGebra becomes important to represent and analyse the task from visual, dynamic, and graphic approaches. In addition, online resources (WolframAlpha and Wikipedia) are used to deal with algebraic operations involved in the algebraic model of the task, and to introduce information needed to review or comprehend embedded concepts. Finally, in order for the tools to be instrumental for students, it is important to take into account information related to the learners' tool appropriation in which they transform an artefact into a problem-solving tool.

Keywords: Digital tools, mathematical problem solving, tool affordances and appropriation process.

1 Introduction

The developments and availability of digital technologies have been transforming the ways people communicate, obtain information, develop, and comprehend disciplinary knowledge. Schmidt & Cohen [1] pointed out that with more people involved in the virtual world there are more opportunities for all to generate and share human knowledge and creativity. The tendency or pattern in technology development seems to be the continuous appearance of new tools and the need for individuals to quickly learn their use in order to incorporate them into daily activities and practices. Then, the challenge for institutions is clear as Cohen and Schmidt [1] put it "as global connectivity continues its unprecedented advance, many old institutions and hierarchies will have to adapt or risk becoming obsolete, irrelevant to modern society"(p. 11). The coordinated use of digital technologies opens up diverse ways to identify, formulate, represent, explore, and solve problems in different disciplines. Consequently, new routes emerge for learners to construct and comprehend disciplinary knowledge. How do learning environments need to be transformed in order to cope and take advantages of digital developments? The discussion of this question becomes

L. Uden et al. (Eds.): LTEC 2014, CCIS 446, pp. 61–71, 2014.

important to think of learning scenarios in which learners rely systematically on the coordinated use of digital technologies to develop disciplinary knowledge and problem solving skills. To illustrate what the use of technology could bring to learning environments, a mathematical task that involves a variation phenomenon is used to discuss how technology could provide opportunities for learners to engage in mathematical thinking throughout problem solving experiences. The article includes a brief review of the field of engineering design and its relation with science developments. An emerging theme in this review is that the design of an artefact does not finish when the product fulfills technical specifications and leaves the designer office; it involves paying attention to users' appropriation process of the artefact to transform it into a problem-solving tool.

2 The Design of Artefacts and Users' Appropriation Process

Engineering design is a purposeful activity bound by specifications and constraints and an eminently collaborative enterprise. It involves an interactive process in which the design is tested and modified and it often offers several solutions to a particular problem [2]. In general, the design and construction of artefacts are tasks that require the participation of experts in several fields including science of materials, control, ergonomics, mathematics, and others disciplines. Any design is framed around a set of technical standards that any artefact needs to fulfil in order to be realised and available to user communities. However, as Béguin [3] pointed out the design of artefacts does not finish when the tool or object fulfils material and technical requirements; it should include how users transform the artefact into an instrument. Then, how do individuals develop the needed expertise to use those artefacts efficiently in problem solving activities? This question becomes important to identify and delve into a research area that examines ways in which subjects transform an artefact (physical devise) into an instrument to solve problems. Then, what information and actions are important to characterize the process to transform and artefact into an instrument? Hadolt, Hörbst & Müller- Rockstroh [4] cited a four-phase model [5] that includes appropriation, objectification, incorporation, and conversion activities. The authors stress that the incorporation of artefacts into practices depends on social, cultural, and economic conditions. Trouche [6] pointed out that "an instrument can be considered an extension of the body, a functional organ made up of an artefact component (an artefact, or the part of an artefact mobilized in the activity) and a psychological component" (p. 285). The artefact's characteristics (ergonomics and constraints) and the schemata developed by the students during the activities are important for them to transform the artefact into a problem-solving instrument. In this respect, Trouche [6] related the students' psychological component to the construction of a scheme with three functions: "a pragmatic function (it allows the agent to do something), a heuristic function (it allows the agent to anticipate and plan actions), and an epistemic function (it allows the agent to understand what he is doing)" (p. 286). Then, tool appropriation depends on cognitive schemata that students or users develop while using the tool to represent and explore problems.

3 Mathematical Learning Environments and Technologies: The Role of Tasks

The aim in using digital technology is to empower learners with affordances that amplify and enhance their ways to construct knowledge. Teachers play an important role in providing conditions for students to use technology in problem solving approaches. Tasks are key elements for teachers to guide, foster, and analyse the students' processes involved in comprehending and constructing mathematical knowledge. "The purpose of a task is to initiate mathematically fruitful activity that leads to a transformation in what learners are sensitise to notice and competent to carry out" [7] (p. 25). Similarly, Blum [8] pointed out that "...tasks are the substance for the cognitive activities of leaners. For teachers, tasks are a crucial element to orchestrate lessons and to clarify the aims of instruction as solving these tasks requires the competencies that students are to acquire" (p. 3). The use of digital technology offers learners an opportunity to extend ways of reasoning about the problems; however, representing and exploring mathematical tasks through the use of digital technologies bring in new challenges for teachers that include the development of an expertise in the tools use in order to identify and analyse what changes to contents and teaching practice are fostered through its use. As Ren [9] pointed out "the accelerated development in technology makes more acute the shortage of instructor knowledge about the effective use of technologies; good teachers who are well prepared are always in short supply" (p. xi). "The point of setting tasks for learners is to get them actively making sense of phenomena and exercising their powers and their emerging skills" [7] (p. 69). Thus, tasks are the vehicle for learners to focus on fundamental concepts that are developed through one's own actions and social interactions [10]. With the use of digital artefacts, learners become active participants in the learning process since these artefacts offer a rich diversity of opportunities to represent and explore the tasks from distinct perspectives. Learners also could share and discuss their ideas via communication technologies such as FaceTime, Tweeter or Facebook, and consult online information to contrast or extend their mathematical concepts comprehension.

With the use of technology learners could search for online information and resources to complement, extend or contrast what they have studied in their regular class. This information includes consulting online resources such as textbooks, Wikipedia, WolframAlpha computational knowledge engine, and online ad hoc videos. What criteria should students apply or follow in order to select and discriminate online information? How should students analyse the available information? It is evident that the existence and the learners' easy access to multiple online resources do not warrantee that students can select and use them efficiently in their learning experiences; students need to critically assess and monitor what information is pertinent or relevant and ways to use online resources. "Any task, particularly problem solving and modelling tasks, can focus learners' attention to the immediate "doing" (calculations, representation, etc.); but unless special steps are taken to promote further engagement, there is seldom motivation for abstraction, rigor, or conceptualization beyond that necessary for the current problem" [11] (p. 94).

Recently, the coordinated use of multiple purpose technologies (internet, or communication technology) and mathematical action technologies (GeoGebra) has provided basis to transform learning materials such as textbooks into e-books that incorporate interactive text, audio, video and animation. An e-book can be read with e-book readers, with a tablet, a smartphone or a computer and offers diverse opportunities for students to develop their learning experiences. Davidson & Carliner [12] mentioned that e-books not only are part of the most recent publishing revolution; but also their use will challenge instruction. In accordance to Roschelle et, al. [13] "The goal in the design of new digital texts must be to cue a stronger, more active relationship between a reader and the text and to support the reader's development of skills and strategies for engaging productively with big ideas" (p. 36).

3.1 Fostering the Formulation of Problems and the Use of Technology

Different digital technologies offer distinct opportunities for learners to engage in mathematical thinking. Thus, the existence of different types of technologies makes necessary to identify what a particular technology can offer to learners during the process of comprehending mathematical ideas and solving problems. In this context, the coordinated use of digital technologies appears relevant throughout all problem-solving episodes including problem formulation, comprehension, representation, exploration, generalization, and communication.

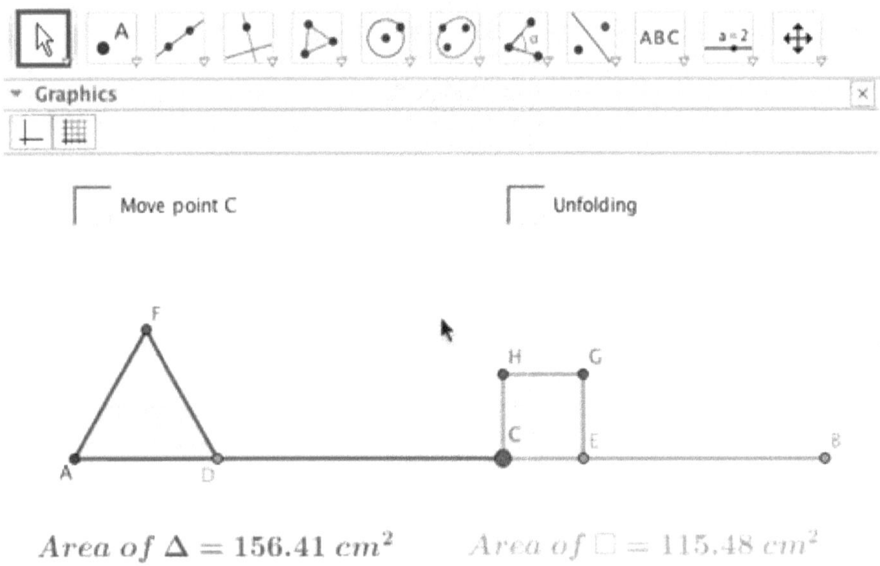

Fig. 1. What happens to both figures when point C is moved along segment AB?

For instance, with the coordinated use of dynamic geometry environments (GeoGebra) and YouTube videos, students can observe the behaviours of mathematical objects and pose questions to identify possible relations among those objects. For example, Fig. 1 shows a dynamic representation involving an equilateral triangle, a square, and a fixed segment. Learners can measure directly the sides and angles of each figure and discuss what properties they have. Then, Students are asked to focus their attention to what happens to the behaviour of the figures when point C is moved along the segment. What mathematical questions can they pose? Students can explore the objects properties by analysing the configuration directly in YouTube (http://www.youtube.com/watch?v=iScN_j3Cdh0). In addition, students can consult online resources to review properties of the involved figures (http://en.wikipedia.org/wiki/Equilateral_triangle).

Comment. In this dynamic configuration, students can observe that point C divides segment AB in two segments AC and CB. Then, a question they might pose is how to draw an equilateral triangle and a square with the lengths of those segments. Thus, the idea in providing a dynamic configuration is to encourage students to observe mathematical behaviours and properties of involved objects and express them in terms of questions or problems that eventually need to be solved. That is, the questions they pose become a platform to engage them in mathematical thinking.

3.2 The Use of a Spreadsheet Tool

Students can rely on different tools to explore the mathematical behaviour exhibited by the involved objects. For example, they can use a spreadsheet tool to quantify and explore properties and possible relations among those objects. Fig. 2 shows a table where the position of point C and length of AC is used to find areas of the involved figures and other relationships between the figures. Based on the table data, learners can explore the extent to which some of parameters change as a result of moving point C along segment AB.

By changing the position of point C (first column: Triangle P) it is observed that when point C is close to point A, then the area of the formed triangles are smaller than the area of the squares; however, when point C is close to point B then the area of the squares become larger than the triangles. Here, some questions can be posed "Is there a position for point C where both areas (of the triangle and the area of the square) are the same?" or how does the sum of both areas (triangle & square) behave when point C is moved along segment AB? Does the sum of the areas have a minimum value?

The table becomes a tool for students to explore these questions, for instance, they can refine the interval, making the variation of point C small, to identify where the area of the figures gets close. Fig. 2 shows results of the variation of parameter (first row) when segment AC change 10 units (first column) each time. It is observed that the point where the areas are equal lies on interval [50, 60].

Triangle Perimeter	Side Triangle	Square Perimeter	Side Square	Height Triangle	Area Triangle	Area Square	Dif of Areas	Sum of Areas	Delta
0.000000	0.00	100.000000	25.00	0.00	0.00	625.00	-625.0000	625.00000	10.000000
10.000000	3.33	90.000000	22.50	2.89	4.81	506.25	-501.4387	511.06125	
20.000000	6.67	80.000000	20.00	5.77	19.25	400.00	-380.7549	419.24500	
30.000000	10.00	70.000000	17.50	8.66	43.30	306.25	-262.9487	349.55127	
40.000000	13.33	60.000000	15.00	11.55	76.98	225.00	-148.0199	301.98003	
50.000000	16.67	50.000000	12.50	14.43	120.28	156.25	-35.96869	276.53130	
60.000000	20.00	40.000000	10.00	17.32	173.21	100.00	73.205081	273.20508	
70.000000	23.33	30.000000	7.50	20.21	235.75	56.25	179.50136	292.00136	
80.000000	26.67	20.000000	5.00	23.09	307.92	25.00	282.92014	332.92014	
90.000000	30.00	10.000000	2.50	25.98	389.71	6.25	383.46143	395.96143	
100.000000	33.33	0.000000	0.00	28.87	481.13	0.00	481.12522	481.12522	

Fig. 2. A table showing length of segment AC as the perimeter of triangle ADF, its side, perimeter of square CEGH, etc. Changing the position of point C 10 units each time.

By focusing on the interval [50, 60] and making the variation of point C smaller, a better approximation to get the position for C to get both areas equal. Fig. 3, shows an approximation for the position of C at the interval [53.265, 53.266].

Triangle Perimeter	Side Triangle	Square Perimeter	Side Square	Height Triangle	Area Triangle	Area Square	Dif of Areas	Sum of Areas	Delta
53.265000	17.76	46.735000	11.68	15.38	136.50	136.51	-0.007079	273.01294	0.000100
53.265100	17.76	46.734900	11.68	15.38	136.50	136.51	-0.005982	273.01287	
53.265200	17.76	46.734800	11.68	15.38	136.50	136.51	-0.004886	273.01280	
53.265300	17.76	46.734700	11.68	15.38	136.50	136.51	-0.003789	273.01273	
53.265400	17.76	46.734600	11.68	15.38	136.50	136.51	-0.002692	273.01266	
53.265500	17.76	46.734500	11.68	15.38	136.51	136.51	-0.001595	273.01259	
53.265600	17.76	46.734400	11.68	15.38	136.51	136.51	-0.000499	273.01251	
53.265700	17.76	46.734300	11.68	15.38	136.51	136.51	0.000598	273.01244	
53.265800	17.76	46.734200	11.68	15.38	136.51	136.51	0.001695	273.01237	
53.265900	17.76	46.734100	11.68	15.38	136.51	136.50	0.002791	273.01230	
53.266000	17.76	46.734000	11.68	15.38	136.51	136.50	0.003888	273.01223	

Fig. 3. Shows a position for C where the areas are almost equal

Comment. The use of the spreadsheet tool offers learners an opportunity to quantify some figure attributes in order to examine the variation of those attributes or parameters. A key conceptual issue here is to capture an interval where the variation of the parameters shows a particular behaviour. For instance, by making the variation of point C smaller and smaller, it was observed that the differences between the area of the triangle and square became small and therefore the both areas become almost equal. (http://www.youtube.com/watch?v=NlXrzjDXJkE).

3.3 A Dynamic Exploration

With a Dynamic Geometry Environment such as GeoGebra is possible to graph the area behaviours of the family of triangles and squares that are formed when point C is moved along segment AB. Fig. 4 shows the graphs of triangle and square areas and the graph of the sum of those areas.

The graphs show at what position of point C (approximate solution) the area of both figures gets the same value and where the sum of those areas reaches its minimum value. It is important to observe that the graphs of involved relations were achieved without making explicit an algebraic model of the situation. In addition, students can analyse how certain parameters behave by observing the information provided by the dynamic, graph, and table approaches (Fig. 4). (http://www.geogebratube.org/student/m90726).

Comment. The use of diverse digital technologies offers learners different angles to analyse variation phenomena. The visual approach shows how the areas of the figures change for different position of point C and it became important to focus on finding where both areas area equal. The use of the table was important to explore quantitatively the parameters' behaviours and to engage in an approximation process through the idea of limit. The continuous approach showed graphically rates of change associated with both areas and provides useful information to contrast for example the sum of the areas and the point where both became equal.

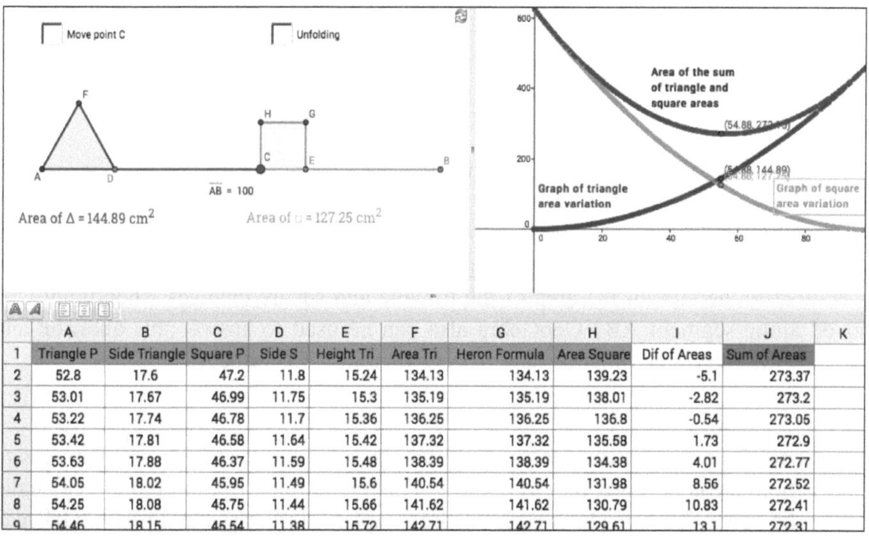

	A	B	C	D	E	F	G	H	I	J	K
1	Triangle P	Side Triangle	Square P	Side S	Height Tri	Area Tri	Heron Formula	Area Square	Dif of Areas	Sum of Areas	
2	52.8	17.6	47.2	11.8	15.24	134.13	134.13	139.23	-5.1	273.37	
3	53.01	17.67	46.99	11.75	15.3	135.19	135.19	138.01	-2.82	273.2	
4	53.22	17.74	46.78	11.7	15.36	136.25	136.25	136.8	-0.54	273.05	
5	53.42	17.81	46.58	11.64	15.42	137.32	137.32	135.58	1.73	272.9	
6	53.63	17.88	46.37	11.59	15.48	138.39	138.39	134.38	4.01	272.77	
7	54.05	18.02	45.95	11.49	15.6	140.54	140.54	131.98	8.56	272.52	
8	54.25	18.08	45.75	11.44	15.66	141.62	141.62	130.79	10.83	272.41	
9	54.46	18.15	45.54	11.38	15.72	142.71	142.71	129.61	13.1	272.31	

Fig. 4. Three representations of the problems to analyse area variation of a family of equilateral triangles and squares

3.4 An Algebraic Model

Given the perimeter of an equilateral triangle/square, how to find its area? In the problem, segment AB measures 100 units, and if x is the length of segment AC, then the length of segment CB will be *100-x*. Based on this information, the area of equilateral triangle and the square having those corresponding perimeters are:

$$A_T(x) = \frac{x^2}{12\sqrt{3}} \text{ and } A_S(x) = \frac{(100-x)^2}{16} \tag{1}$$

Thus, to determine the value of x for which both areas are equal implies to solve

$$\left(\frac{x}{3}\right)^2 \frac{\sqrt{3}}{4} = \left(\frac{100-x}{4}\right)^2 \tag{2}$$

Fig. 5 shows, the solution provided by WolframAlpha.

Input

$$\frac{x^2}{12\sqrt{3}} = \frac{1}{16}(100-x)^2$$

Solutions

$$x = \frac{300}{3-2\sqrt[4]{3}}$$

$$x = \frac{300}{3+2\sqrt[4]{3}}$$

Fig. 5. What x determines the same areas?.

By using GeoGebra, it is possible to find the solution geometrically. Fig. 6 shows the points where the graphs of the area get intersected.

How does the sum of the area of the triangle and square changes when point C is moved along segment AB? GeoGebra also can be used to answer this question and Fig. 7 shows where the function sum reaches its minimum value.

Comment. A key aspect in constructing the algebraic model of the problem was to express both areas in terms of a variable x. This model then is explored algebraically to find the value of x for which both areas are equal. Similarly, both area models can be graphed to find the intersection points. In the context of the problem only one solution is considered.

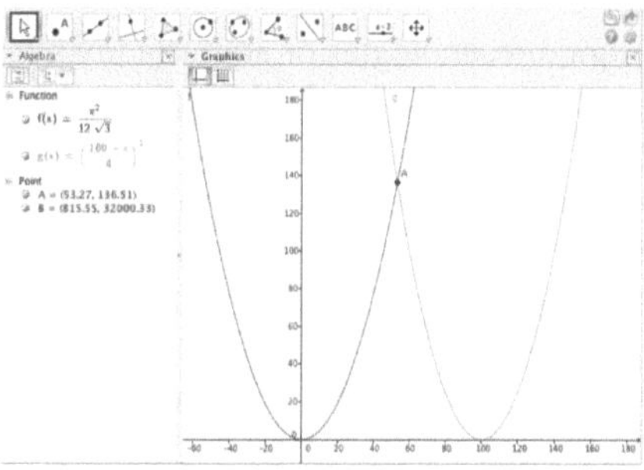

Fig. 6. A geometric solution showing where the function areas of the triangle and square are equal

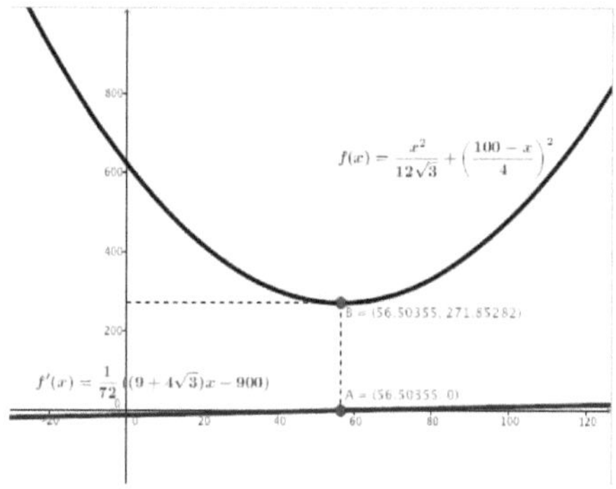

Fig. 7. Finding the minimum value of the function sum of the area of the triangle and square

4 Concluding Remarks

To what extent could technology developments and available digital tools provide conditions to structure robust learning environments to engage students in knowledge construction? Throughout this contribution, it is argued that the coordinated use of several digital tools could offer learners distinct opportunities to develop mathematical thinking. For instance, the YouTube platform can be used to exhibit different ways to discuss problem or task statements including situations where learners can formulate their own mathematical questions. At this stage, learners can rely on online resources (Wikipedia or WolframAlpha) to clarify or extend their own ideas or concepts understanding. Likewise, during the process of representing and exploring the tasks, students can use other tools to examine embedded concepts. For instance, the use of a spreadsheet tool becomes important to quantify the behaviour of particular parameters and then to observe how they change. In the task, the table approach became useful to quantify and explore the area behaviour of both figures and the sum/difference of those areas. This table information was key to identify when the area of both figures gets equal values (when the difference of both areas gets close to zero) or the point where the sum of those areas reaches its minimum value.

Similarly, a dynamic geometry environment provides affordances to approach the task from three perspectives, the actual model that provides a visual change of the figures, the graph representation, and the record of data through a table. In the same way, the use of WolframAlpha tool or GeoGebra became important to deal with algebraic models of the situation.

In this context, the coordinated use of several digital technologies offers diverse opportunities for learners not only to communicate and discuss mathematical task and ways to formulate problems; but also to represent and explore the tasks from diverse angles and perspectives. In this perspective, learners could choose initially what problem approach or tool to use to represent and explore the tasks. It is also important to implement a research programme to investigate what type of mathematical reasoning and knowledge learners construct as a result of using different tools in their learning experiences.

Finally, it is recognized that the design of digital technologies or artefacts involves the collaboration of experts' communities working on different fields and an important element in the design is the users' appropriation process of the tool. Thus, designers should include or rely on information about how users transform an artefact into an instrument to solve problems. Users appropriation tools include ways in which subjects develop cognitive schemata to incorporate the tool into their practices. In addition, the design of materials for learners to foster the coordinated use different digital technologies requires the participation of a multidisciplinary team to make explicit a didactic proposal to frame learning environments.

Acknowledgement. The authors would like to acknowledge the support received from projects Conacyt-168543 and Plan Nacional I+D+I del MCIN, Reference EDU2011-29328 during the preparation of this article.

References

1. Schmidt, E., Cohen, J.: The new digital area. Reshaping the future of people, nations and business. Random House and Google Inc., NY (2013) (eBook version)
2. National Research Council, NRC (2009). Engineering in K-12 education. The National Academic Press, Washington, DC (2009)
3. Béguin, P.: Design as a mutual learning process between users and designers. Interacting with Computers 14, 709–730 (2003)
4. Hadolt, V., Hörbst, V., Müller-Rockstroh, B.: Biomedical techniques in context: On the appropriation of biomedical procedures and artifacts. Medical Anthropology 31, 179–195 (2012)
5. Hahn, H.P.: Global goods and the process of appropriation. In: Probst, P., Spittler, G. (eds.) Between Resistance and Expansion: Dimensions of Local Vitality in Africa, pp. 213–231. Lit Verlag, Münster (2004)
6. Trouche, L.: Managing the complexity of human/machine interactions in computerized learning environments: Guiding students' command process through instrumental orchestration. International Journal of Computers for Mathematical Learning 9, 281–307 (2004)
7. Mason, J., Johnston-Wilder, S.: Designing and using mathematical tasks. Tarquin Publications, St. Albans (2006)
8. Blum, W.: Introduction: Content related research on PISA. In: Prenzel, M., Kobarg, M., Schöps, K., Rönnebeck, S. (eds.) Research on PISA. Research Outcomes of the PISA Research Conference 2009. Springer, NY (2013)
9. Ren, Y.: Foreword. Information and communication technologies in education. In: Spector, J.M., Merrill, M.D., Elen, J., Bishop, M.J. (eds.) Handbook of Research on Educational Communications and Technology, 4th edn., pp. vii-xi. Springer, NY (2014)
10. Santos-Trigo, M.: A mathematical problem-solving approach to identify and explore instructional routes based on the use of computational tools. In: Yamamoto, J., Kush, J., Lombard, R., Hertzog, J. (eds.) Technology Implementation and Teacher Education: Reflective Models, pp. 296–313. IGI Global, Hershey (2010)

11. Watson, A., Mason, J.: Seeing an exercise as a single mathematical object: Using variation to structure sense-making. Mathematical Thinking and Learning 8(20), 91–11 (2006)
12. Davidson, A.L., Carliner, S.: E-books for educational uses. In: Spector, J.M., et al. (eds.) Handbook of Research and Educational Communication and Technology, Springer Science+Business Media, New York (2014), doi:10.1007/978-1-4614-3185-5_57
13. Roschelle, J., Courey, S., Patton, C., Murray, E.: Dynabooks: Supporting teachers to engage all learners in key literacies. In: Mouza, C., Lavigne, N. (eds.) Emerging Technologies for the Classroom, Explorations in the Learning Sciences, Instructional Systems and Performance Technologies, pp. 31–46. Springer, New York (2013)

Co-regulation in Technology Enhanced Learning Environments

Jonathan Kaplan

CHArt-UPON –*Cognitions Humaine et Artificielle*– lab (EA 4004)
Department of Psychology
West Paris University (Université Paris 10), France
kaplan@kaplan-consultants.org

Abstract. This paper discusses the importance of strategy use in regulating cognitive processes, with a particular interest in co-regulation of the learning by peers in technology enhanced learning environments. Research on self-regulated learning has focused on cognitive, motivational and emotional regulation in relation to academic achievement. Co-regulation is an important facet of the regulatory processes taking place in communication-intensive learning environments that are geared towards peer interaction and social networking. This paper succinctly presents Self- and Co-Regulation (SCoR) general concepts and research and elaborates on why SCoR is particularly relevant to learning environments such as MOOCs that are designed with reference to connectivist learning theory. The paper discusses difficulties inherent to the field and stresses the need for commitment to designing environments that are effective for learners.

Keywords: Self-regulated learning, Co-regulation of learning, SCoR, e-Learning, Massive open online course, MOOC.

1 Introduction

One of the main issues that regularly plague the introduction of any 'new' technology, is, and should be: How would it make things better, and for whom? In present times educational contexts, this could be put in terms such as: How would Massive Open Online Courses (MOOCs) make *learning* better? Putting the question this way points to the choice of making education better for learners. This is the concern of this paper. Looking into facets of learning that involve the use of Internet-based applications for e-learning is burgeoning when it comes to MOOCs. There is another level, inherent to online learning, which is its social dimension. The social dimension of learning which is drawing growing interest among some researchers requires that attention be paid to interactions between learners in studying the learning process.

Cognition has long been considered from the individual level. This is mainly true within twentieth century epistemology which developed in conjunction with the then massively industrialised economies led by capitalism. This epistemology

L. Uden et al. (Eds.): LTEC 2014, CCIS 446, pp. 72–81, 2014.

has been one of competitiveness and the individualistic outlook that this has produced. This article focuses on an approach to understanding learning on the level of collective processes. It is somewhat a renewal of an interest dropped soon after the previous century began.

As access to the Internet became public from the beginning of the 1990s onward and ignited new ideas for education, the trend has been to explore Internet-based technologies that could serve educational endeavours. The evolutionary process of human technologies, as Marchal McLuhan [17] describes it, is one in which first a new technology is used to do what was previously done without it. Then, through its use, perceptions of one's environment shift and are reshaped. The next step in this cyclic process comes about when one's changed perceptions inspire new ideas for uses of the technology. It is at this point that new applications develop and are experimented, and so the process goes on. If we focus on a technology at one point in time, we should be able to tell at which stage the technology is evolving in. Perhaps more accurately said: at which stage we are in, in relation to the technology we are using. An example can be given from the way MOOCs are being used now, as the race to adopt them has commenced. Most experimentation is taking place within the stage of using MOOCs to do what we did in the past, hopefully bettering it as one's power to act grows with the use of the new human "extension" [17]. MOOCs follow from the general concept of open education, though what is open may be conceived differently [19]. Apart from the understanding of what is open, MOOCs have been classified according to two major tendencies, each related to a separate paradigm, which inevitably is also related to what is being conceived of as open. The first are c-MOOCs. In these, knowledge is thought of as being constructed through interaction among peers forming communities of learners. c-MOOCs have been referred to as MOOCs congruent with connectivist theory. The second type are x-MOOCs. In these, knowledge is believed to be acquired by integrating knowledge established by authoritative others. x-MOOCs are congruent with a paradigm based on knowledge transmission from instructor to student [7,15,19]. Referring back to the stage in the evolutionary process of usage of MOOC educational technologies, x-MOOCs appear as a form of powered-up lectures. This is a case of using new technology to do what was done in the past without it. c-MOOCs are affixed to student driven learning. Student driven learning relies on learner self-direction; an educational ideal that has been marginal in some realms albeit its longstanding history and fervent proponents. As Bady states "the pro-MOOC argument is always that it's cheaper and almost never that it's better" [3]. This article discusses and suggests directions that can be taken to ensure that wherever technology enhanced education ventures to go its concern with learner affordances and the quality of the learning be prime.

2 Background

For learner self-direction to thrive, motivation needs to be autonomous. Autonomous motivation is linked to autonomous regulation of one's learning [18,20,21]. The autonomous character of interactions in c-MOOCs, on which learning in these relies on, brings forth the concept of co-regulation of the learning process. Co-regulation was first studied in pioneering research on self-direction in communities of learners [11,12,13]. The research demonstrated that Self- and Co-Regulation (SCoR) take place when adults learn cooperatively. The research also demonstrated that two regulation strategies: Group Processing Anticipation (GPA) and Co-Evaluation, were more salient where no person was designated as a reference person to the field of study (i.e. groups to which no facilitator or instructor were assigned). GPA was also more collective vs. individual in these types of groups. Several other regulation strategies were perceived by learners to be more often the result of collective activity than of individual activity. More self- and co-regulation is assumed to characterise self-direction in learning. It logically follows that more frequent and thorough regulation of learning takes place when there is less a feeling of someone else leading and directing one's learning. One does not feel as autonomous and therefore regulates one's learning less when control is taken over by the instructor. This does not necessarily mean that stronger learning outcomes will correlate positively with enhanced self- and co-regulatory activity. Nonetheless, it has been pointed to the need in studying self-regulation (and co-regulation as it may be) to also link it to academic achievement, lest there would be little point in researching it [28].

Regulating one's learning, in particular co-regulating the process with peers, should be of particular interest when learners form communities when studying online. Learners who are low on self-regulation and have control in computer-based instruction need Self-Regulated Learning (SRL) strategies to achieve success [29]. Having control refers to learning environments that afford sufficient latitude for making choices that enable to structure one's learning. Environments that are restrictive in the sense that they direct learners to use resources chosen by the course designers and that impose learning paths or enforce methods, are examples of environments that do not afford high levels of control. In hypermedia environments students have difficulties "because they fail to engage in key mechanisms related to regulating their learning" [2]. According to Winters, Greene and Costich [28] "individuals that can effectively plan, monitor, and control their learning are best positioned to take advantage of multiple representations and learner control afforded" in computer-based learning environments. MOOCs that are designed around connectivist epistemology are environments that, in principle, should afford such control.

3 Overview of Research

SRL research has been conceptualised in various ways by authors, though a consensual definition can perhaps be the one encapsulated by Greene and Azevedo when they state that "in general self-regulated learning research focuses upon how students actively monitor and control their cognition, motivation, and context to effectively learn" [9].

In SRL research, links are often sought between strategies that learners' use to regulate their learning and academic achievement. SRL strategies that were initially studied borrowed from categories in social learning theory that include goal setting, structuring the environment, self-consequences and self-attributions, as well as self-evaluation. Several researches developed models that coalesce cognitive, motivational or emotional strategy use, while others offering to differentiate between them, e.g. Boekaerts [6] separates cognitive and motivational self-regulation. Nevertheless, most models that stemmed from Zimmerman and Martinez-Pons's seminal work [30], somewhat mingle strategies of quite different nature.

Sitzmann and Ely [24] offer a meta-analysis of SRL research with correlations to learning. Moderate to strong predictors of learning are goal level and self-efficacy beliefs. Although goal level is not a strategy per se, setting goals is. It has been demonstrated that setting goals can play a role, in particular when goals are proximal. As to self-efficacy beliefs, they are not strategies; rather, they are dispositions that subjects have that are in fact linked to goal setting. Learners with high self-efficacy beliefs tend to set goals that are more demanding, persist, exert more effort and achieve higher on standards [4,5]. Accordingly, perceived self-efficacy contributes to volition but cannot be considered a strategy one can deploy when learning.

SRL can be qualified as a nebulous field of study encompassing vast sub-domains of interest. Put in practical terms, concern should be with what can be done to enable learners to deploy strategies that will contribute to performance (the learning process) and to achievement (the learning outcome). Interest in the processual aspect of SRL has led to grouping strategies within phases, considered as repeating cyclically. Schunk and Zimmerman [23] conceptualised them as: forethought, performance (or volitional control), and self-reflection phases. Inspired by a somewhat similar cybernetic conception, Kaplan [11,13] separates monitoring, which encompasses strategies that a learner may use to promote metacognition and consciousness of emotions, volition, metacognition (meta-metacognition), plus adds a decisions-making phase (see Fig. 1). Making decisions substantiates adjustments that are made to the cognitive system, or the need to maintain things as they are (a decision to make no adjustments), without which there would be no evidence of learning from metacognitive input (as well as cognition of emotions, volition, etc.) that was used to assess learning by the subject during the last phase of a cycle. Decisions denote the intention formation, the moment of "crossing the Rubicon" [1] that precedes planning for action to come. Regarding monitoring, there is consensus that it is a salient characteristic of successful self-regulation [25]. Greene and Azevedo [9] in a study with middle-school and high-school students found that "only monitoring statistically significantly affected the likelihood of having a more sophisticated mental model at posttest [...], supporting the importance it has been given in SRL models (Winne, 2001; Winne & Hadwin, 1998)".

Co-regulation among self-directed learners was introduced as a concept and studied by Kaplan [11,12,13] in small groups with learners meeting in a room on

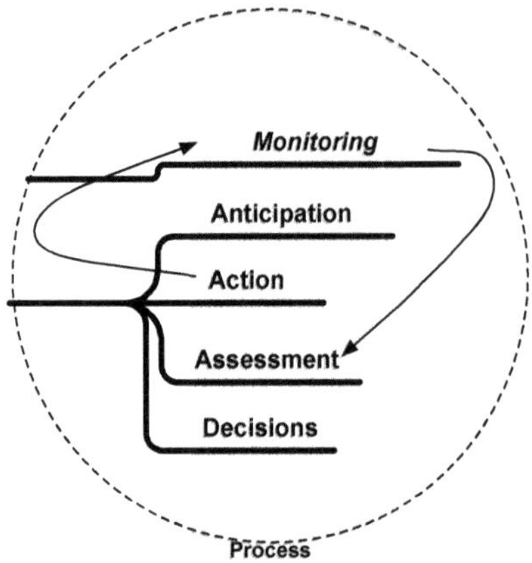

Fig. 1. Regulation of Learning Phases Model (Kaplan, 2009)

a regular basis. In order to study SCoR in large groups with particular interest in those learning together at a distance, such as is the case in MOOCs, Kaplan, Fenouillet and de Montalembert [14] developed ERICA (*Échelle de la Régulation Individuelle et Collective de l'Apprentissage*)–an inventory to measure individual and collective regulation of learning. Following from Kaplan's model (see Fig. 1), the research programme that led to refining the inventory involved large cohorts of students in undergraduate and postgraduate programs. In these, instruction was predominantly organised around lectures, various class-based activities and apprenticeships to gain practical skills.

The ways learners regulate their learning, individually and collectively, depend on the instructional environments, instructional designs, topics being learned, goals being pursued, learning activity types, as well as a myriad of other variables that affect the ways learners tackle a learning task at any one time. Because of the specific contexts in which the study was conducted, certain learning regulation strategies had to be dropped, leading to a smaller set that proved robust through statistical analyses. Testing the inventory in technology enhanced environments will enable determining the validity of the tool to measure SCoR in these contexts too.

There has been some budding of ideas around the concept of co-regulation related to metacognition [8,22,27], primarily focused on affective and motivational regulation. Reference is made by some authors to co-regulation in terms of how individuals regulate each other's learning [26]. These authors use the term 'other-regulation' to designate the effects of interaction with others on self-regulation, therefore pleading for a socio-cognitive perspective in which reciprocal regulatory processes are taken into account. Volet, Vauras and Salonen [27] nevertheless propose distinguishing the term 'coregulation' by considering regulations at the dyadic or group level in which a joint task and goal are pursued and in which participants share reference values and norms.

Conceptualising co-regulation in terms of a joint task such as studying a particular topic in which reference values and norms are shared applies well to the groups that Kaplan [11,12,13] studied. In these groups, metacognitive awareness was identified by learners to be more often than not on the 'we' level, but both self- and co-regulation coexisted.

On the basis of these findings, and in accordance with the emerging literature in the domain, The SCoR inventory ERICA comprises four individual regulation and two collective regulation macro-level strategies [14]. Using the inventory will enable investigating variations in tendencies and features of regulation of learning in e-learning implementations such as those used in MOOCs.

4 Challenges and Practical Suggestions

The challenges facing online education in respect to learners' capabilities to manage their learning is particularly critical in MOOC implementations that do not follow from a peer-managed autonomous learner approach. This is the case in x-MOOC designs that follow from a knowledge transmission paradigm. Persistence in MOOCs has been pointed to as a weakness [10]. This may be the result of lesser ability for learners to regulate their learning in such massive courses in which tutors cannot be present to help each learner. Furthermore, trying to reproduce the way universities dispense courses on campus on an even more massive scale by delivering MOOCs omits taking into account chat that takes place everywhere on campus outside of classrooms and lecture halls. A great deal of co-regulation takes place among peers through informal discussion [14]. Virtual spaces for these are not adequately accounted for in some MOOC designs.

What can be done to overcome the challenges that educational environments pose in relation to potential deficiencies in affording learners control requires paying attention to successive layers in the design of such environments. I will highlight these before offering some principles that would be helpful when choosing a platform and designing online courses.

In order to overcome limitations imposed by these environments, what might first be studied is the front-end software interface and its ergonomics, including the services available to users through modules that are or can be added to the Learning Management System (LMS). For example, does the LMS in use enable adding a module to provide learners with the ability to interact and form small communities in which co-regulation can take place? If so, does the module materialise on the screen on various devices in a way that makes it accessible at all times? Is it easy to locate on the screen and use? etc. If a course is already set up on an LMS, the next step would be to study that specific setup. Obviously, options will need consideration if designing a new course were underway. Choices involve not only modules that can be integrated into an LMS, but also the way services, areas for activities and the placement of contents are laid out by the instructor or others involved in the course design. For example, are there personal tracking tools of learning activities? Are learners able to add notes related to these activities? Does the LMS enable prompting learners to remind them to keep notes or a journal of their learning activities and this only if they are not already doing so? Scaffolding regulation in this way can be helpful for learners who do not tend to use self-regulation strategies to monitor their learning. Content placement, the ability to access content non-linearly but still contiguously, specific cues and directions that are related to the instructional design that was chosen need to be considered as well, as all these elements conjointly form a learning environment that affords learners with varying levels of choice that in turn affect learning strategy use. Not all considerations can be covered by the examples given here. However, these examples illustrate there is no simple answer as to what works best. This is particularly true when considering the diversity of learning habits, cultural influences, prior learning experiences and so on, that shape each and everyone's ways of managing one's learning. Furthermore, as the learning environment is also shaped to an extent by the learners themselves as they interact, this requires taking the learner into account as well. All these facets of the learning make for unique situations that require being studied on a case-by-case basis. Principles though can be followed when designing learning environments such as MOOCs. These principles follow from research in educational psychology. Although related research spans many branches of knowledge that have seldom been studied in conjunction, taking into account what we do know should enable better affordances of technologically enhanced learning environments. I offer 10 principles to support learners' regulation of their learning:

1. Support phases of anticipation, monitoring, assessment and decision making by learners. This can be done by implementing modules (services) on LMSs and recommendations to cyclically use them or other means to Anticipate, Monitor, Assess and Decide (AMAD). For example, announce the aims of a learning sequence, enable learners to state their goals and how they practically intend to carry out the learning in respect to these goals.
2. Scaffold systematic use of the various services available for learners to AMAD; however, without constraining learners to use them. For example, advise learners to keep track of their activities (monitor) or make sure the LMS does and that the learner can access records.
3. Facilitate metacognition by providing tools and services that can be used by learners to stop and reflect on their learning. One such tool is an individual or a collectively edited journal that learners maintain, in which they recount what they are doing to progress towards their goals. A blog-like page for each learner to use or for a group of learners that can be made public or kept private is a good example.
4. Prompt learners or have the LMS prompt them to enact regulation phases e.g. to periodically go through their automated tracking records or read their group diary. Make sure prompts go away if the learner does enact monitoring strategies or if she or he deactivates the prompt.
5. Inform about norms including those that will be used for accreditation in relation to course objectives so that learners can measure their progress against these standards when self- and co-assessing.

6. Provide learners with tools to self-assess and co-assess the process they are carrying out to attain their learning goals, not only their attainments, and invite them to do so.
7. Enable communication channels for peers so as to enhance co-regulation. Include feedback mechanisms and enable keeping track of discussions. A peer borne frequently asked questions and answers area, online forums and areas where learners can share documents are some examples of such channels.
8. Design courses by breaking them down to well paced sequences that are neither too long nor too short. Proximal goals enhance feeling in control and help perceiving oneself as efficacious.
9. Bolster learner autonomy by pointing learners to tasks and activities to be carried out in a manner that is non constraining. This does not mean not providing guidelines and instructions. Rather, it entails offering flexibility so that learners can choose means and feel in control when striving to attain expected outcomes.
10. Study individual and collective regulation strategies used by learners within each of the phases that are being supported on the LMS to learn about what works and how best to implement courses to cater to learners' needs.

5 Discussion

There are a number of difficulties inherent to studying self-regulation. Co-regulation adds a layer to these difficulties. Firstly, regulation strategies are highly contextual, making inferences and generalisations difficult; secondly, they are hard to observe as they are most often internal processes taking place in the mind; thirdly, not enacting a strategy is a valid regulatory decision, making direct observation impossible; fourthly, requesting subjects to tell about their regulatory processes invokes metacognition, an important dimension of regulation. How then does the researcher know that the subject is able to remember often subconscious or automated cognitive, metacognitive and emotional meandering and not mistake for these metacognition invoked at present by the researcher's question? In other words, how well the subject can distinguish between the actual past experience and present thought on it (as memory is a reconstruction), remains open (cf. Kitsantas and Zimmerman [16] for an attempt to circumvent this problem). Furthermore, co-regulation involves perceptions and strategies that are the result of interaction among co-learners. Trying to capture such ethereal collective moments is a daunting task. Nevertheless, following the track of exploration of the relationship between interfaces used as mediators in education and the quality of the learning, as well as outcomes, is necessary, as education has been endlessly experimenting with technology in a quest for efficiency and hopefully, quality too.

6 Conclusions

Learning environments that include contemporary technological interfaces, enable access to resources, provide for interaction among peers, contain a myriad of means to form communities through which building up knowledge can be facilitated. These learning environments need to support autonomy, contribute to feeling in control of one's learning and enable cooperative interaction with others to enable learners to engage, persist and perform effectively. For example, users of a MOOC are subjected to environmental constraints and affordances. They also participate in shaping the environment. When a c-MOOC approach is being strived for this is of particular concern. The learning management system and the MOOC design need to support through online services and end-user ergonomics co-regulation of the learning in reference to the regulation phases.

Self-regulation and co-regulation in particular, are relevant to learning situations in which learners are expected to cooperate in the process of knowledge acquisition and are essential to knowledge generation. The domain merits attention in order for learners to benefit fully from technology mediated forms of learning, in particular those that rely on participants directing their learning process.

References

1. Achtziger, A., Gollwitzer, P.M.: Motivation and volition in the course of action. In: Heckhausen, J., Heckhausen, H. (eds.) Motivation and action, pp. 275–299. Cambridge University Press, Cambridge (2010)
2. Azevedo, R., Cromley, J.G.: Does training on self-regulated learning facilitate students' learning with hypermedia? Journal of Educational Psychology 96(3), 523–535 (2004)
3. Bady, A.: The MOOC moment and the end of reform. Liberal Education 99(4) (2013)
4. Bandura, A.: Perceived self-efficacy in cognitive development and functioning. Educational Psychologist 28(2), 117–148 (1993)
5. Bandura, A.: Self-efficacy: the exercise of control. W.H. Freeman, New York (1997)
6. Boekaerts, M.: Self-regulated learning: A new concept embraced by researchers, policy makers, educators, teachers, and students. Learning and Instruction 7(2), 161–186 (1997)
7. Boyatt, R., Joy, M., Rocks, C., Sinclair, J.: What (use) is a MOOC? In: Uden, L., Tao, Y.H., Yang, H.C., Ting, I.H. (eds.) The 2nd International Workshop on Learning Technology for Education in Cloud. pp. 133–145. Springer, Dordrecht (2014)
8. Efklides, A.: Metacognition: Defining its facets and levels of functioning in relation to self-regulation and co-regulation. European Psychologist 13(4), 277–287 (2008)
9. Greene, J.A., Azevedo, R.: A macro-level analysis of SRL processes and their relations to the acquisition of a sophisticated mental model of a complex system. Contemporary Educational Psychology 34(1), 18–29 (2009)
10. Heutte, J., Kaplan, J., Fenouillet, F., Caron, P.A., Rosselle, M.: MOOC user persistence - lessons from french educational policy adoption and deployment of a pilot course. In: Uden, L., et al. (eds.) The 3rd International Workshop on Learning Technology for Education in Cloud, pp. 13–24. Springer, Dordrecht (2014)
11. Kaplan, J.: Self-Direction in Cooperative Learning - The Case of Study Circles. Ph.D. thesis, Paris 10 University, Nanterre (2009)

12. Kaplan, J.: From self-direction to co-direction in adult cooperative learning. In: Brigham, S.M., Plumb, D. (eds.) Connected Understanding: Linkages Between Theory and Practice in Adult Education, pp. 176–180. Adult Education – Congresses, Montreal, Quebec (2010)
13. Kaplan, J.: L'autodirection dans les apprentissages coopératifs: Le cas des Cercles d'Étude. Éditions Universitaires Européennes, Sarrebruck (2010)
14. Kaplan, J., Fenouillet, F., de Montalembert, M.: ERICA - an instrument to assess individual and collective regulation of learning (forthcoming)
15. Karsenti, T.: The MOOC - what the research says. International Journal of Technologies in Higher Education 10(2), 23–37 (2013)
16. Kitsantas, A., Zimmerman, Barry, J.: Comparing self-regulatory processes among novice, non-expert, and expert volleyball players: A microanalytic study. Journal of Applied Sport Psychology 14, 91–105 (2002)
17. McLuhan, M.: Understanding media - The extensions of man. Routledge, London, New York (1964)
18. Reeve, J., Ryan, R., Deci, E.L., Jang, H.: Understanding and promoting autonomous self-regulation: A self-determination theory perspective. In: Schunk, D.H., Zimmerman, B.J. (eds.) Motivation and Self-Regulated Learning : Theory, Research, and Applications, pp. 223–244. Lawrence Erlbaum Associates, New York (2008)
19. Rodriguez, O.: The concept of openness behind c and x-MOOCs (massive open online courses). Open Praxis 5(1), 67–73 (2013)
20. Ryan, R., Deci, E.L.: Intrinsic and extrinsic motivations: Classic définitions and new directions. Contemporary Educational Psychology 25, 54–67 (2000)
21. Ryan, R., Deci, E.L.: Self-determination theory and the facilitation of intrinsic motivation, social development, and well-being. American Psychologist 55(1), 68–78 (2000)
22. Salonen, P., Vauras, M., Efklides, A.: Social interaction - what can it tell us about metacognition and coregulation in learning? European Psychologist 10(3), 199 (2005)
23. Schunk, D.H., Zimmerman, B.J.: Self-Regulated Learning - From Teaching to Self-Reflective Practice. Guilford Press, New York (1998)
24. Sitzmann, T., Ely, K.: A meta-analysis of self-regulated learning in work-related training and educational attainment: What we know and where we need to go. Psychological Bulletin 137(3), 421–442 (2011)
25. Steffens, K.: Self-regulated leaning in technology-enhanced learning environments: lessons of a european peer review. European Journal of Education - Research, Development and Policies 41(3-4), 352–379 (2006)
26. Volet, S., Summers, M., Thurman, J.: High-level co-regulation in collaborative learning: How does it emerge and how is it sustained? Learning and Instruction 19(2), 128–143 (2009)
27. Volet, S., Vauras, M., Salonen, P.: Self- and social regulation in learning contexts: An integrative perspective. Educational Psychologist 44(4), 215–226 (2009)
28. Winters, F., Greene, J., Costich, C.: Self-regulation of learning within computer-based learning environments: A critical analysis. Educational Psychology Review 20(4), 429–444 (2008)
29. Young, J.D.: The effect of self-regulated learning strategies on performance in learner controlled computer-based instruction. Educational Technology Research and Development 44(2), 17–27 (1996)
30. Zimmerman, B.J., Martinez Pons, M.: Development of a structured interview for assessing student use of self-regulated learning strategies. American Educational Reasearch Journal 23(4), 614–628 (1986)

The Relationship between Group Awareness and Participation in a Computer-Supported Collaborative Environment

Jorge Chávez[1,*] and Margarida Romero[2]

[1] University of Santiago de Chile (Chile)
Department of Educational Innovation
Jorge.chavez@usach.cl
[2] Université Laval (Canada)

Abstract. The objective of this research is to analyze the relation between Group Awareness (GA) and participation from the introduction of a visualization tool that permits to evaluate different dimensions of the proper interaction of a collaborative process that is carried out in Computer-Supported Collaborative Learning (CSCL) environments. The study considers that Group Awareness can contribute considerably to the processes of interaction in CSCL environments. Along this research line there are increasing numbers of reports that consider GA as a crucial factor for the success of collaboration, since it allows the activities and intentions of other members that collaborate in a virtual learning environment to be perceived and understood. In the present study we analyze group awareness with a quasi-experimental methodology, in which a group of participants have a computer tool that allows them to declare group awareness. Half of the students had an extended version of a tool that permitted them to evaluate and visualize assigned results in pairs, while the other half could evaluate but not visualize the assessments of other group members. The results show that there is better group awareness in groups with greater participation. Nevertheless, the use of a GA tool would not have a direct impact on students' participation. The results point out the GA can be considered as a product of participation, and not exactly a by-product of a GAW tool.

Keywords: Group awareness, Online learning, Participation, Group awareness, Higher education.

1 Introduction

Computer-supported collaborative learning (CSCL) has undergone important development over the last decades (Dillenbourg, Järvelä, & Fischer, 2009). This development is based largely on the increase in the use of Information and

* Corresponding author: University of Santiago of Chile, Building Citecamp, Las Sophoras 175, Central Station, Santiago, Chile.

L. Uden et al. (Eds.): LTEC 2014, CCIS 446, pp. 82–94, 2014.

Communication Technology (ICT) to improve the efficiency and the quality of group working and learning processes (Stahl, Koschmann, & Suthers, 2006).

One of the main objectives of these environments is to facilitate synchronous and asynchronous communication exchange or a combination of both. In the case of CSCL, the best known manifestation is that of Virtual Learning Environments (VLE). These environments can be characterized as support media for information transfer, application and clarification of concepts, exchange and development of ideas, exploration of shared resources, collaboration in the building of knowledge, and development of awareness and skills processes (Lameras, Levy, Paraskakis, & Webber, 2012). These characteristics make these environments become collaborative work spaces particularly adequate for facilitating group teaching and learning processes (Choitz & Lee, 2006).

However, and in spite of the increasingly extended use of these kinds of environments (VLE), more and new questions keep arising on the process of computer mediated learning. In short, the main objective of this research line (CSCL) is to analyze how people can learn jointly with the help of computers, with the purpose of improving the learning processes (Stahl et al., 2006). On the other hand, there is agreement on the need to advance in the studies of VLEs that will allow the potential of these tools to support the teaching and learning processes to be offered, based largely on increased social interaction between the group members (Linden, Erkens, Schmidt, & Renshaw, 2002).

Dehler, Bodemer, Buder & Hesse (2011) point out that there is sufficient evidence to state that the quality of the interaction is a determining factor in the learning results. However, for this to happen it is necessary to facilitate the processes of participation in the different activities so that the students can perform tasks that facilitate that interaction. Along the same ideas, Fransen, Kirschner & Erkens (2011) mention that the collaboration is not always efficient, and that to remedy this situation it is necessary to determine and understand the variables that affect the team's efficiency. Among the variables that can have an influence on those collaborative processes we can point out, for example, the complexity of the task, the time assigned to each participant for reading the contributions of the others, the individual and team characteristics, or the characteristics of the environment, among others. However, there is increasing agreement (Engelmann, Dehler, Bodemer, & Buder, 2009; Janssen, Erkens, Kanselaar, & Jaspers, 2007) that GA may be playing a primary role in the development of the interaction among the participants as a facilitator of the knowledge construction processes, in the understanding that people need sufficient context or reference of the presence, activities and intentions of others in order to carry out effective and efficient cooperation activities, i.e., information on the different aspects of the interaction that allow becoming aware on how the others perceive the participation or behavior of the rest of the participants (Bodemer & Dehler, 2011).

In agreement with the above, our research states that the students who participate more actively can condition the formation of GA, since involvement in the activity arises from the different actions that a participant carries out during the collaboration process, contributing to the generation of greater GA. Therefore, insofar as the participants contribute actively to the collaboration process, their GA will be greater. The above has led us to bring up the need to study the relation that there is between PA and GA, from the so-called group awareness *widgets*, or GAW, computer tools whose purpose is to provide information on a number of aspects of the interaction (Chavez & Romero, 2012).

2 Participation in CSCL

Participation is one of the key factors for understanding collaborative learning processes (Wenger, 1998). In a review of the literature on participation, Hrastinski (2008, p.1761) proposed a definition of the concept of online participation as "...learning by taking part and maintaining relations with others. It is a complex process comprising doing, communicating, thinking, feeling and belonging, which occurs both online and offline. Student participation in online discussions therefore involves students' actions such as joining and contributing ideas to the group formation process, sharing ideas with colleagues on how to execute group tasks and taking individual responsibility to complete share of group tasks".

The idea of this definition is based on the fact that students who participate actively in a collaborative situation generate more efficient interactions, and this can improve their learning results (Dillenbourg, 1999; Hrastinski, 2008), increase productivity and the quality of the results (Fredericksen, Pickett, Shea, Pelz, & Swan, 2000), and also improve the perception of the student's satisfaction and retention rate in a positive way (Rovai, 2002).

However, in spite of the importance of participation in collaborative learning, not all the students participate actively, and in many cases, even if their participation is high from a quantitative standpoint, the quality of the debates in those environments can be very low (Kirschner, Buckingham-Shum, & Carr, 2003; Stahl, 2004). Moreover, the lack of participation can also compromise the development of GA among the group members, because an important part of the available information is based on the traces of interaction resulting from the participation. Because of that, the need to improve participation to allow the development of GA in online learning environments is brought up (Bodemer & Dehler, 2011).

3 Group Awareness a Relation with Participation

Insofar as participation increases, the probability of generating group awareness increases. If on the one hand a greater participation can allow the development of better GA due to the fact that more interaction trails can be generated that allow the development of GA, the use of GAW to facilitate the visualization of participation must be considered, because it can increase the development of GA (Buder, 2011; Engelmann, Dehler, Bodemer & Buder , 2009; Janssen, Erkens, Kanselaar, & Jaspers, 2007).

The visualization of participation can serve to reveal and express the thoughts on the collaboration processes, providing adequate information with respect to type and mode of participation developed by the rest of the participants (Janssen et al., 2007).

In the same way, the visualization of participation can also be used to discuss how well the group is functioning and/or how the group's processes can be improved (Bodemer & Dehler, 2011).

The above makes us point out that visualization of PA from GAW devices can increase or modify the ways of acting with the purpose of increasing the team effectiveness , providing information that is not available in those environments, thereby constituting one of the greatest challenges of CSCL (Buder, 2011).

In short, GAW have been developed to overcome the deficiencies of the online expression of the context of the CSCL, providing the students with the information relative to the interaction and with that the auto- and co-regulation of the collaboration activities, increasing the effectiveness of the processes and the results of learning (Janssen, Erkens & Kirschner, 2011; Phielix, Prins, & Kirschner, 2010). This has made us consider GA as the mediator variable between participation and the results of learning, in the understanding that it can contribute considerably to the collaborative construction of knowledge.

4 Operationalization and Measurement of the Variables

4.1 Measurement of Participation

Participation is analyzed on the basis of three structural activity indicators which, as pointed out by Dimitracopoulou (2008, p.4) "constitute variables indicating 'something' related to the mode or the 'quality' of individual activity, the mode or the quality of the collaboration, the process or the quality of the collaborative product." In our case, the focus is centered on the activity mode, from an analysis of the amount of total contributions (ATC) of the participants, the length of the messages or total words spoken (TWS), and the number of answers (NA).

These indicators can be used together or separately, with their use determined by the objective of the analysis that it is desired to approach in each of the hypotheses presented. In some cases they have been used individually and in others jointly, from the use of the global participation rate (GPR), which weights each of these indicators as a function of the theoretical importance given in the literature, and it incorporates as a factor the time taken by the activity or the duration of the instruction process.

$$GPR = \frac{ATC * 3 + TWS * 2 + NA}{\text{Days of Activity duration}}$$

4.2 Measurement of the Group Awareness

The study of GA corresponds to the classes proposed by Buder (2011), each of which operates from the comments or assessments proposed by the peers with the purpose of facilitating information not available in a CSCL environment, that can be classified from three dimensions or variables considered important for the study of the relation between awareness and learning. These three dimensions are organized from a series of indicators used to measure GA. With respect to the operationalization of GA we have used the classification proposed by Buder (2011), with three dimensions organized from a number of indicators used to measure GA.

GAp, or participative awareness, uses five indicators: *a) Communication:* It evaluates the effectiveness of the way in which the participants have contributed to the debate, and it refers basically to the positive or negative perception of how a student has contributed to the debate. *b) Time organization*: It evaluates the degree to which the participants have distributed efficiently the time that they have used during the collaboration process. *c) Conflict management*: It evaluates the way in which the participants overcome the difficulties that arise during the collaboration process. *d) Number of contributions during the last week:* It evaluates the degree of participation in a given time period. *e) Number of hours devoted to the activity:* It evaluates the actual time invested in the collaboration process.

GAc, or cognitive awareness, reports on four indicators: a*) Preparation of the guideline:* It reports on the quality of the degree to which the participant designs an analysis and evaluation guideline for a given ICT-based formative scenario on participation in the debate and from the proposed dimensions of analysis. *b) Review of the guideline:* It evaluates the students' ability to analyze the quality of the prepared guideline and whether it fulfills the criteria required for its design. *c) Analysis of the scenarios*: It evaluates the students' ability to analyze critically the educational potential of the formative scenarios and of ICT-based teaching, with the purpose of recovering and synthesizing all the contents that have been dealt with throughout the course. *d) Use of the guideline:* In this synthesizing activity the participants must apply the guideline that they have made to each of the cases that make up the subject content. *e) Writing*: It evaluates a formal criterion considered for the quality of the writing of the document that was prepared.

GAs, or social awareness, has been analyzed using three indicators: *a) Prior knowledge of the group members:* This indicator reports on the knowledge level of the peers before beginning the activity. b) *Degree of pleasure or satisfaction with the work done with the peers:* This indicator analyzes the attitude toward the work, the surroundings and the collaborators, or in other words it analyzes the student's general attitude toward the work done during the collaboration activity. *c) Existence of a friendship relation:* It analyzes whether throughout the collaborative activity the participants consider the possibility of having developed some friendship relation with a team member.

An example of this operationalization can be seen in Figure 1, where student B evaluates himself with a score of 5 (on a 1 to 7 scale) while his peer, student A, considers that B should get a score of only 3. That is, student A considers that B's participation level is 42%, compared with 71% assigned by B during self-evaluation. In other words, student A considers that student B participated 29% less than considered by B himself. Therefore, the reliability or the probability of a good functioning that can be reached by the group consciousness is a difference between the perceived consciousness and the maximum awareness possible, which in this case is 71%.

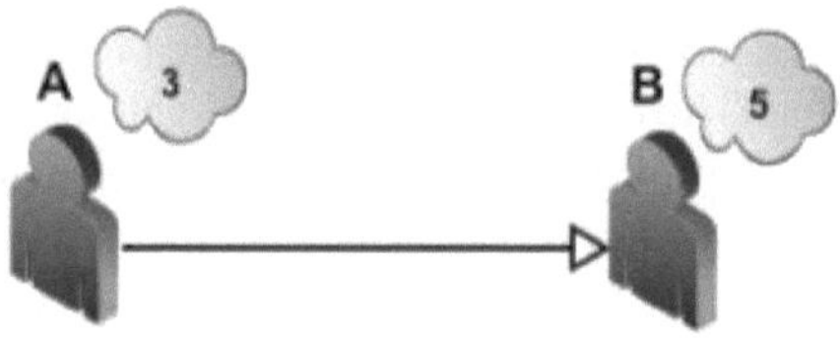

Fig. 1. Example of GA calculation

In our case we have considered GA not only as the distance between the evaluation of a student A and that of a student B, but we have also examined the distances of the remaining members of the team (Fig. 2). In other words, we have considered GA as the evaluation that a group of students (A, D, C) makes on the performance of a given partner (B).

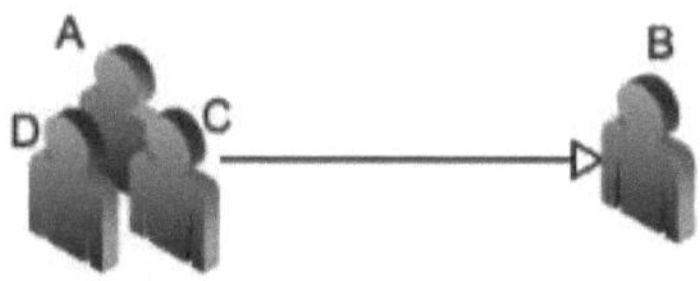

Fig. 2. Evaluation of GA

An example (Table 1) of the group analysis is the following: The student identified as IdUser 1250 (B) considers that his participation deserves a score of 5 (self-evaluation), while the student identified as IdUser 1251 (A) considers that the participation of student B deserves a score of 3. Student 1252 (C) considers that student 1250 (B) deserves a 5, and finally student 1253 (D) considers that student 1250 (B) deserves a 4, which represent reliabilities of 71.4%, 100% and 85%, respectively.

Table 1. Example of the calculation of GAp for each of the indicators performed by the different participants in the group

Group	idUser	Evaluated idUser	Indicator 1	% reliability	Indicator 2	% reliability	Total
G1	1250	1250	5		6		
	1251	1250	3	71.4	3	57.1	71.4
	1252	1250	5	100.0	5	85.7	96.4
	1253	1250	4	85.7	0	14.3	42.9
				M=85.7		M=52.4	M=70.2
							14.2

The calculation of GA generates an individual reliability index for that indicator equivalent to 85%. Then the same procedure is applied for each indicator (indicator 1, indicator 2, up to 4 for GAp) with the purpose of getting a Global Index of Group Awareness for each of the different typologies or dimensions, therefore considering each of the subdimensions of GA (GAp; GAs; GAc).

5 Methodology

5.1 Research and Participant Design

The research that is presented was developed in an online university training context at the Universitat Oberta de Catalunya (UOC), specifically in a master of technologies applied to education. The design used is of the quasi-experimental type and it involved a total of 56 students, 39 of whom were female and 17 were male. The average age of the participants was 26 years. The students were divided into two study groups, and they were randomly assigned to an experimental group (EG, n=26) and a control group (CG, n=30). The composition of the groups in terms of gender was heterogeneous. Students of both the EG and the CG had access to the tool, but only the EG students could visualize the assessments made by the other students.

5.2 Description of the Learning Task

The tasks refer basically to collaborative writing of documents, in which the students must develop a topic or solve a case study. The final idea of this activity is for the students to succeed in preparing an analysis guideline that will allow them to analyze a given formative scenario based on ICT. The duration was five to six weeks and the work groups had four to six students (M = 4.5, SD = 0.60, min = 4, Max = 6). The interactions among the students took place on the common tools of the UOC virtual campus, whose main function is related to the discussion forum. However, there is the probability that at the same time many of them had used their electronic mail as a communication medium, but we did not have access to that information.

5.3 Group Awareness Tool

At the level of the GA tool it was decided to include a tool called EURO-CAT that, among other things, allows the group members to facilitate the information on their own activity from their group's evaluation or perception (see section 5.4.3). Each group member evaluated his own activity as well as that of the other group members from different indicators related to different aspects of the GA on a Likert scale from 1 to 7 points. At the same time, the students can visualize the tool that allows them to compare easily both their own results and those of their group partners (Romero, 2012). Fig. 2 shows the tool that permits students to examine the participation of different analyzed indicators and the modality by which a group of students evaluates the activity of the members of this group.

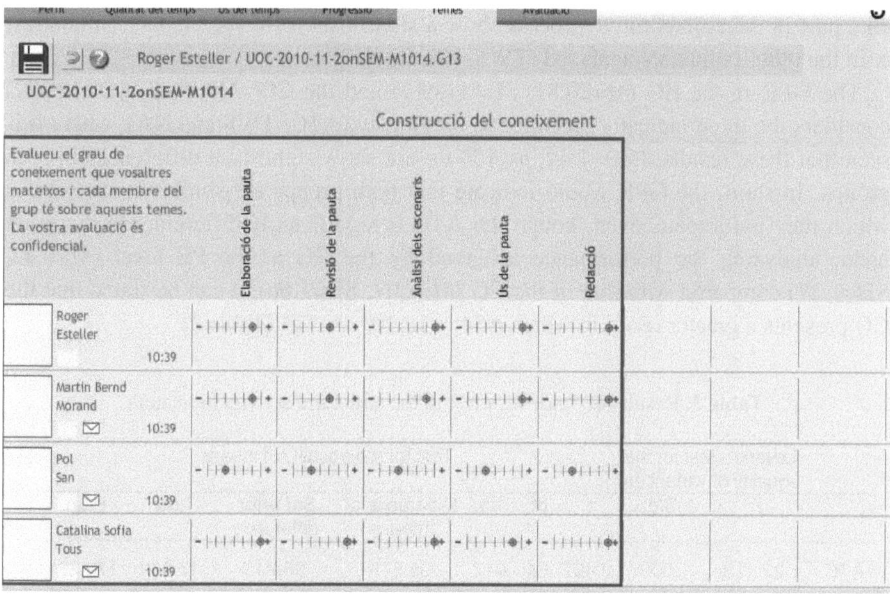

Fig. 3. Screenshot of the GA Tool

6 Results

Analyzing the initial results (Table 2) we can see that the structural PA indicators are quite similar. However, CG does not show better results in all the analyzed indicators. With respect to the ATC indicator in CG (*M*=140.50, DS=171.86), it was quite better than EG (*M*=44.92, DS=104.38). In view of this considerable difference, *Student's t* tests were applied between the groups with the purpose of contrasting the mean differences seen in each of these indicators and finding if these differences can be considered significant (Table 3).

Table 2. Descriptive statistics of the structural indicators of PA and PE achieved by the groups

	EG (N=26)				CG (N=30)			
	Min.	Max.	M	SD	Min.	Max.	M	SD
ATC	2	431	44.92	104.387	2	525	140.50	171.861
TWS	386	2849	1565.69	778.127	278	3770	1697.67	868.466
NA	1	69	17.96	18.021	0	69	18.20	18.430
GPR	3	39	20.81	11.617	4	50	25.43	12.322
PE	4	9	6.42	1.270	1	9	7.07	1.660

The results show that CG performs better in all the indicators (Table 1). However, the only indicator that shows significant differences is ATC, in which t (54)= 2.467, p=.017. The above leads us to point out that ATC or the times that the participants take part in the collaborative process show a significant difference in CG, in contrast with the other indicators analyzed (TWS, NA and GPR).

The GPR in the EG (*M*=20.81, SD=11.617) and the CG (*M*=25.43, SD=12.322) considers the three indicators mentioned previously (ATC, TWS and NA), where it is seen that these results $t(54)=1.44$, $p=.156$ do not show significant differences in both groups. In short, the GPR would indicate that both groups are similar in the way in which they participate, even though the ATC is significantly different. On the other hand, analyzing the performance achieved by the EG at the PE level (*M*=6.42, SD=1.27) compared with that of the CG (*M*=7.07, SD=1.66), it can be stated that the CG presents a greater result in which $t(54)=-1.610$, $p= .113$ (Table 3).

Table 3. Results of *Student's t* test in the structural activity indicators

	Levene's test for the equality of variances		Test for the equality of means						
	F	Sig.	t	df	Sig.	Difference of means	Std.error difference	Low	High
ATC	22.473	.000	2.467	54	.017	95.577	38.743	17.902	173.251
TWS	.013	.910	.595	54	.554	131.974	221.824	-312.756	576.704
NA	.208	.650	.049	54	.961	.238	4.888	-9.561	10.038
GPR	.032	.858	1.438	54	.156	4.626	3.216	-1.821	11.073
PE	.003	.955	1.610	54	.113	.644	.400	-.158	1.445

*p>0.05.
**p<0.01.

For the analysis of the results of the set of indices of GA (IGAp, IGAs and IGAc) we have calculated the descriptive statistics that are represented in Table 4. On the other hand, and with the purpose of analyzing the differences between the EG and the CG shown by the participants in each of these indices, *Student's t* test was applied to the groups.

Table 4. Descriptive statistics of the GA indicators achieved by the groups

	EG (*N*=26)				CG (*N*=30)			
	Min.	Max.	*M*	SD	Min.	Max.	*M*	SD
IGAp	64	98	80.56	9.385	57	100	84.57	12.746
IGAs	67	90	80.40	5.998	60	95	77.99	6.016
IGAc	66	100	81.36	6.599	67	95	87.84	5.253

**p>.05.*
***p<.01.*

The null hypothesis for the analysis of the global indices is based on the nonexistence of differences between the results of the EG and the CG with respect to the different GA dimensions analyzed (IGAp, IGAs and IGAc). However, when the significance of the relations of the different indices is analyzed (see Table 5), it is found that IGAc, where $t(54)= 4.093$, $p=.000$, present significant differences in both groups, so the null hypothesis is rejected for this index. Meanwhile, with respect to the IGAp, where $t(54)=-1.32$, $p=.192$, and the IGAs, where $t(54)=-1.497$, $p=.140$, it is seen that there are no significant differences, so we accept the null hypothesis for IGp and IGAs. The total results are shown in Table 5, which reports the different indices analyzed in both groups.

Table 5. Results of *Student's t* test for the different GA indices

	Levene's test for the equality of variances		Test for the equality of means						
	F	Sig.	t	df	Sig.	Difference of means	Std. error difference	Low	High
IGAp	6.458	.014	1.322	54	.192	4.007	3.032	-2.072	10.085
IGAs	.045	.834	-1.497	54	.140	-2.410	1.610	-5.637	.818
IGAc	1.405	.241	4.093	54	.000	6.486	1.585	3.309	9.664

*$p>.05$.
**$p<.01$.

7 Discussion and Conclusions

With respect to the most important conclusions on the behavior of the structural participation indicators, we can state that in a first level of analysis there is a significant difference in the number of contributions (ATC) in favor of the CG. The rest of the indicators present a similar behavior, both in the control (CG) and in the experimental group (EG).

Most of the work along this line uses this (ATC) indicator as the most important aspect for measuring the participation of the students in a CSCL environment (Lipponen, Rahikainen, Lallimo, & Hakkarainen, 2003). Therefore, if we consider the ATC as the only indicator to determine the level of activity of the participants, we can point out that the results reveal that the CG participates more actively than the EG, although the CG had no access to a GAW tool.

The initial results associated with the difference between both groups indicate that the students who most contributed were not necessarily those that could visualize the GAW tool. On the other hand, it should be mentioned that recent work reports the usefulness of visualizing the participation, which may be stimulating sending longer messages (Janssen et al., 2007). However, when we analyze the length of the messages obtained, the experimental group had a low average length of its messages.

Although these results may contradict previous studies by Michinov and Primois (2005) and Zumbach, Hillers and Reimann (2004), it is necessary to point out that those studies used different types of visualizations.

Another element to be considered in this analysis is that the number of contributions or the length of the messages can constitute an important indicator of participation. However, it should be noted that greater participation is not a guarantee of learning (Stahl, et al., 2006). The above has led us to propose a Global Participation Rate (GPR) with the purpose of grouping a set of indicators that reflect the collaborative activity associated not only with a given action such as the number of times that a participant contributes in a virtual environment, because that contribution can have very dissimilar characteristics (Choitz & Lee, 2006; Kirschner, et al., 2003) .

In brief, the initial results with respect to the differences that may exist in both groups (EG and CG) on the kind of participation of the students in an instructional process that differs in the use of a GAW tool, indicate that the only indicator that shows a significant difference in both groups is the ATC in favor of the CG. On the other hand, it must be pointed out that when using the GPR the groups do not present a significant difference.

In the former case we can assume that the use of a GA tool does not have an incidence on the number of contributions made by the participants. In the second case, when using the GPR, although that index does not show a significant difference between both groups, it is still greater in the CG, reinforcing the idea that if we associate this difference with the visualization of a GA tool, we can assume that the use of widgets has no incidence on the participation of the students throughout the collaboration process.

By analyzing the different indices of GA (GAp, GAc and GAs) in both the EG and the CG, the initial results indicate that there is a significant difference in the IGAc in favor of the CG, in agreement with the results of the structural participation indicators, which would be pointing to a relation between this kind of group awareness and the number of contributions (ATC) that the participants make in a collaboration process. At the IGAs level, the GE shows a higher result in this dimension, which even though not significant, must be considered since it can be a factor that may be affected by the collaboration tool.

On the other hand, if we consider the GPR we can point out that this index in relation to the control group also shows differences, which though not significant, have higher results than those obtained for the experimental group. Along the same order of ideas, it can be stated that the students that contribute more to the collaboration process acquire greater cognitive awareness of their activity, or in other words, they acquire greater awareness of the content of the learning that is taking place. In brief, we can assume that the participation of the students is often centered on the development of the task and not necessarily on other aspects of the interaction, in agreement with the results of research along this line (Bodemer & Dehler, 2011; Engelmann et al., 2009; Kirschner et al., 2004).

The above can be explained from the idea that information on the extent to which the participants can value the interventions or activities performed by the other participants throughout the collaboration process depends basically on the number of times that they contribute to a given activity. On the contrary, it is very difficult for the participants to develop an awareness of the degree or level of quality of the work done if they do not achieve an active participation that can be demonstrated and can be put in evidence from those central aspects or dimensions that the students use to evaluate the activity of their peers, which in this case, as we had already pointed out, tend to concentrate on the evaluation associated with the tasks or with the content of what they are learning.

In relation to the Global GA indices, we can conclude that there is a significant difference in the IGAc in favor of the CG. This result makes us consider the importance of the already mentioned idea, related to the type of attention or activity focus on which the students center their attention while they collaborate. On the other hand, and since different types of GA were analyzed, we can state that the participation of the students can be associated with one type of GA and not necessarily with all the dimensions of analysis or types of GA studied. This becomes of great importance with respect to the other dimensions that are being analyzed, since although the students had a tool that allowed the assessment of the activity in other action dimensions, the main attention focus is centered on the development of the task, although they do not have a visualization tool.

The above leads to the idea that GA can be considered as a by-product of the participation and not exactly a by-product of a tool of the GAW. Although GA cannot necessarily be associated as a tool of the GAW, our differences suggest that such a relation can be reflected in structural activity indicators that would lead to the conclusion that the greater the activity in an EVA, the more the participants' orientation would be centered on awareness with respect to the knowledge (GAc), i.e., from assessing the kind of task or the way in which the participants carry out a given activity.

References

1. Bodemer, D., Dehler, J.: Group awareness in CSCL environments. Computers in Human Behavior 27(3), 1043–1045 (2011), doi:16/j.chb.2010.07.014
2. Buder, J.: Group awareness tools for learning: Current and future directions. Computers in Human Behavior 27(3), 1114–1117 (2011), doi:10.1016/j.chb.2010.07.012
3. Chavez, J., Romero, M.: Group Awareness, Learning, and Participation in Computer Supported Collaborative Learning (CSCL). Procedia - Social and Behavioral Sciences 46, 3068–3073 (2012), doi:10.1016/j.sbspro.2012.06.012
4. Choitz, P., Lee, D.: Designing Asynchronous, Text - Based Computer Conferences. Performance Improvement Quarterly 19(3), 55–71 (2006), doi:10.1111/j.1937-8327.2006.tb00377.x
5. Dehler, J., Bodemer, D., Buder, J., Hesse, F.W.: Guiding knowledge communication in CSCL via group knowledge awareness. Computers in Human Behavior 27(3), 1068–1078 (2011), doi:10.1016/j.chb.2010.05.018
6. Dimitracopoulou, A.: Computer based interaction analysis supporting self-regulation: achievements and prospects of an emerging research direction. Technology, Instruction, Cognition and Learning (TICL) 6(4), 291–314 (2008)

7. Dillenbourg, P.: What do you mean by collaborative learning. In: Collaborative learning: Cognitive and Computational Approaches, pp. 1–16. Elsevier Science, Amsterdan (1999)
8. Dillenbourg, P., Järvelä, S., Fischer, F.: The evolution of research on computer-supported collaborative learning, pp. 3–19 (2009)
9. Engelmann, T., Dehler, J., Bodemer, D., Buder, J.: Knowledge awareness in CSCL: A psychological perspective. Computers in Human Behavior 25(4), 949–960 (2009), doi:10.1016/j.chb.2009.04.004
10. Fransen, J., Kirschner, P.A., Erkens, G.: Mediating team effectiveness in the context of collaborative learning: The importance of team and task awareness. Computers in Human Behavior 27(3), 1103–1113 (2011), doi:10.1016/j.chb.2010.05.017
11. Fredericksen, E., Pickett, A., Shea, P., Pelz, W., Swan, K.: Student satisfaction and perceived learning with on-line courses: Principles and examples from the SUNY learning network. Journal of Asynchronous Learning Networks 4(2), 7–41 (2000)
12. Hrastinski, S.: What is online learner participation? A literature review. Computers & Education 51(4), 1755–1765 (2008)
13. Janssen, J., Erkens, G., Kanselaar, G., Jaspers, J.: Visualization of participation: Does it contribute to successful computer-supported collaborative learning? Computers & Education 49(4), 1037–1065 (2007), doi:16/j.compedu.2006.01.004
14. Janssen, J., Erkens, G., Kirschner, P.A.: Group awareness tools: It's what you do with it that matters. Computers in Human Behavior 27(3), 1046–1058 (2011)
15. Kirschner, P.A., Buckingham-Shum, S.J., Carr, C.S.: Visualizing argumentation: Software tools for collaborative and educational sense-making, pp. 25–47. Springer, Heidelberg (2003)
16. Kirschner, P., Strijbos, J.-W., Kreijns, K., Beers, P.: Designing electronic collaborative learning environments. Educational Technology Research and Development 52(3), 47–66 (2004), doi:10.1007/BF02504675
17. Lameras, P., Levy, P., Paraskakis, I., Webber, S.: Blended university teaching using virtual learning environments: conceptions and approaches. Instructional Science, 1–17 (2012)
18. Linden, J., Erkens, G., Schmidt, H., Renshaw, P.: Collaborative learning. New Learning, 37–54 (2002)
19. Lipponen, L., Rahikainen, M., Lallimo, J., Hakkarainen, K.: Patterns of participation and discourse in elementary students' computer-supported collaborative learning. Learning and Instruction 13(5), 487–509 (2003)
20. Michinov, N., Primois, C.: Improving productivity and creativity in online groups through social comparison process: New evidence for asynchronous electronic brainstorming. Computers in Human Behavior 21(1), 11–28 (2005)
21. Phielix, C., Prins, F.J., Kirschner, P.A.: Awareness of group performance in a CSCL-environment: Effects of peer feedback and reflection. Computers in Human Behavior 26(2), 151–161 (2010)
22. Rovai, A.P.: Sense of community, perceived cognitive learning, and persistence in asynchronous learning networks. The Internet and Higher Education 5(4), 319–332 (2002)
23. Stahl, G., Koschmann, T., Suthers, D.: Computer-supported collaborative learning: An historical perspective. Cambridge Handbook of the Learning Sciences (2006)
24. Zumbach, J., Hillers, A., Reimann, P.: Supporting distributed problem-based learning: The use of feedback mechanisms in online learning. Online Collaborative Learning: Theory and Practice 86 (2004)
25. Stahl, G.: Building collaborative knowing. What we know about CSCL, pp. 53–85 (2004)
26. Wenger, E.: Communities of practice: learning, meaning, and identity. Cambridge University Press (1998)

The Usage of Google Apps Services in Higher Education

Ali Mahdi Owayid[1] and Lorna Uden[2]

[1] Computer Center, Al Buraimi University College, Sultanate of Oman
admin@buc.edu.om
[2] Faculty of Computing, Engineering and Technology,
Staffordshire University, Stafford, UK
l.uden@staffs.ac.uk

Abstract. Google Apps, as one of cloud computing applications, is gaining popularity and can be effectively used in education for communication between academic staff and their students. This paper reports on the use of Google Apps services for higher education. It investigates the use of Google Apps services (Mail, Docs/Drive, Calendar, and Sites) as a package among information department staff themselves and the use of Google Apps services package between academic staff and their students at ABC academic institution. The research aims to find out whether there was a significant difference in the use of Google Apps services by the IT staff and their students. The finding reveals that despite the frequent use of Google Apps services package by IT staff, the usage of the same group with their students was less than normal. The results also show that the differences were significant. Analysis of results shows that there are factors that contribute to the differences.

Keywords: Google Apps Services, Cloud Computing, Communication channel, Usage.

1 Introduction

The rapid growth of digital technologies such as the use of email, e-learning, the internet, and multimedia for instructional programs was the reason behind the growing number of academic institutions [1]. Communication between academic staff and their students is playing a key role in achieving these objectives. Technology such as email presents new way in communication. The influence of new technologies on education is increasing proportional to the development in technologies that offer new options for communication [2].

Since the recession, most academic institutions have started to find new ways to obtain and control computing resources with low expense [3]. Cloud computing or software-as-a-service (SaaS) is a web technology. It is a computing model that IT applications are provided as a service and enable users to reach applications from the cloud internet [4]. By using cloud computing, clients do not have to buy and own extra hardware network equipment as well as worry about maintenance costs [5]. Many academic institutions are offloading the cost of infrastructure and maintenance efforts and investing the savings on other IT initiatives [4]. Google Apps as one of cloud computing applications has becomes popular and it is our belief that it can be

L. Uden et al. (Eds.): LTEC 2014, CCIS 446, pp. 95–104, 2014.

effectively used in educational institutions for communication between academic staff and their students. Google Apps, as an on line service, is easy to use, reliable, useful and productive to enhance communication in academic institutions. It can thus be considered as one of the teaching tools [4]. In addition, Google Apps services are cloud computing technology where users can reach Google Apps services anywhere and at any time via the internet.

Academic institutions are paying more attention and priority to acquire specific hardware, software, and advanced network rather than developing their information systems and academic staff skills to use the available technologies. For optimal use of technologies in academic institutions, it is important to help staff to be more comfortable and confident in using these technologies. To achieve this, a developed strategy is required to help academic staff to be comfortable with involving computers in their teaching or communication activities [1]. Much research is available about cloud computing and most of it is concerned with taking Google apps as an example of cloud computing or SaaS [6]. However there is little research focused on discovering the undergraduate students' perceptions of Google Docs / Drive as a communication tool [7]. This paper aims to evaluate the use of Google Apps services (Mail, Docs / Drive, Calendar, and Sites) among ABC's information technology department staff and with their students.

2 Literature Review

Since 1990, major IT companies have invested billions of dollars in cloud computing. For instance, Salesforce.com has been offering and providing on-demand Software as a Service (SaaS) for clients since 1999. Subsequently, IBM and Microsoft started to provide cloud computing services since 2000s. [8] suggested that there are six advantages of cloud computing for education. These include: backup, storage, accessibility, collaboration, resource and time conscious, and assignment. An example of the use of cloud computing in education is Virtual Computing Lab (VCL). VCL is a cloud infrastructure that pools the IT resources of several sites (servers, storage systems, and software authorities at North Carolina State University. The VCL enables the pupils from the various primary and secondary schools in the State, as well as the students using the different university campuses to access a highly developed and up-to-date pool of technical and learning resources wherever they happen to be (including at home).

Google Docs / Drive software provides Web-based word-processing, spreadsheet, and presentation applications [3]. It is a collection of web-based programs and file storage that run in a web browser, without requiring users to buy or install software. It consists of Google Apps suite Mail, Docs / Drive, Calendar, and Sites - that offer useful and attractive options for clients who are seeking for free or low-cost, easy to use, and flexible ways to manage the electronic communication services and resources [9]. Google Apps offer collaboration tools to improve communication for academic staff by sharing documents at any time and from any location. Figure 1 shows the free Google Apps services.

Email: Gmail is a free electronic mail service from Google with two important tools: virus protection and spam filters. It allows the users to use labels instead of folders where emails can have multiple labels. Multiple emails in a single conversation will be grouped as a single email thread [4].

Fig. 1. Google Apps Services

DOCS / Drive: DOCS / Drive in Google Apps allows users to share documents, spreadsheets, and presentations. Collaboration in real-time is possible with the team or with the whole school. Users can publish final documents to the entire world, too.

Calendar: Calendar is a free web based time management application that allows the user to store his events on line and can be accessed from any place provided by internet access. The user can add and share multiple calendars with different permission levels. Therefore, schedules can be collaborated and shared between groups [4].

Google Sites: Google Sites is a very important part of the Google Apps. With Google Sites, an academic staff member can create his / her web site and include documents, forms, presentation documents, pictures, calendars etc. by using easy page templates without the need for professional knowledge in designing web sites [6]. The main goal of Sites in Google Apps is to create a team-oriented site. The files in the Google Apps site can be used collaboratively and shared by multiple users.

3 The Case Study

ABC - a private academic institution - moved to a new campus. The new campus is built with advanced infrastructure in order to be able to handle the latest technologies. All classrooms are provided with smart boards and are connected to the ABC local area network and internet. Besides that, areas outside and inside the campus are covered by wireless network. ABC strives to have the latest electronic information services for use by staff and students.

For many years, ABC used Microsoft Outlook Exchange server licensed under Microsoft Outlook application for their staff and students as its electronic mail service. Today, most academic institutions have changed their mail server from Microsoft Outlook to Google Apps. This change saves money for the intuitions as well as administering time [10]. For instant, Arizona State University (ASU) relocates 450,000 dollars per year to other core activities when shifting from IMAP email client to Gmail using Google Apps [11]. Because of this, ABC in 2009 migrated its Microsoft Exchange server to Google Apps services.

The network department at ABC is responsible for providing information technology services to the academic and administrative staff as well as to the students. Google Apps have the potential to provide effective communication between staff and students at ABC. It is chosen because the software is freely available to students and all partners. This research aims to investigate the effectiveness of the use of Google Apps by staffs and students at ABC. It also investigates the relationship between the usage of Google Apps services among IT department staff and the usage of the same service by IT department staff and their students.

4 Related Works

Most of the published papers describe the facilities and features in Google Apps package [10] or discuss the migration process from a mail server to Google Apps server [12]. Only [4] investigated Google Apps services as a solution for communication in educational institutions. However, there is very little research that studied the perception of academic staff about Google Apps. [5] conducted quantitative and qualitative surveys and interviewed elementary school teachers using Docs/Drive service inside schools and [2] studied Email service as one of the communication channels that used by academic staff in interacting with their students.

5 Methodology

Determining sample size and managing the bias of non-response is crucial for designing a quantitative survey. Using smaller groups of people to generate inferences about larger groups is one of the real advantages of quantitative methods. Normally, these surveys are designed in order to decrease both; alpha error unreal difference in population and beta error undiscovered real difference in population [13].

The response sample included all the academic staff of the information technology department at ABC. The information technology department staff was chosen because they are keen and interested to use electronic services more than other academic departments' staff and Google Apps services particularly. Since the selected participants belong to the same department at the same organization, the number of nonresponse is zero.

This study used a survey research method by distributing a group administered questionnaire to the respondents [14]. The questionnaire was designed by the network director in collaboration with head of quality assurance department. The first version of this questionnaire was revised and updated according to the feedback of the research method modules instructor about the proposed research hypotheses. The study was guided by the following three hypotheses:

H1: The use of Google Apps services among IT staff is frequent.

H2: The use of Google Apps between IT staff and their student is frequent.

H3: The use of Google Apps services among IT staff and between IT and their students differs significantly.

The last version was sent for a last check with the Head of foundation unit and the Head of information technology department at ABC. After that, the questionnaires were distributed among academic staff in information technology at ABC. The reliability of the questionnaire was evaluated by measuring the internal consistency of the scales using Corobachs alpha.

6 Results and Discussion

The five point Likert-type scale with 1 = Never, 2 = Rarely, 3 = Normal, 4 = Frequently, and 5 = Most Frequently, IT staff were asked to respond to the 9 items. Question one of the questionnaires, 'How often do you use ABC Mail service of Google Apps with your colleagues?', was used to find out among IT faculty members the usage of email service with colleagues. Likewise, question two to four asked the IT faculty member about the usage of Docs/Drive, Calendar, and Sites services with his colleagues respectively. Similarly, questions five to eight were concerned with the usage of Google Apps package (Mail, Docs/Drive, Calendar, and Sites) between IT staff and their students. Question nine asked IT staff about their suggestions to increase the usage level of Google Apps at ABC. By using Spss release 16.0, questions one to four were grouped together to one variable called F-package-F(the use of Google Apps services among IT staff themselves), where questions five to eight are grouped together to be one variable called F-package-S (the use of Google Apps between IT staff and their student is frequent).

6.1 IT Staff Usage Google Apps among Themselves Frequently

To answer RQ1, the responses to the (F-package-F) package including Mail, Docs/Drive, Calendar, and Sites services would be investigated after discussing the responses to each service individually. Table 1 shows that IT staff found themselves using the mail service more frequently (Mean = 4.42) among themselves likewise for using Docs/Drive service (Mean = 4.17). In spite of the mean of Calendar and Sites services (Mean = 3.66, Mean = 3.83) less than frequent in level 4, the usage is closer to frequent and more than normal.

By calculating the frequency use of all services as a package (F-package-F), (67%) of IT staff use these services frequently and only (33%) of them use these services more than normal and close to frequently use level. To prove this statistically, the one sample T-test method with test value (4) was used to find the mean value of the usage of this package of (4.02). It shows the probability of sampling error for the resulting p-value - (Sig. 2-tailed) -is (0.795) which is greater than the used threshold value of (0.05) of confidence interval of (95%). In other words, (0.795) was greater than (0.05) and this concludes that the null hypothesis is not rejected. This is supported by the result that the mean is by different only (0.02) from the mean of the hypothesized value [15] as shown in Table 2.

Based on these findings as shown in the histogram Figure 2 below, the first hypothesis was found to be supported, suggesting that IT staff emphasize on Mail service than Calendar service in communication between each other and use shared documents and files in Docs / Drive service in their collective work frequently while their use of Site service was more than normal and very close to frequent.

Table 1. Descriptive statistical for F-package-F

	N	Range	Minimum	Maximum	Sum	Mean		Std. Deviation	Variance
	Statistic	Statistic	Statistic	Statistic	Statistic	Statistic	Std. Error	Statistic	Statistic
How often do you use BUC Mail service of Google Apps with your colleagues?	12	1.00	4.00	5.00	53.00	4.4167	.14866	.51493	.265
How often do you use Shared Docs service of Google Apps with your colleagues?	12	2.00	3.00	5.00	50.00	4.1667	.16667	.57735	.333
How often do you use Calendar service of Google Apps with your colleagues?	12	2.00	3.00	5.00	44.00	3.6667	.18803	.65134	.424
How often do you use Site service of Google Apps with your colleagues?	12	2.00	3.00	5.00	46.00	3.8333	.24100	.83485	.697
Valid N (list wise)	12								

Table 2. One Sample T-Test Results of (F-package-F)

One-Sample Test

	Test Value = 4					
					95% Confidence Interval of the Difference	
	t	df	Sig. (2-tailed)	Mean Difference	Lower	Upper
Usage of Google Apps package among IT Staff	.266	11	.795	.02083	-.1513	.1930

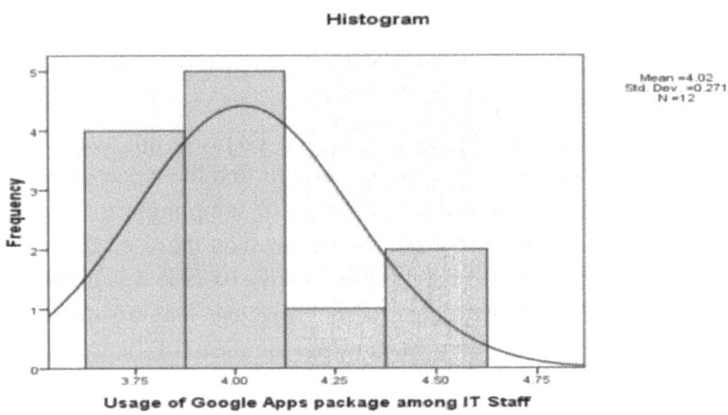

Fig. 2. F-package-F Histogram

6.2 IT Staff Usage Google Apps with Their Students Frequently

By following the same strategy described above, the mean value for the usage of mail service in F-package-S between IT staff and students was (Mean = 2.41) which is slightly differ than the usage of Site service (Mean = 2.58). The usage of Docs/Drive service mean was (Mean = 2.16) in the third rank while the IT staff usage of Calendar service with their student was (Mean = 1.91) as shown in table 3.

In other words, (66.7%) of the IT staff used the Google apps services with their students less than normal and they used it rarely or never use it at all while (33.3%) of them used these services normally but not frequently. By applying the sample T-test on F-package-S as shown in Table 4, the mean value of the usage of Google services Package between IT staff and their students was (2.27) and the p-value (Sig. 2-tailed) was (0.000) while the mean difference was (1.72). Because the p-value was less than the threshold value (0.05) and the mean was different from the hypothesized value, the null hypothesis is rejected and not supported.

Table 3. Descriptive statistical for F-package-S

	N	Range	Minimum	Maximum	Sum	Mean		Std. Deviation	Variance
	Statistic	Statistic	Statistic	Statistic	Statistic	Statistic	Std. Error	Statistic	Statistic
How often do you use BUC Mail service of Google Apps with your students?	12	3.00	1.00	4.00	29.00	2.4167	.31282	1.08362	1.174
How often do you use shared Docs service of Google Apps with your students?	12	4.00	1.00	5.00	26.00	2.1667	.32177	1.11464	1.242
How often do you use Calendar service of Google Apps with your students?	12	2.00	1.00	3.00	23.00	1.9167	.22891	.79296	.629
How often do you use Site service of Google Apps with your students?	12	4.00	1.00	5.00	31.00	2.5833	.35799	1.24011	1.538
Valid N (listwise)	12								

Table 4. One Sample T-Test Results of (F-package-S)

	Test Value = 4					
					95% Confidence Interval of the Difference	
	t	df	Sig. (2-tailed)	Mean Difference	Lower	Upper
Usage of Google Apps package between IT Staff and their Students	-7.833	11	.000	-1.72917	-2.2150	-1.2433

According to these results and as shown in the histogram Figure 3, the second hypothesis is rejected and supports the alternative. In other words, the usage of Google Apps services between IT staff and their students is not frequent and normal. These results highlight that there are serious problems in using Google Apps services between IT staff and students.

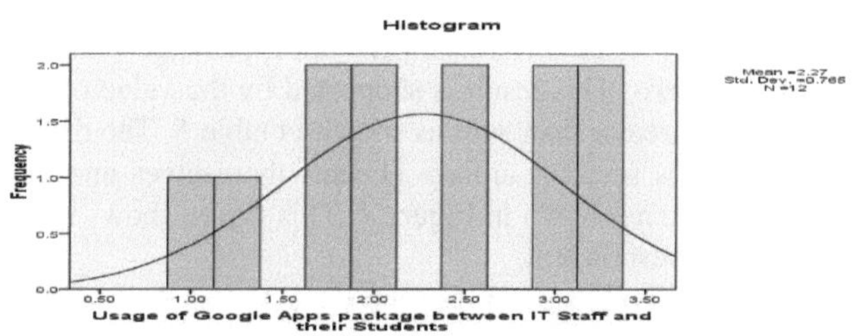

Fig. 3. F-package-S Histogram

6.3 The Usage Level of Google Apps Differ Significantly

In order to discuss the hypothesis H3, we need to investigate the difference between the usage of Google Apps among IT staff themselves and IT staff with their students by comparing the responses to both packages F-package-F with and F-package-S by the same respondents respectively. Because the two packages are not independent of one another, a paired sample T-test was used to compare between F-package-F and F-package-S. As SPSS does not tell us straightforwardly which package is larger, we need to look at the differences in the values of the two packages and see if the mean of these differences is equal to zero.

Table 5. Paired Samples T-Test Results

	Paired Differences							
				95% Confidence Interval of the Difference				
	Mean	Std. Deviation	Std. Error Mean	Lower	Upper	t	df	Sig. (2-tailed)
Pair 1 Usage of Google Apps package among IT Staff - Usage of Google Apps package between IT Staff and their Students	1.75000	.69085	.19943	1.31106	2.18894	8.775	11	.000

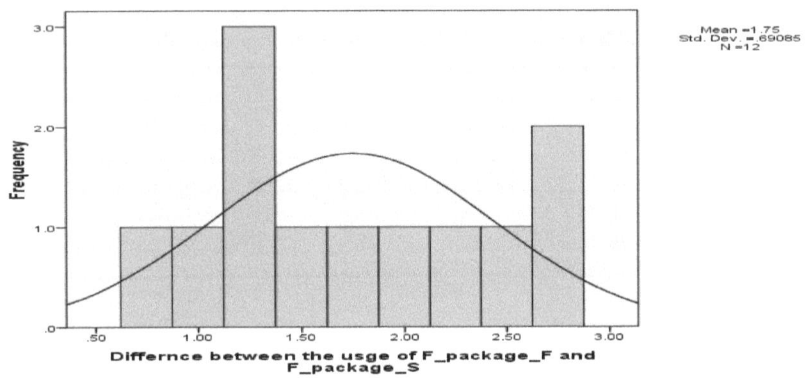

Fig. 4. Difference between F-package-F and F-package-S

The probability of p-value is less than the prespecified alpha value (usually .05) and this concludes that the mean difference between F-package-F and F-package-S is statistically differs than zero. This result is supported by the value of the mean (mean = 1.75) and this value is greater than zero as shown in table 5. The difference between the usage of Google Apps services among IT staff themselves and their students is explained in the histogram as shown in Figure 4. This figure shows the frequencies of the mean values for each respondent.

The finding reveals that hypothesis H3 is supported. That is the usage of Google Apps (F- package-F) is more than the usage of Google Apps (F-package-S). This evidence shows that findings of H1 and H2 are statistically supported. According to the Corobachs alpha value (0.606) which was calculated for the 8 items of frequent usage of the Google Apps services; this makes the study statistically acceptable and the data reliable.

Although cloud computing using Google Apps has great potential for education, the main concern is Security breaches. security risks includes compliance risks, the loss of governance, data protection , lock - in issues, isolation failure, management interface compromise, incomplete or insecure data deletion and malicious insiders. There are also the issues of privacy, data integrity, intellectual property management, regulation issues and audit trails. Apart from the security concerns, there are certain other issues like maintaining the integrity of data, ensuring access is limited to authorized users and maintaining the availability of data and services.

7 Conclusion and Future Work

The purpose of this study is to investigate the use of Google Apps at ABC. These results indicate that the IT staff at ABC use Google Apps services package frequently as the main communication channel among themselves. However, the use of Google Apps between IT academic staff and their students is less frequent. It is our belief that there is a lack of trust in the use of online tools by the students. Trust facilitates cooperative behavior. There was a lack of trust in sharing between staffs and students. Trust is the most important precondition for sharing. Although sharing is a voluntary behavior, we often need to share values and/or establish a common shared objective with someone before we are willing to share. Conversely, trust is also voluntary especially to trust initially is a voluntary act of faith.

This study supports hypothesis H3 that the usage of Google Apps services package among IT staff differs significantly from the usage of Google Apps services package between IT staff and their students. The underlying reasons can be attributed to: students have limited use of electronic information services particularly in their first and second years at university and poor interaction of IT staff with their students. This was because IT staff preferred to use face to face communication rather than using the mail service. At the same time, IT staff also preferred the use of traditional ways of transferring files rather than using Docs/Drive services. IT staff did not share important events with students through Calendar service but preferred to use other method. Finally, it is obvious that IT staff did not interact with students through their websites. These above results conclude that students at ABC were not using Google Apps services as main communication channel.

Although the study sheds light on the reasons why ABC did not produce the potential benefits of using Google apps as predicted. It is important to realize the study has limitations. This study only involves only one institution. There may be other variables that would impact the use of Google apps by institutions. Further studies with other variables are required.

In order to enhance the communication level between staff and students, the management of the academic institute should instructing students to use the available electronic facilities like using ERP system at the college. Instructors should encourage their students to use Google Apps services through using Drive service for sharing an assignment with them and by uploading some materials on their websites. Furthermore, instructors should use Calendar for announcing important activities and events.

References

1. Kagima, L.K., Hausafus, C.O.: Integration of electronic communication in higher education: Contributions of faculty computer self-efficacy. The Internet and Higher Education 2(4), 221–235 (2001)
2. Baghestan, A.G., Zavareh, M.A., Hassan, M.A.: Communication Channels Used by Academic Staff in Interacting with Their Students. Journal of Social Sciences and Humanities 17(2) (2009)
3. Han, Y.: On the clouds: a new way of computing. Information Technology and Libraries 29(2), 87–92 (2010)
4. Sviridova, T., Sviridova, L., Tymoshenko, B.: Google Apps as solution of communication issues in educational process. In: 2011 IEEE Proceedings of VIIth International Conference Perspective Technologies and Methods in MEMS Design (MEMSTECH), pp. 183–184 (2011)
5. Kaimuloa Bates, B.: Using Google Apps in Professional Learning Communities (2011)
6. Wang, Y., Jin, B.: The application of SaaS model in network education-take Google apps for example. In: 2nd International Conference on IEEE Education Technology and Computer (ICETC), vol. 4, pp. V4–191 (2010)
7. Edwards, J.T.: A Case Study: Using Google Documents as a Collaborative Writing Tool in Undergraduate Courses. The Texas Speech Communication Journal Online (2012), http://www.etsca.com/tscjonline/0911-google (accessed December 7, 2012)
8. Weaver, D.: Use Six Advantages of Cloud Computing in Education (2014), http://www.pearsonschoolsystems.com/blog/?p=1507#sthash.kICqfKNL.dpbs (accessed April 13, 2014)
9. Hartnett, E., Koury, R.: Using Google Apps Through the Electronic Resource Life Cycle. Collection Management 37(1), 47–54 (2012)
10. Hastings, R.: A Year with Google Apps. Computers in Libraries 30(4), 12–16 (2010)
11. Barlow, K., Lane, J.: Like technology from an advanced alien culture: Google apps for education at ASU. In: Proceedings of the 35th annual ACM SIGUCCS fall Conference, pp. 8–10. ACM (2007), 2007
12. Klein, R., Orelup, R., Smith, M.: Google apps for education: Valparaiso University's migration experience. In: Proceedings of the ACM SIGUCCS 40th Annual Conference on Special Interest Group on University and College Computing Services, pp. 203–208. ACM (2012)
13. Bartlett, J.E., Kotrlik, J.W., Higgins, C.: Organizational Research: Determining Appropriate Sample Size in Survey Research Appropri-ate Sample Size in Survey Research. Information Technology, Learning, and Performance Journal 19(1), 43 (2001)
14. Trochim, W.M.: Types of Surveys. Research Method Knowledge Base (2012), http://www.socialresearchmethids.net/kb/survtype.php (accessed December 9, 2012)
15. R. T. IDRE, SPSS Annotated Output, http://statistics.ats.ucla.edu/stat/spss/output/Spss-ttest.html

The Key Factors of Knowledge Sharing in Online Community

Liang-Cheng Huang[1], I-Hsien Ting[2], and Seng-Cho T. Chou[3]

[1] Department of Information Management, National Taiwan University
Institute of Statistical Sciences, Academia Sinica
d95725010@ntu.edu.tw
[2] Department of Information Management, National University of Kaohsiung
iting@nuk.edu.tw
[3] Department of Information Management, National Taiwan University
chou@ntu.edu.tw

Abstract. In web 2.0 social network services also provided many attached tools for help social communication, for example, photo sharing and comment mechanism. According to above mentioned, Web 2.0 facilitated web-based information sharing, even knowledge sharing. However, less study examined that knowledge sharing about online users. In this paper, we aim to examine the users' content and social value in knowledge platform impact on knowledge sharing and use. Finally, the study develops a KMO 2.0 success model. In the model, we have proposed 13 hypotheses for testing. From the results, the hypotheses H1, H3, H5, H6, H7, H8, H9, H10, H11, H12, and H13 have been supported.

1 Introduction

1.1 Background

Due to technology development and internet widespread, the new term of "Web2.0" was emerged. The concept "Web 2.0" began with a brainstorming session between O'Reilly and MediaLive in a conference (O'Reilly, 2007). Web 2.0 has many characteristics such as the web as platform, user participation, information with personality, and interactivity responsiveness (Kim, Yue, Hall, & Gates, 2009). Based on the characteristics, Web 2.0 developed two elements: user generated content (UGC) and social networks services (SNS). In Web 1.0, all information on the Internet was provided by the webmaster. For example, users received information passively through the news portal websites or firm official website. In Web 2.0, information could be generated by users like the concept of user generated content. The kinds of platform are such as blog website, Wikipedia, and Youtube. For the concept of social network services, users could maintain offline friendship and meet new one through social network sites such Facebook and Myspace. In addition, social network services also provided many attached tools for help social communication, for example, photo sharing and comment mechanism. According to above mentioned, Web 2.0 facilitated web-based information sharing, even knowledge sharing.

L. Uden et al. (Eds.): LTEC 2014, CCIS 446, pp. 105–113, 2014.

1.2 Motivation

About knowledge management, the past literatures mostly focused on the organization field. For example, the knowledge success model displayed that factors how impact on knowledge use in the organization (Kulkarni, Ravindran, & Freeze, 2006). Moreover, the organization culture influenced the knowledge management (Alavi, Kayworth, & Leidner, 2005). In spite of web-based research, it showed that employees utilized web technology such as forum and community to promote knowledge sharing. But less study examined that knowledge sharing about online users. Based on the gap, the study investigates that the features of user generated content (content value) and social network services (social value) influence on knowledge sharing and use.

1.3 Research Question

This study aims to examine that users' content and social value in knowledge platform impact on knowledge sharing and use. Finally, the study develops a KM 2.0 success model.

2 Literature Review

2.1 Content Value and Social Value

Based on the study of Helen and Wagner (2006), this study investigates the influence of two important factors—content and social values—on knowledge sharing. Kulkarni, Ravindran, and Freeze (2006) tried to define content value as various qualities including its relevance, accuracy, timeliness, applicability, comprehensibility, presentation formats, extent of insight, availability of expertise and advice, and so on. Moreover, there is an abundance of research showing that social value plays an important role in knowledge sharing in the internet. For instance, bloggers hope to link with popular blogs so that more people will view and rate their own (Wagner & Bolloju, 2005).

2.2 Knowledge Sharing

Knowledge sharing is a communication process that includes two parts: (1) the knowledge owner externalizes the knowledge; (2) the knowledge demander internalizes the knowledge (Hendriks, 1999). The knowledge conversion includes both transmission and absorption; therefore an enterprise should not merely absorb knowledge, but also acquire knowledge channels (Davenport & Prusak, 1998). Nonaka (1995) argued that the some of the main obstacles to converting knowledge could be resolved as follows: lack of trust can be improved through face-to-face conversation, lack of learnability can be solved by hiring more competent and open-minded workers, and cultural gaps can be bridged through education, team work, and interactive discussions. Since to knowledge is unlike products, which are easy transferable, during the process of learning new knowledge, a person should be able to rebuild knowledge and equipped his or herself with the basic knowledge that allows for effective learning and sharing.

2.3 User Satisfaction

According to the research of Kulkarni et al. (2006), user satisfaction can be defined as subjective evaluation of the various outcomes due to the knowledge sharing and retrieval capabilities existing within the organization, including ease of getting the information and knowledge needed, satisfaction with the access to knowledge, adequacy of the information/knowledge to meet one's needs.

3 Research Model

H1: Norms of reciprocity is positively related to information value.
H2: Norms of voluntarism is positively related to information value.
H3: Norms of social trust is positively related to information value.

H4: Norms of reciprocity is positively related to social value.
H5: Norms of voluntarism is positively related to social value.
H6: Norms of social trust is positively related to social value.

Knowledge management in open source proveds user to serach, compose and edit contents according to soe basic rules, and absorb knowledge through the knowledge sharing process. People can collaborate with each other to create and share knowledge (Richards, 2009). Blau (1964) asserted that when socializing, every individual expects for feedback. For example, in pair or group interaction individuals want to participate and maintain an important role in the activity (Jones, Hesterly, & Borgatti, 1997). This implies the social value of such platform would effect the knowledge sharing. Besides, Seddon (1997) also claimed in IS success model that if the quality of knowledge content is high, then a knowledge worker is more likely to perceive that knowledge management initiatives contribute to him/her self-efficiency.

H7: Information value is positively related to perceived usefulness of knowledge sharing.
H8: Social value is positively related to perceived usefulness of knowledge sharing.

In line with the IS success model, we propose that content value, social quality, and perceived usefulness of knowledge sharing together determine the level of overall user satisfaction, which, like its equivalent in the IS success model (Rai, Lang & Welker, 2002), is a subjective measure of the various outcomes of the knowledge sharing, retrieval, and knowledge reuse capabilities existing within the firm as a result of the knowledge management initiatives undertaken.

H9: Information value is positively related to user satisfaction.
H10: Social value is positively related to user satisfaction.
H11: Perceived usefulness of knowledge sharing is positively related to user satisfaction.

Comaring model proposed by DeLone & McLean (2003) with Seddon (1997), it is interesting to note the difference between D&M and Seddon in the treatment of IS use. The D&M model includes a causal path from user satisfaction to system dependence (same as IS use), as well as one from system dependence to perceived usefulness. Seddon (1997) includes only one causal relationship leading from user Satisfaction to IS use; the model does not propose that perceived usefulness causes IS use or vice versa. In line with Seddon's IS success model, we propose that user satisfaction causes intention of knowledge use. Further, we argue that a relationship between usefulness and use is entirely possible in the knowledge management context.

H12: Perceived usefulness of knowledge sharing is positicely related to intention of knowledg use.
H13: User satisfaction is positively related to intention of knowledge use.

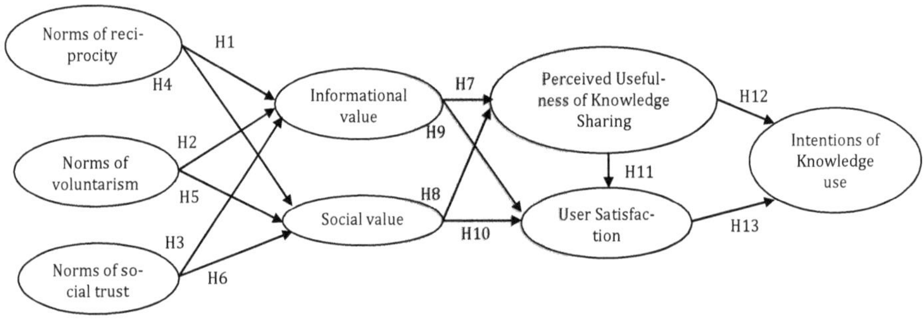

Fig. 1. Research model

4 Methodology

This study used survey method to test the hypothesis. The detail information of methodology is in the following sections.

4.1 Measurement

Social capital consisted of three dimensions: norms of reciprocity, norms of voluntarism, and norms of social trust. This study used a two-item scale which was developed by Wasko and Faraj's (2000) to measure norms of reciprocity. To measure norms of voluntarism, this study adopted Podsakoff, Ahearne, and MacKenzie's (1997) three-item scale. This study utilized norms of social trust scale. The three-item scale was developed by Moorman, Zaltman, and Deshpande (1992). Moreover, this study adopted a three-item scale for informational value and a four-item scale for social value. These scales were developed by Mathwick and Klebba (2003).

For perceived usefulness of knowledge sharing, this study used a six-item scale which developed by Kulkarni, Ravindran, and Freeze (2006). This scale was originally adopted in the organization condition. Therefore, this study deleted one item to further measure. And this study also adopted Kulkarni, Ravindran, and

Freeze's (2006) three-item to measure user satisfaction. Finally, this study utilized a three-item which was developed by Goodhue and Thompson (1995) to measure intentions of knowledge use.

All items of three dimensions of social capital, information value, social value, perceived usefulness of knowledge sharing, user satisfaction, and intentions of knowledge use were the seven-point Likert-type, with a measuring range of from 1 (strongly disagree) to 7 (strongly agree).

4.2 Participant

This study recruited in total 305 subjects which were from the online community. After deleted subjects without using online community experiences, the remaining 298 completed responses were accepted for data analysis. The subjects consisted of 146 (49.00%) students and 152 (51.00%) non-students. The subjects included 154 (51.68%) males and 144 (48.32%) females. The age of subjects ranged from 16 to 56 years (Mean = 25.76, SD = 4.66). In the amount of education, 50.67% of the subjects had university degrees and 44.97% of the subjects had master degrees. The subjects have adopted online community averagely 4.48 years (SD = 2.16). The subjects averagely used 12.18 hours (SD = 8.94) per week.

4.3 Procedure

This study recruits voluntary participants in an online community. This study posts messages of call for voluntarily subjects on questionnaire boards about two weeks. The participants can click the hyperlink which posts in the call for voluntarily subjects to join this study. This study builds an online questionnaire web page to collect data. Each participant is provided 50 p coins as souvenirs for complete responses.

4.4 Reliability and Validity

Factor analysis was conducted by using the principal component factor analysis with the varimax rotation. The results displayed that loadings of items were higher than .73 and considered significant (Hair, Jr., Tatham, & Black, 1998). Cronbach's α was usually used to estimate the reliability of a construct. This study calculated Cronbach's α to estimate reliabilities for all measurement scales. In the study, Cronbach's α value range for all measurement scales was from .74 for intention of knowledge use to .91 for perceived of usefulness knowledge sharing. All Cronbach's α values were over .70 and in the commonly acceptable range of reliability (Nunnally, 1978). In addition, this study employed average variance extracted (AVE) and composite reliability (CR) to evaluate convergent validity. For all measurement scales, the range of average variance extracted (AVE) value was from .65 for intention of knowledge use to .80 for norms of reciprocity. Moreover, composite reliability value range was from .85 for intention of knowledge use to .93 for perceived of usefulness knowledge sharing. All average variance extracted (AVE) values exceeded .50, and composite reliability (CR) values was over .70. They were in the commonly acceptable range of average variance extracted (AVE) and composite reliability (CR) (Fornell & Larcker, 1981).

5 Results

Due to our sample being medium-sized, this study used SmartPLS 2.0 to estimate the research model. After analyzing the data, figure 2 presents the PLS model estimation output. The explanatory power of the constructs were 48% for informational value, 44% for social value, 55% for perceived usefulness of knowledge sharing, 60% for user satisfaction, and 65% for intentions of knowledge use. Except that the path linkages from norms of reciprocity to social value and norms of voluntarism to informational value were not significant, other path linkages were significant. The results supported hypotheses H1, H3, H5, H6, H7, H8, H9, H10, H11, H12, and H13.

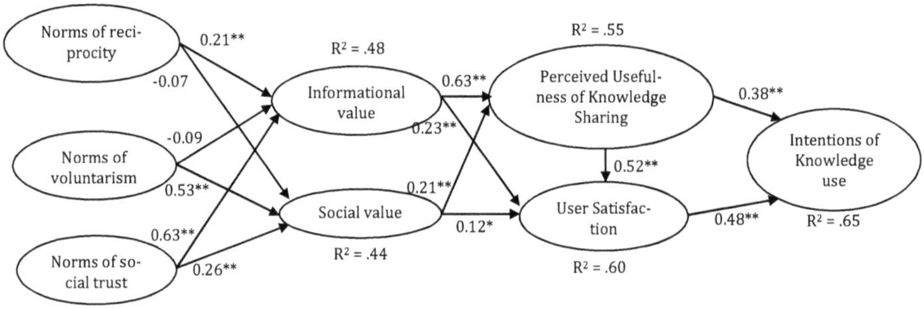

Fig. 2. Results of PLS analysis $*p < .05$, $**p < .01$

In order to observe the gender effect, the data were divided into two groups, male and female, to compare the different results. Figure 3 revealed the PLS model estimation outcome for male group. The explanatory power of the constructs were 57% for informational value, 45% for social value, 59% for perceived usefulness of knowledge sharing, 69% for user satisfaction, and 68% for intentions of knowledge use. Except that the path linkages from norms of reciprocity to informational and social value and norms of voluntarism to informational value were not significant, other path linkages were significant. Moreover, figure 4 shows the PLS model estimation results for the female group. The explanatory power of the constructs were 42% for informational value, 44% for social value, 50% for perceived usefulness of knowledge sharing, 49% for user satisfaction, and 62% for intentions of knowledge use. And the path linkages from norms of reciprocity to social value, norms of voluntarism to informational value, and social value to user satisfaction were not significant. The other path linkages were significant. Comparing the PLS results for male and female groups, the relationship between norms of reciprocity and informational value was significant for female group whereas it was not significant for male group. In addition, the path coefficient from norms of social trust to social value was higher for female group than for male group. On the contrary, the path coefficient from norms of voluntarism to social value was less for female group than for male group. Based on the results, female group were more willing to reciprocity with other community members than male group. On the other hand, male group preferred to more voluntarism than female group in online community.

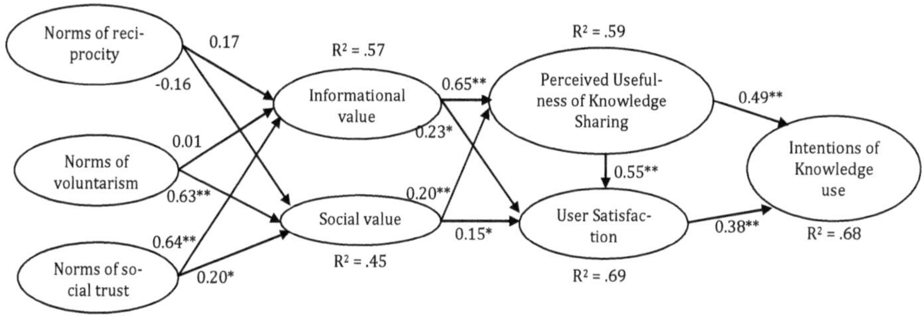

Fig. 3. Results of PLS analysis for male group $*p < .05$, $**p < .01$

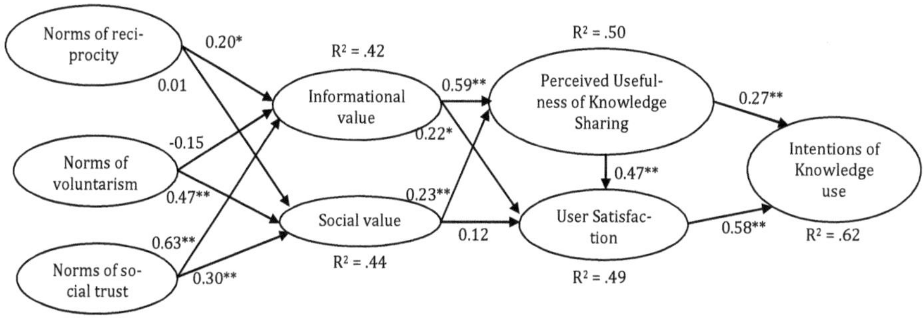

Fig. 4. Results of PLS analysis for female group $*p < .05$, $**p < .01$

In addition, this study also wanted to test the occupation effect. Therefore, the data were divided into two groups, student and non-student, to compare the different results. Figure 5 revealed the PLS model estimation outcome for student group. The explanatory power of the constructs were 48% for informational value, 43% for social value, 53% for perceived usefulness of knowledge sharing, 64% for user satisfaction, and 60% for intentions of knowledge use. Except that the path linkages from norms of reciprocity and norms of social trust to social value, norms of voluntarism to informational value, and social value to user satisfaction were not significant, other path linkages were significant. And figure 6 shows the PLS model estimation results for the non-student group. The explanatory power of the constructs were 49% for informational value, 48% for social value, 56% for perceived usefulness of knowledge sharing, 58% for user satisfaction, and 70% for intentions of knowledge use. Furthermore, the path linkages from norms of reciprocity to social value, norms of voluntarism to informational value, and informational value to user satisfaction were not significant. The other path linkages were significant. Comparing the PLS results for student and non-student groups, the relationship between norms of social trust and social value was significant for non-student group, but for student group it was not significant. Furthermore, the path coefficient from norms of social trust to informational value was higher for non-student group than for student group. Conversely, the path coefficient from norms of reciprocity to informational value was less for non-student group than for student group. According to the results, non-student group had more social trust than student group in online community. On the contrary, student group would like to reciprocity with others than non-student group.

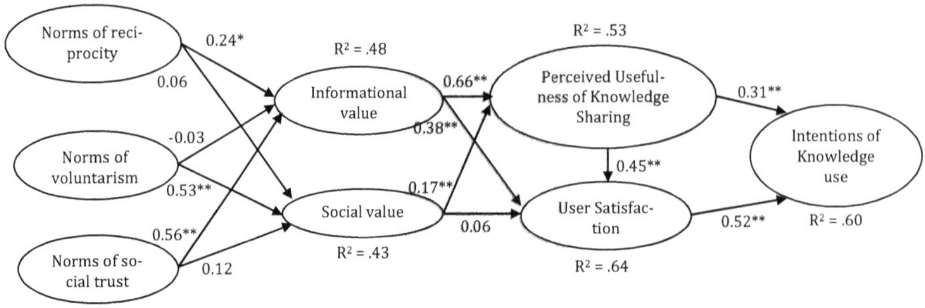

Fig. 5. Results of PLS analysis for student $*p < .05$, $**p < .01$

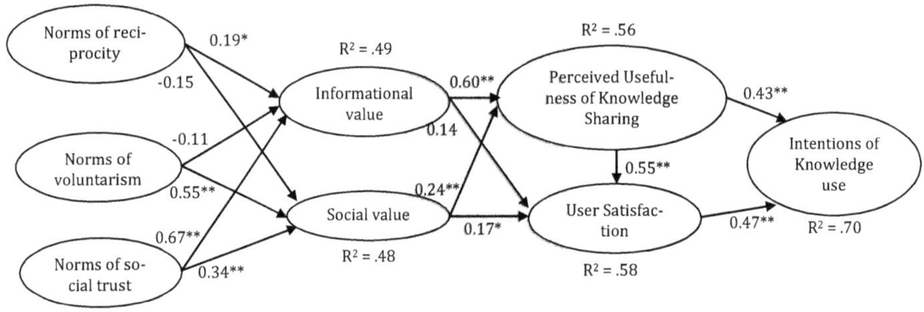

Fig. 6. Results of PLS analysis for non-student $*p < .05$, $**p < .01$

References

1. Alavi, M., Kayworth, T.R., Leidner, D.E.: An Empirical Examination of the Influence of Organizational Culture on Knowledge Management Practice. Journal of Management Information Systems 22(3), 191–224 (2005)
2. Blau, P.M.: Exchange and power in social life. John Wiley and Sons, New York (1964)
3. Davenport, T.H., Prusak, L.: Working knowledge: How organization manage what they know? Harvard Business School Press, Massachusetts (1998)
4. DeLone, W.H., McLean, E.R.: The DeLone and McLean model of information systems success: A ten-year update. Journal of Management Information Systems 19(4), 9–30 (2003)
5. Fornell, C., Larcker, D.: Evaluating structural equation models with unobservable variables and measurement error. Journal of Marketing Research 18(1), 39–50 (1981)
6. Goodhue, D.L., Thompson, R.L.: Task-technology fit and individual performance. MIS Quarterly 19(2), 213–236 (1995)
7. Hair Jr., J.F., Anderson, R.E., Tatham, R.L., Black, W.C.: Multivariate Data Analysis, 5th edn. Prentice Hall, Upper Saddle River (1998)
8. Helen, S.D., Wagner, C.: Weblog success: Exploring the role of technology. International Journal of Human–Computer Studies 64(9), 789–798 (2006)
9. Hendriks, P.: Why share knowledge? The influence of ICT on motivation for knowledge sharing. Knowledge and Process Management 6(2), 91–100 (1999)

10. Jones, C., Hesterly, W.S., Borgatti, S.P.: A general theory of network governance. Exchange conditions and social mechanisms. Academy of Management Review 22(4), 911–945 (1997)
11. Kim, D.J., Yue, K.B., Hall, S.P.: Global Diffusion of the Internet XV: Web 2.0 Technologies, Principles, and Applications: A Conceptual Framework from Technology Push and Demand Pull Perspective. Communications of the Association for Information Systems 24, 657–672 (2009)
12. Kulkarni, U.R., Ravindran, S., Freeze, R.: Knowledge Management Success Model: Theoretical Development and Empirical Validation. Journal of Management Information Systems 23(3), 309–347 (2006)
13. Mathwick, C., Klebba, J.: The Nature and Value of Virtual Community Participation. Paper presented at the American Marketing Association Summer Educators' Conference, Chicago (2003)
14. Moorman, C., Zaltman, G., Deshpande, R.: Relationships between Providers and Users of Market Research: The Dynamics of Trust within and between Organizations. Journal of Marketing Research 29, 314–328 (1992)
15. Nonaka, I., Takeuchi, H.: The knowledge-creating company. Oxford University Press, New York (1995)
16. Nunnally, J.C.: Psychometric Theory, 2nd edn. McGraw-Hill, New York (1978)
17. O'Reilly, T.: What Is Web 2.0: Design Patterns and Business Models for the Next Generation of Software. Communications & Strategies 65(1), 17–37 (2007)
18. Podsakoff, P.M., Ahearne, M., MacKenzie, S.B.: Organizational Citizenship Behavior and the Quantity and Quality of Work Group Preferences. Journal of Applied Psychology 8(2), 262–270 (1997)
19. Rai, A., Lang, S.S., Welker, R.B.: Assessing the validity of IS success models: An empirical test and theoretical analysis. Information Systems Research 13(1), 50–69 (2002)
20. Seddon, P.B.: A respecification and extension of the DeLone and McLean model of IS success. Information Systems Research 8(3), 240–253 (1997)
21. Wagner, C., Bolloju, N.: Supporting knowledge management in organizations with conversational technologies: Discussion forums, weblogs, and wikis. Journal of Database Management 16(2), 1–8 (2005)
22. Wasko, M., Faraj, S.: It Is What One Does: Why People Participate and Help Others in Electronic Communities of Practice. Journal of Strategic Information Systems 9(2/3), 155–173 (2000)

Can the Online Social Networks Be Used as a Learning Tool? A Case Study in Twitter

Luciana A.M. Zaina, Tiago A. Ameida, and Guilherme M. Torres

Federal University of São Carlos – Sorocaba - Rdv João Leme dos Santos, Km110 – Sorocaba – SP – Brazil
{lzaina,talmeida}@ufscar.br, guimato@gmail.com

Abstract. The Web 2.0 has provided a significant increase in the use of online social networks. In this scenario, Twitter has being used for collaborating, communicating and to exchange ideas between users who share common interests. Consequently, it can be observed an increasing adoption of social networks as a resource to support learning outside the classroom. They can provide mechanisms for sharing ideas and discussions about the studing subjects. However, as far as we know, there is no consensus in the literature whether users indeed efficiently employ these resources for such purpose. An important question is: can the online social networks be used as an efficient learning tool? Helping us to find the answer, this paper presents empirical results of an experiment performed to evaluate the effectiveness of Twitter for supporting learning and also to identify the common behavior of its users.

1 Introduction

Although social networks are not a new concept, its popularity has grown with the increasing interation on virtual communities and electronic environments. Within the context of learning, we observe a raising adoption of social networks for supporting the classroom activities. These environments are being used as an extension of the classroom, providing mechanisms for sharing ideas and to discuss important topics [6].

Among the available online social networks, Twitter has become well-known for using the concept of microblogging, which allows just short messages (limited to 140 characters) to convey information, and for being perform on different devices [16].

Recent reports indicate that about twenty million users produce more than fifty million messages on Twitter daily. The analysis of such messages can help in gathering information about users. Beyond simply numerical checks, as the num ber of user's followers, we can also parse the messages and employ pattern recognition algorithms and text mining techniques in order to offer a deep analysis [20].

Text mining techniques have been adopted in the e-learning area aiming to supply the teacher on identification about the successes and failures during the process of teaching and learning, and on recommendation of issues that may contribute to the process of learning.

L. Uden et al. (Eds.): LTEC 2014, CCIS 446, pp. 114–123, 2014.

Observing the trend of using the electronic social networks to support learning, the goal of this work is to empirically examine the effectiveness of employing Twitter to support the outside classroom discussions. To do that, we have collected data trought text mining techniques to find terms commonly used by teachers and students. In this way, we have collected and analyzed messages posted by two professors about subjects that were taught in an undergraduated course of Computer Science in a Brazilian University. These messages were compared to the messages sent by students who followed the teachers and also attended the courses. After that, we have examined whether students forwarded messages or even sent new posts about the theme proposed by the teachers. Additionally, we applied a questionnaire to the involved students in order to compare both the results obtained from the text mining analysis and the students.

The remainder of this paper is organized as follows: Section 2 presents the theoretical background need to perform this work. The related work is presented and compared in Section 3. Section 4 discusses the methodology and presents the experiment results. Finally, Section 5 outlines the main conclusions.

2 Theoretical Background

This study is based on three different contexts: the online social networks, e-learning environments and text mining tools. A briefly theorical background of each one is described in the following.

2.1 E-learning and Online Social Networks

The main characteristics of Web 2.0 have improved the spreading of applications of Online Social Networks (OSN) in recent years [2]. Communication and collaboration tools such as blogs, wikis and social networks have attracted billions of users, and online social networks has surpassed the email popularity [3]. Many OSN have emerged with different purposes, such as: professional contacts (LinkdIn[1]), short message sharing (Twitter[2]), video sharing (YouTube[3]), sharing of general purpose (MySpace[4], Facebook[5], Orkut[6]), among many others. Many fields like commercial (marketing and political campaigns), sociology (human behavior and communication), security and privacy, internet (traffic and volume data), user experiece (UX) and e-learning demand efforts into studies of the OSN adoption [4].

An e-learning environment should support the process of teaching and learning using some electronic tool for learning purposes (wikis, blogs and OSN). Although an e-learning environment does not need an Internet connection, with the spread of the use of the Web, there is a major trend in the development of web environments to

[1] http://www.linkedin.com/
[2] http://twitter.com/
[3] http://www.youtube.com/
[4] http://www.myspace.com
[5] http://www.facebook.com
[6] http://www.orkut.com/

assist the learning process [5]. This way, the OSN can be used to encourage learning as a social process, based on the idea that knowledge is continuing under construction. Furthermore, users may express and share ideas with different users who have the same interests [6].

Among different OSN environments, Twitter has stood out for supplying the users' communication, collaboration and sharing ideas from short messages (140 characters or less). According to Cormode, Krishnamurthy and Willinger [8], about twenty million users post more than fifty million messages daily in Twitter from different devices.

Twitter implements the conception of microblogging service in Web 2.0, providing API (Application Programming Interface) with a set of features to handle and post the message, including updates, data status and data of user profile, and so on [7,9]. In addition to texts, the user can add into his messages Web site links, and photos. Due to the size limit, the Twitter employs link shorteners to create a smaller URL from the original message, in order to minimize the describer URL [10].

2.2 Text Mining Process

Text mining techniques can be applied to analyze words and expressions in messages posted in Twitter in order to find important information about the users. Such techniques is generally used to looking for patterns in texts written in natural language. The searching process is driven by the goal of the analysis. Thus the identification of the problem and the context in which it is applied should be decided before the text mining application. The success of the mining process usually depends on this initial phase where is defined the set of data that will be handled, and the constraints related to data and to the context [1].

The first step is the pre-processing which involves the preparation of the texts to the mining. Usually the data are not structured which imposes restrictions on the use of machine learning tools. The data may be structured into an array of attribute-value. The array is built after the step of tokenization, which parses the unstructured text, identifies important characteristics, and separates the text into tokens (called words or terms) by applying regular expressions. The tokenization is a process of lexical analysis that verifies an input of lines of characters and generates a sequence of symbols. During this step it is possible to remove characters without a context semantic, as marks, syllabic separations, special marks and numbers [1].

After pre-processing the texts, the patterns are extracted producing word and expression groups of interest. The main goal of this step is to sort out the groups that have common interest in patterns extracted from the database. Subsequently, it is necessary to perform a post-processing step, applying statistical index to validate the obtained patterns and to indicate the quality of the results. The resulting set and context support the final analysis.

3 Related Work

There are few papers in the literature that present studies about the employment of online social networks to support learning. In the folloing, we briefly discuss the most important of them.

Dunlap & Lowenthal (2009) [11] analyzed the use of Twitter to share ideas for extra classroom. Students were asked to use the tool to clarify issues and doubts. The main purpose of such work was to check if Twitter could be used as an extension of the communication that occurred in the classroom. According to the authors, the participants were able to write concisely the new findings on a specific topic and to share ideas with colleagues. Another relevant point reported in the paper is the insertion of Twitter as a natural communication media.

Borau et . al. (2009) [12] evaluated the efficacy of using Twitter as a support tool to develop skills for reading and writing in English. The experiments were performed with Chinese students who participate in an online language course. A questionnaire was applied and 62 % reported that they enjoyed the experience. Data analysis tools have found that the most common activities performed by users were posting links and messages of doubts.

Cheong & Lee (2009) [13] listed the most mentioned terms on Twitter comparing them with those ones presented in the user's profile who posted messages (age, sex, geographic location, etc). To review the posts and identify user profiles, the authors employed the Kohonen self-organizing maps [17] by means of the Viscovery Somine tool [18]. The authors concluded that the most mentioned terms are directly related to some characteristic of the user's profile that posted the message.

In another study, Vieweg et . al. (2010) [14] analyzed the effectiveness of Twitter to disseminating information on natural disasters. The experiments were performed during two natural disasters when the users had posted different messages with relevant tags to geographical location. Based on the formation of groups that characterize a relevant category to the natural phenomenon, the authors concluded that the shared information could help victims to take important decisions during such events. However, the authors highlight the need for the user to understand the syntax that should be used to build messages which are adherent to a context.

4 The Experiment

We have conducted an empirical experiment with undergratuated computer science students of a Brazilian University aiming to answer the question: is the Twitter a native learning tool? The experiment was performed to check if the OSNs are good environments to exchange information, as pointed out by the envolved students. In this way, our goal is to certify that the students are active agents in the learning process. To do that, professors have adopted Twitter as a complementary learning tool outside the classroom. The messages posted by two teachers who have taught the courses "Web Development", "Software Engineering" and "Entrepreneurship" were collected using the Twitter API. After that, the messages were analyzed and compared with the tweets posted by 52 students enrolled in the courses who followed the professor on Twitter. After 4 months, 1,794 messages were collected: 118 posted by professors and 1,676 by the students. Any kind of recommendation regarding the messages format were made by the professors, since we aimed to observe the natural behaviour of the students in the social network without any kind of guidance.

Before the messages analysis, the professors have pointed out the most relevant keywords to the teaching objectives and consequently to guide the text mining process. From the collected messages we applied the text mining techniques considering the pointed relevant keywords. This way, we first tokenized the messages and constructed arrays to track the occorrence and frequency of each relevant keyword. The method we have used is based on the proposal of Almeida and Yamakami [15] that works with similar scenarios in e-mails. The algorithm was implemented in Matlab [19] and the text mining process is described in the following.

First, a matrix of occurrences is created from the list of tokens extracted from each message. In Twitter messages is frequent the occurrence of links, and the words delimitors contain marks that are used in links. So, two different sets of words delimiters were used to split the messages in tokens. The first set specifies only the most common delimiters like newline, blank and tab; while the second consists of the most common characters in written texts, such as semicolons, colons, dash, among others. Thus, the tokenization of message was performed in two steps. First, each character has been parsed and the delimiters of the first set were ignored. When a common character was found, it is started the step of creating the token: each parsed character is concatenated until a general delimiter is found again.

During the process of tokenization, it is applied a regular expression to check if each extracted term is a link. Another step of tokenization is performed using the second set of delimiters if the token is not considered a link. As Twitter employes a mechanism to reduce the size of the links, for the same original link, different shortened links can be created in different moments. Aiming to verify the relevance of the links on the analysis, we use an API to get the original link before perform the text mining process again.

Two matrices of relevant terms are built with tokens extracted from two sets of messages: one from the messages posted by the teachers and other from the students ones. After that, we calculated the intersection of these sets to verify how often students and teachers used the same terms in the posted messages.

By the intersection set, it is observed that there was a low frequency of messages forward by the students from the teachers' original messages or even posting messages that contained the relevant terms. To be more specific, from 36 terms considered relevant only 2 were mentioned by the students in new posts or in forwarding messages. Therefore, we can safe conclude that the students acted as receivers of messages.

To validate the found results and to better understand our findings, a questionnaire composed by eight questions was elaborated and applied to the envolved students. Basically, the questions were created to answer i) what relevant terms most interested to the students; ii) the weekly frequency of access to Twitter; iii) if the messages posted by professors contributed to learning the issue addressed in the classroom; among others.

The responses were analyzed comparing with the results observed by the text mining process. The main objective was empirically verifying the behavior of students from the messages sent by the professors and we tried to prove if they were indeed just receivers or, on the opposite side, they are senders. The applied questions are:

1. What of the listed terms are you interested in reading about? (The set of terms considered relevant by professors was presented).
2. What is the frequency that you access Twitter weekly?

3. How many tweets do you post in a week (in avarege)?

4. Considering the terms that you marked in question 1, how often do you retweet messages that contain such terms?

5. Do you usually access the links you receive on Twitter messages?

6. Considering the terms that you marked in question 1, do you usually access the links presented in tweets that you have received?

7. After reading a tweet, do you usually search in the Web for more information about the topic?

8. Considering the tweets with terms that you marked in question 1, did they motivated you to acquire new information about the topic?

From the 52 students who participated of the experiment, 38 (73%) filled the questionnaire, considering a good sample size to draw conclusions about the students behavior, the use of Twitter and the relevant terms.

Taking into account the responses for the Question 1: the students are interested and considered relevant the terms indicated by professors that appear in several messages. Table 1 shows the frequency (%) of the terms chosen by the students. Such terms differ from the data obtained by mining the messages since the students retweeted only messages containing the word "job".

Table 1. The relevant terms according to the responses of students

Term	Frequency (%)
Web	66
Android	63
Mobile	61
Google	55
Inovação	53

According to the responses, more than half of the students point out that the week frequency of accessing Twitter is from zero to twice (Question 2) (Figure 1a). It matchs with the results extracted from the process of text mining where 26% of participants access more than ten times per week the online social network. About 80% of students indicate that they post less than two messages per week (Question 3) (Figure 1b). Moreover, almost 80% of respondents report that they forward less than twice a week the messages containing the terms that were previously marked as relevant (Question 4) (Figure 1 (c)). Based on the answers, we can observe the passive behavior of the students in Twitter, acting as receivers of messages.

Regarding the questions about the use of the links: 71% of respondents indicate they click on links to read them (Question 5) (Figure 2 (a)), and 87% report they access the links related to relevant terms (Question 6) (Figure 2 (b)). After reading some news about these terms, 68% of students point out that they look for more information about the topic on the Web (Question 7) (Figure 2 (c)). Finally, all the respondents have answered that the messages they received helped to acquire new information about the topic of interest (Question 8).

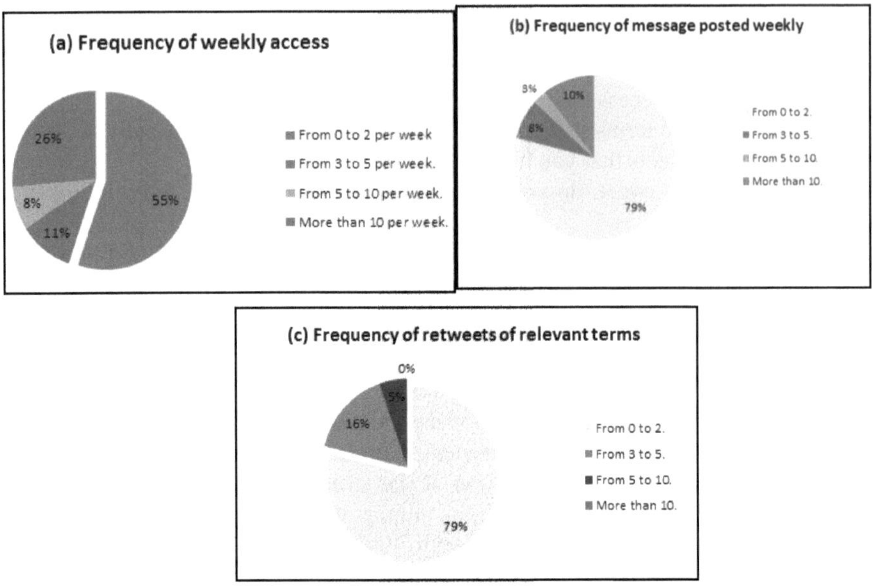

Fig. 1. Access of Twitter and messages sending

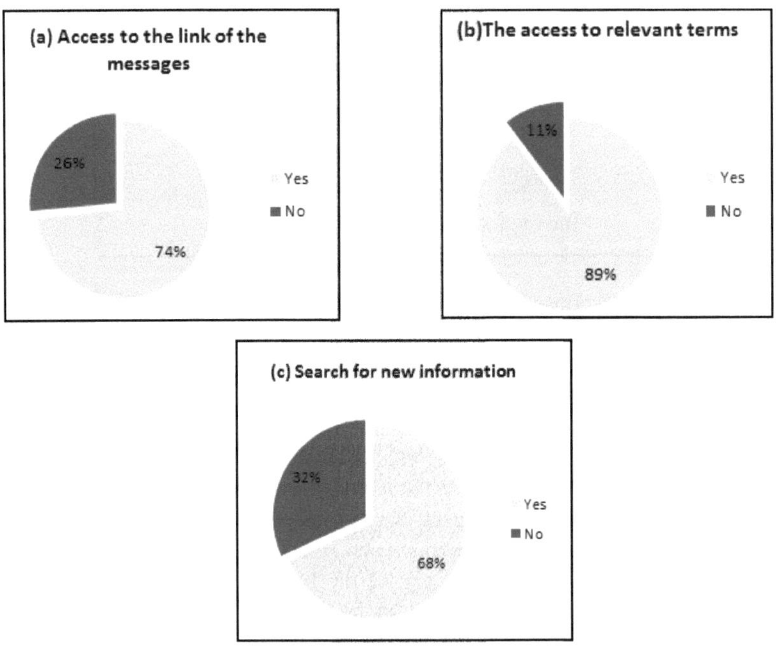

Fig. 2. Access and relevance of the links

Comparing the results found by text mining techinique with the questionnaire responses, we can observe that the students behaved as receivers of information. Although the most of students did not send or forward messages with the relevant terms, they have agreed that the posts contributed to the acquisition of new and interesting information. So, we evidenced that despite the messages posted by the professors have motivated the students, they usually not exchange the information with their collegues.

It is important to highlight that in this work, we have not recommended to the students to use any patterns or rules for sending messages, differing to other works presented in the literature that employed Twitter as a learning environment. The teachers have just informed that they would post messages on Twitter about topics related to the courses. The main goal would be observating the students' behavior as active agents in the search and sharing process of information. Nevertheless, at this moment we have concluded, based on the found results, that the Twitter environment did not motivate students to share the messages they received, even though the messages' content br considered relevant for them.

Comparing Twitter with other e-learning environments such as forums, chats or even LMS (Learning Management System), we observe that online social networks currently do not have enough resources that motivate the students to use the environment as a learning space. So, it is necessary to provide resources to improve the motivation, such as recommendation of relevant information, in order to the students explore the full potential of the social networks for learning purposes.

5 Conclusions and Further Works

The employment of online social networks for sharing and exchanging information and ideas has been growing in recent years and many of them have used for different purposes, including for e-learning.

In this work we reported the analysis of an empirical experiement conducted to analyze the effectiveness of using Twitter as a resource to support classroom for sharing and disseminating information. To do that, we looked for patterns of interest in postings, from a set of keywords considered relevant within the context of learning. Apart from mining the text of the messages, the method performed the analysis of the links presented in posted messages.

First, we collected and analyzed messages posted by professors and their students on Twitter. This way, the professores have listed a set of keywords that they consider relevant to the topics addressed in their courses. The analysis of the messages clearly indicated that students do not forward messages and even posted new messages that contained the terms considered relevant.

Currently, we are working in the field of social networks for learning. One project is referred to search of learning resources on the Web and tagging them in a collaboratively way. So, to estimulate the student participation, the developed system can recommend data or information that it considers of the students' interest. Furthermore, other project in progress is related to a social network for ideas that employs concepts of gamification to motivate students to participate and share information.

As a future work, we intend to investigate semantic-based approaches, such as Latent Semantic Analysis in order to ensure more accurate results about the terms that share the interests of students and professors.

Acknowledgments. We thank the Brazilian agency FAPESP for the financial support.

References

1. Maulik, U., Bandyopadhyay, S., Mukhopadhyay, A.: Data Mining Fundamentals - Multiobjective Genetic Algorithms for Clustering, pp. 51–70 (2011)
2. Benevenuto, F., Rodrigues, T., Cha, M., Almeida, V.: Characterizing User Navigation and Interactions in Online Social Networks. Elsevier Information Sciences 195(15), 1–24 (2012)
3. Nielsen Online. Social networks & blogs now 4th most popular online activity, ahead of personal email, http://www.nielsen-online.com/pr/pr_090309.pdf (accessed in January 20, 2012)
4. Cha, M., Benevenuto, F., Haddadi, H., Gummadi, K.: The world of connections and information flow in Twitter. IEEE Transactions on Systems, Man and Cybernetics - Part A 42(4), 991–998 (2012)
5. Zaina, L.A.M., Bressan, G., Ruggiero, W.V.: Learning Management System of Tidia-Ae Project. In: Proceedings of the 9th IASTED International Conference on Computers and Advanced Technology in Education (2006)
6. Dabbagh, N., Reo, R.: Back to the future: tracing the roots and learning affordances of social software. In: Lee, M.J.W., McLoughlin, C. (eds.) Web 2.0-Based e-Learning: Applying Social Informatics for Tertiary Teaching (2011)
7. Stevens, V.: Trial by Twitter: The Rise and Slide of the Year's Most Viral Microblogging Platform. TESLEJ: teaching english as a second or foreign language, V. 12, N. 1 (2009), http://tesl-ej.org/ej45/int.html (accessed in: February 1, 2012)
8. Cormode, G., Krishnamurthy, B., Willinger, W.: A Manifesto for Modeling and Measurement in Social Media. First Monday 15(9) (Online) (2010), http://firstmonday.org/htbin/cgiwrap/bin/ojs/index.php/fm/article/view/3072 (accessed in: October 19, 2012)
9. API TWITTER, http://dev.twitter.com/doc (accessed in: March 1, 2012)
10. API LONGURL, http://api.longurl.org/v2/expand (accessed in: April 1, 2012)
11. Dunlap, J.C., Lowenthal, P.R.: Tweeting the night away: Using Twitter to enhance social presence. Journal of Information Systems Education 20(2), 129–136 (2009)
12. Borau, K., Ullrich, C., Feng, J., Shen, R.: Microblogging for Language Learning: Using Twitter to Train Communicative and Cultural Competence. In: Spaniol, M., Li, Q., Klamma, R., Lau, R.W.H. (eds.) ICWL 2009. LNCS, vol. 5686, pp. 78–87. Springer, Heidelberg (2009)
13. Cheong, M., Lee, V.: Integrating web-based intelligence retrieval and decision-making from the Twitter trends knowledge base. In: Proceedings of The 2nd ACM Workshop on Social Web Search and Mining (SWSM 2009) (2009)

14. Vieweg, S., et al.: Microblogging during two natural hazards events: what twitter contribute to situational awareness. In: Proceedings of the 28th International Conference on Human Factors in Computing Systems (CHI 2010) (2010)
15. Almeida, T.A., Yamakami, A.: Facing the Spammers: A Very Effective Approach to Avoid Junk E-mails. Expert Systems with Applications 39(7), 6557–6561 (2012)
16. TWITTER, `https://twitter.com/` (acessed in: February 1, 2012)
17. Kohonen, T.: Self-Organizing Maps. 3a. edição (2001)
18. VISCOVERY SOMine, `http://www.viscovery.net/somine/` (acessed in: April 20, 2012)
19. O'Reilly, T.: What is Web 2.0: Design patterns and business models for the next generation of software (2010), `http://oreilly.com/web2/archive/what-is-web-20.html` (accessed in: October 16, 2010)
20. Nielsen Online, 2013th edn. Social media report 2012: social media comes of age (2012), `http://www.nielsen.com/us/en/newswire/2012/social-media-report-2012-social-media-comes-of-age.html` (accessed in: July 2, 2013)

Use of Moodle Platforms in Higher Education: A Chilean Case

Darío Liberona and Darcy Fuenzalida

Universidad Federico Santa María, Santiago, Chile
{jose.liberona,darcy.fuenzalida}@usm.cl

Abstract. The vast majority of universities in the western world have integrated an online learning platform in their campus, to help teachers and to go with the times, the most used technology is a learning management system (LMS by the acronym in English learning management system), being Moodle the most used LMS platform in the world, because, compared with other web applications is more effective and feasible for educational use , besides is an open source platform that is mostly free.

Thus, the objective of this article is to analyze and compare the perceptions of students, teachers and find out the advances in one particular case. For this , we used a survey design with a sample of 178 students and 87 teachers of different majors at the Universidad de Santiago de Chile. The results highlight the importance giving to the use of Moodle for both, the university teaching to display the organization of courses material, and the use to exchange information. Students show a high degree of satisfaction with the technology but recognize very little use of the tools. The migration of the site version represented a setback in the use of the platform.

Keywords: Distance learning, Moodle, ICT (Information and Communication Technologies), Education technology, E-learning, LMS platforms.

1 Introduction

By 2004 almost a decade ago E-learning seemed like a new education paradigm in Chile, at the time, distance learning have not jet evolve at all in the country, a great difference from establish distance learning programs in United States at the State University of Pensylvania (1886) or the University of Chicago (1889) that were implemented more than a hundred years ago, and had a very long tradition before any e-learning platforms were incorporated [11], [6]. By the beginning of the XXI century many institutions were developing their e-learning programs and the question about what their future incorporation and contribution to the traditional university education was going to be was made, also by that time some expected or predicted that an important part of higher education was going to be taught through new learning technologies, but has this really happen?.

During this decade, Social networks were created, the mobile revolution came, and so many technologies have been incorporated to enterprises and educational

L. Uden et al. (Eds.): LTEC 2014, CCIS 446, pp. 124–134, 2014.

institutions, but the questions about how we have taken advantage of these new learning technologies in education are still not clear. There are no studies regarding the advance in Chile. Complete online programs have been developed by the Universidad Uniacc (Computes Sciences and Management, Psychology) and Universidad Mayor (Management, Public Managment), there is no cases like the University of Umea in Sweden were from a traditional University switched over time to 75% online enrolment [13].

The research idea is to evaluate the use and effectiveness of e-learning education platform (LMS) using the model case. E-learning comprises all forms of electronically supported learning and teaching activities [12]. Surveys were conducted to find out what is the real contribution of e-learning platforms to the education system in a particular case, in the opinion of students and teachers, some questions were made in order to check if the platform potential is fully developed and to know what is the relative use or maturity of this technology at the University.

Using google analytics, surveys and personal interviews to analyze the use of this educational and communication platform at the University of Santiago in Chile, 87 teachers and 158 students that use the Moodle platform were surveyed in order to evaluate its use and perception of the contribution to education.

There has been a clear convergence between Knowledge Management strategy and technology over the last few years [2], there is a transformation from general information from a learning object to a reusable learning context, and from individual learning to collaborative learning through e-learning platforms [8], in this case we are analyzing how is this trend being addresses by traditional universities in Chile in the particular case of the University of Santiago.

1.1 The LMS and Moodle Platform

E-learning could simply be defined as learning using some electronic means: such as computer and Internet-based courseware and local and wide area networks. You can learn via a range of learning technologies such as internet, WAP (Wireless Application Protocol), teleconferencing, mobile platforms, SMS (Short Message Service), multimedia, teleconferencing, videoconferencing and computer-based learning platforms such as LMS (Learning Management Systems) [9], [3].

There are several Learning Management Systems for distance education or e-learning being use in educational institutions and enterprises.

There are many LMS platforms, about 20 platforms have more than 1 million users (Fig. 1), some are free inniciatives and others are pay plataforms. Moodle is the most used one [5], it is an open source free platform, others popular platforms are Edmodo, ConnectEdu, Balckboard and Sumtotal Systems with various pricing models and functionalities [10].

		Customers	Users
1	Moodle	87.084	73.753.015
2	Edmodo	120.000	20.000.000
3	ConnectEDU	135.000	20.000.000
4	Blackboard	20.000	20.000.000
5	SumTotal Systems	1.851	38.541.032
6	Schoology	35.000	2.000.000

Source: Capterra.com

Fig. 1. The Most used LMS platforms in the world

The University of Santiago de Chile and most of Chilean Universities use Moodle has their working e-learning platform.

Moodle

Moodle is a PHP-platform (open source) that allows the creation of educational portals and virtual classroom software.

Moodle ' is a Virtual Learning Environment, course management system , with free distribution (open-source), which helps educators create online learning communities . This type of technology platforms is also known as LMS (Learning Management System).

Moodle was created by Martin Dougiamas , who was administrator of WebCT at Curtin University of Technology in Australia . He based his design on the ideas of constructivism in education who claim that knowledge is constructed in the mind of the student rather than be passed unchanged from books or teaching and collaborative learning [3]. A teacher who operates from this point of view creates a student-centered environment that helps you build that knowledge based on their own skills and knowledge rather than simply publish and transmit the information he believes that students should know.

The first version of the tool appeared on August 20, 2002 and from there have been new versions regularly. Until July 2008, the registered user base includes over 21 million , spread over 46,000 sites worldwide and is translated into more than 75 languages, this happen on the first six years of the initiative. By 2013 the sites using moodle were about 70.000, wiht a user base of around 70 million, in 235 countries, accounting for about 7 million courses with about 1.2 million teachers, more than triple in another six years [4].

The following chart displays the total records you have in each month, in addition to the accounts that are included throughout 2010.

We can infer that 40% of the sites are devoloping sites or projects with less than 10 students each, and there is about 10.000 sites with more than 1.000 registered students, about 14% of the total sites. There are about 2.500 moodle instalations with more than 10.000 students each, wich clearly shows the potential of this tool for academic institutions in terms of capacity [10].

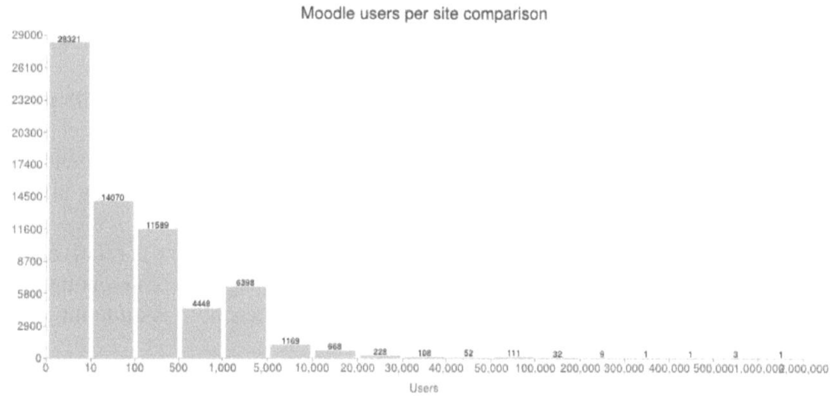

Source: moodle.org

Fig. 2. Number os user range per Moodle site

This software is used by and estimated of over 1,500 educational institutions worldwide. The professionals in charge of the educational process are members of the communities of Moodle in Spanish and English respectively in pedagogical and technical forums [3].

In terms of their use in countries, the ones that use it more are in the western hemisphere, and represent around 55% of the total users. Chile is in the 17 position with 938 sites. The top 20 (8.5%) of the 235 countries, account for 70% of the installations.

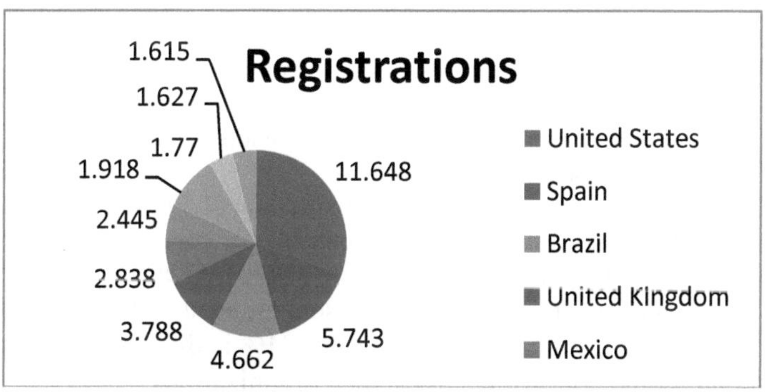

Fig. 3. Registration of the 10 most active Moodle user countries

Moodle has the following features:

• Management fees : free (visitors enroll) payment (prepayment students enrolled) or linked to a closed list.
• Creating collaborative environments forums, chat rooms , queries .
• Multiple forms of activity. Supports media formats, activities SCORM packages.

Moodle is basically designed to help distance learning, but can be used to reinforce concepts after class, or in the computer lab.
Properties that explain the interest of teachers for Moodle

• Customizable: Its interface can adapt its appearance to be consistent with the corporate image of the company or school.
• Versatility: Moodle can be used to create many different types of content and is equally useful as a teaching tool and as a forum for communication among all members of the educational community.
• Ease of use : Despite its versatility, the course creation software is relatively easy to use. It is not necessary to know any programming language to create enough compelling content . The interface used (for both student and teacher) is quite intuitive to use.
• " Community " Support : The so called " Moodle community " made up of all those who use this educational software and extending around the world , is permanently ready to guide and support any of its members in the use of Moodle. The idea is, " raises your questions, problems , ideas , suggestions, etc. and responds to others when you know the answer to your questions or problems".
• Gratuities : Moodle is provided as an open source or "free software " , under the GNU Public License . This means that , although it has copyrights, may be used freely provided that certain clauses are accepted.
• Open Source: Moodle is a software " open source " , which means that anyone who knows your programming language (php) can modify the program at will , introducing new functions or adapt existing ones to meet the specific needs the school.

1.2 Moodle in Chile

As we know mainly Moodle was created to support the education category, but this has also been and is used by a number of institutions in different fields, so it could be use as a means of communication for all employees belonging to the organization. Also using this system, companies today provide remote training to their employees. There are 938 installations in Chile [8].

In the Chilean case there are about 27 universities out of 59 that have some Moodle platform, some have more than 5 installations in different faculties, representing around 8% of the installations in Chile, there are about 116 school installation (12%), and other 45 installations from professional institutes, about 26% of the Moodle is use directly from educational institutions and 74% is divided into private ventures, companies and educational assistance organizations.

Also Moodle is use to generate instances of collaborative work on e-learning of this system in some companies.

2 Moodle at the University of Santiago de Chile

The University of Santiago de Chile works with Moodle to support distance education and complement the synchronous learning (at the callsroom) with asynchronous learning (virtual). There is a general virtual site for all students in the University since 2006, but there within it, a series of other platforms that work independently of this site (www.usachvirtual.cl), some faculties have their own platforms, and even some teachers who adopt other educational portals to complement their teaching, an example of this can be seen in the Technology Faculty through the website www.usachvirtual.cl

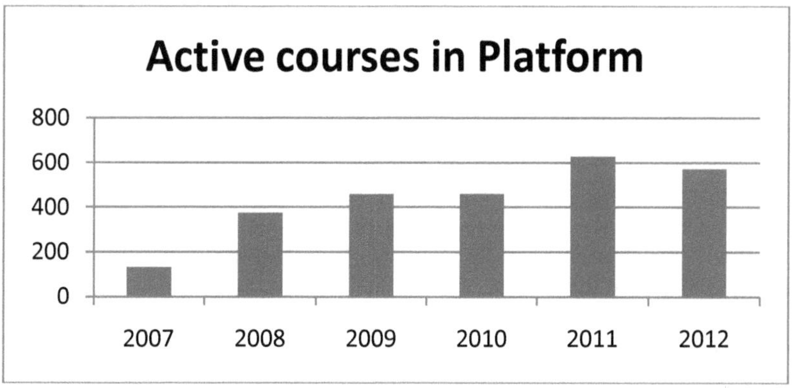

Fig. 4. Active courses in Moodle Platform

It is observed that the number of courses that have been activated have been increasing with the passage of time (with exception of the platform version change period). The main reasons according to the platform managers and the interviews conducted are:

• The increased use of the internet as an indispensable tool for education. The speed , fluidity and ease of use are the main features that have moved the world to such portals .

• Many teachers who used the University moodle platforms (aula.usach.cl and uvirtual.usach.cl, usachvirtual.cl) have changed since the second classroom platform has many variables that did not have the previous platform , and secondly because the University is trying to unify the portal and promoting that all faculties use the same platform (www.usachvirtual.cl) for educational and communication purposes .

• Another variable influencing is that the system includes variables such as forums, site for questions, complementary option to upload videos, images, etc. Therefore communication is not unilateral, but it is bilateral, taking feedback if this is necessary and further support has been extended to all kinds of things, such as the fact of supporting audio visual material.

Also we can note that since 2nd term of 2012 all the courses given in the University have automatically created a course prototype and all the students are automatically enrol in their correspondent courses, raising the number of courses for 2013 to more than 4.599, from which about 12% are active.

Table 1. Number of active teacher and total active courses (2012 figures)

Faculty	Total Active teachers	Total Active Courses
Common Program	6	7
CITECAMP	44	53
Management and Economy faculty	9	23
Sciences	25	53
Medical and Health	26	48
Humanities	14	34
Engineering	98	296
Biology and Chemistry	23	49
Technological	5	6
Elderly program	1	1
Total	251	570

As we observe in fig. 4 there was a little decrease in the number of courses since the migration of the Moodle platform to a new version (upgrade), and 2013 is not show in fig. 4 because now, all the courses of the University have a pre-created e-learning course and all the students are enrolled in this courses.

During 2012 and 2013 a migration platform process has been conducted that it seems to have lowered the number of active courses and teachers, some of the previous user did not continue using the system, having this migration a negative impact at first, many teacher did not went though the trouble of learning how to use another platform at first, but this is rapidly being corrected.

2.1 Students Use of Moodle

What stands out is that it has significantly increased the percentage of students using Moodle, from 1% in 2007 to 31.43 % of them in 2012.

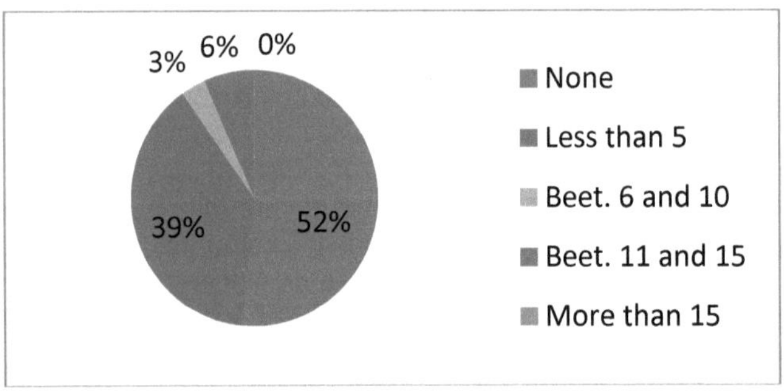

Fig. 5. Number or online courses taking by students during his carrier (4th and 5th year students)

Regarding the students survey, there is clear evidence that they value online courses (88%), and 41% considers that the importance of e-learning courses will be very significant in the future, however only 13% will take a career that is fully online, but 45% one that will have a blended system.

Table 2. Students opinion on contribution of e-learning classes

Students Survey			
Do you consider e-learning a contribution to Education	88%		
E-learning will be very important	41%	E-learning will be more important than traditional education	9,80%
Would you study a careers 100% online	13%	Would you study a career that is 50% online and 50% in a classroom	45%
The courses were what you expected or more	64%		
Students that have taken other e-learning curses outside the University	41%	Were the courses better quality	52%

Table 3. Reasons to use e-learning and promoters of the platform

Most important reason Why e-learning is good in education			
Allows to manage better the time	69%	It is more flexible	54%
Improves de learing experience	52%	Easy to review material and study	44%
A mobile course (celular) will be good or better	16%	A mobile course will be bad or very bad	41%
Who is encouraging the use of E-learning			
Some teachers	53%	The technology departament or Platform administrators	25%
It is not promoted	16%	Some students	15%

3 Conclusions

In the case of University of Santiago there have been a lot of advances over the last three years in terms of using e-learning platforms and interconnecting different systems (i.e. registration data base, traditional courses data base), but the real use of distance education capabilities is still in its infancy and very little advance in terms of using the real advantages of the tools and the collaboration learning environment has been made.

Only 12% of the possible pre-created courses are active and have some content, meaning that the technology is only use in 12% of the lectures that are being taught every semester, and being considered active is a very basic stage into the exploiting of the potential of e-learning functionality, the majority of the teachers that use the platforms, use it as a way of only putting files or sending messages to students, rather that engaging on a collaborative distance learning program, using forums, evaluating services, surveys, or other more complex features. Only a few teachers are using most of the potential of this learning technology (Moodle), basically because of the leadership of a particular head department and the very active participation of a group of young teachers, they have even request the integration of a series of other special educational software packages to be integrated with the Moodle platform.

Only 9,8% of the University students really have been expose to e-learning complements on their traditional lectures (considering more than 3 courses during their studies), and 52% has never had any interaction with the platform at the end of their careers, even that has been fully implemented at least three years before they started their programs at the University.

Taking measures to automate the basic course pre creation and automatic students enrolment in order to facilitate the content edition of all university courses has been a great step forward (2012-2013), this is that the platform is integrated to a series of University systems, students enrolment, classes per semester, teachers names, so students are uploaded every semester and almost all of the campus courses are pre created in the platform since the beginning of the academic term, if you have a class in the University an e-learning class will be created for you, totalling around 4.600 different courses.

Measures have been taken to transfer some of the courses in other systems to this new platform and trying to integrate all the courses into only one platform, since some faculties did have some other platforms or other e-learning projects.

Even though that the surveys were not conducted at Universidad Santa Maria, another well known Chilean university that uses the Moodle platform, many interviews were conducted with the team in charge of the programs, they seem to have a very similar situation than the University of Santiago, in almost every way, they recently migrated the platform versions and have integrated the system to the enrolment and lectures applications given the possibility to every teacher that will teach a course during the semester to use the platform with close to 30% of courses being use by the teachers.

Many questions regarding this learning technology remain, some related to the pedagogical aspects of Moodle itself , such as the relationship between its use and improved education or its impact on the skills development of students others to the adoption of the technology and its use. We did note measure this aspects on the survey, however the opinion of students in more favourable than the one of teachers, in United States a survey to 2,800 colleges and universities show that 77% of academic leaders rates the learning outcomes in online education as the same or superior to those in face-to-face instruction [1].

Other potential use of the Moodle platform is as a CMS (Content Management System), which is intended to be use as a communications and knowledge transfer platform, many companies in Chile have done so, there is a common use of this kind in the world [7], this is not yet in the scope of the Universidad de Santiago or Universidad Santa Maria, the universities are in the process of increasing the basic use of the platform and then go to a more sophisticated use of functions such as online evaluation, rich media usage and more integration with other platforms and educational technology tools.

The real contribution of e-learning LMS systems in the University for now is very marginal, with a few exceptions, the main challenges for now are to create awareness and go to the stage of having only one platform and give services to all faculties integrating a lot of systems.

The perception of the students is very positive and in general 88% of them would like to use a lot more this learning technologies, especially in an asynchronous way and using rich media. However regarding the question if an open university's degree is as valuable as a regular university degree?, only 17% of the students will consider obtaining a degree in a program that is completely online and 76% will be willing to do it in a program that was 50% online and 50% traditional classes.

In terms of quality perceptions, in general courses were perceived with less quality than traditional courses, on the contrary in United Stated 77% of the academic leaders think that online courses are the same or superior than face to face instruction [1].

The quality of the courses delivered by teachers who use this technology is rather poor, the most used in this environment is the posting of files or links and other functionalities like, forums, quiz, surveys, notes, blogs, collaborative work and rich media are not use in general.

There are a lot of opportunities in the future for virtual supported learning, for now there are no plans on using, applying or working on MOOC at the University of Santiago for now.

If traditional universities consider de lifelong learning (LLL) needs of the new modern society, this implies that effort to improve and more rapid advance in the adoption and integration of virtual learning programs and capacities in every University have to be made in the country.

While there is so many completely virtual institutions all over the world, such as UOC (Universidad Oberta de Catalunya), Florida Virtual School, open Universities in England, Portugal, Australia, Pakistan, Canada, Bulgaria to name a few, also many MOOC programs and courses in both new and traditional universities, in Chilean universities there is rather a very slow adoption in the virtual learning arena, there is no open Universities, and only a few Universities have online degree programs.

References

1. Allen, E., Seaman, J.: Grade Change, Tracking online education in the United States. Babson Research Group, Pearson (2014)
2. Al-Sadi, J., Shawar, B.A., Sarie, T.: The Relationship between Knowledge Management and E-learning. In: Proceedings of CSREA EEE, pp. 514–518 (2008)
3. Capterra, `http://www.capterra.com/infographics/top-lms-software` (retrieve on March 2, 2014)
4. Dougiamas, M., Taylor, P.: Moodle: Using Learning Communities to Create an Open Source Course Management System. In: Lassner, D., McNaught, C. (eds.) Proceedings of World Conference on Educational Multimedia, Hypermedia and Telecommunications 2003, pp. 171–178. AACE, Chesapeake (2003)

5. Ferriman, J.: The 20 most popular Learning Management Systems, http://www.learndash.com/20-most-popular-learning-management-systems-infographic/ (accessed on February 10, 2014)
6. Fuenzalida, D.: E-learning una herramienta para la Educación Ejecutiva, Palo Alto, Color House, Santiago (2004)
7. Mahwish, W., Khan, A.: Creative Learning Environment and Knowledge Management. International Journal of Academic Research in Business and Social Sciences 2(1) (January 2012) ISSN: 2222-6990
8. Michalca, R., Uta, A., Andreescu, A., Intorsureanu, I.: Knowledge Management in E-learning Systems. Revista Informatica Economica 2(46) (2008)
9. Miltiadis, D., Meir, R., Maier, R.: Knowledge Management Strategies, Handbook of applied technologies. IGI Publishing, Hershey (2008)
10. Moodle, https://moodle.org/stats/ (accessed on March 10, 2014)
11. Rosenberg: E-learning strategies for delivering Knowledge in the digital age, p. 28. McGraw Hill, United States (2001)
12. Shrestha, S., Kim, J.M.: Bridging the Gap between E-Learning and Knowledge Management (KM): An enhancement of Moodle system by applying KM Functions. International Journal of Science and Technology 2(1) (January 2013)
13. Sordrestrom, T., From, J.: From distance to online Education: Educational Management in the 21st century (2011)

Community of Practice for Knowledge Sharing in Higher Education: Analysing Community of Practice through the Lens of Activity Theory

Andi Bing Sie[1], Anne-Maria Aho[2], and Lorna Uden[3]

[1] School of Graduate Study, Asia e University, Kuala Lumpur, Malaysia
[2] Seinäjoki University of Applied Sciences, Seinäjoki, Finland
[3] Staffordshire University, Stafford, United Kingdom

Abstract. Knowledge sharing is fundamental to learning among students. Learning and innovation occur when students are collaborating and able to share knowledge. Therefore students must be encouraged and be willing to share knowledge with one another. Although there are many benefits to knowledge sharing among students, in practice it is not easy to achieve. Communities of practice (COP) are an ideal platform for students to collaborate and share knowledge as they learn. However, creating and implementing an effective COP is not trivial. This paper describes our experience of using COP to promote knowledge sharing among undergraduate students working in a multicultural setting, analyses COP using activity theory, and outlines a design proposal for a COP using social objects.

Keywords: Knowledge Sharing, Communities of Practice, Activity Theory.

1 Introduction

As twenty-first-century businesses face global expansion, and knowledge management (KM) has become the most valuable asset for both profit and not-for-profit organizations, developing knowledge management and knowledge sharing strategies, particularly those capable of capturing hard-to- document tacit knowledge, is now a critical need. This is true for learning communities in higher education as well. However, despite the growing significance of knowledge sharing and knowledge management practices for organization's competitiveness, several barriers to knowledge sharing make it difficult for knowledge management to deliver a positive return on investment.

Why do people resist sharing knowledge? Sun and Scott [1] conclude there are at least fourteen sources from which barriers to knowledge sharing can arise. A review undertaken by Riege [2] has identified three-dozen barriers to knowledge sharing that managers must consider. These potential barriers can be divided into three categories: individual, organizational and technological.

L. Uden et al. (Eds.): LTEC 2014, CCIS 446, pp. 135–148, 2014.

Potential Individual Barriers

At the individual level, Riege [2] has identified a number of potential barriers to knowledge sharing among undergraduate students, shown below:

1. General lack of time to share knowledge
2. Apprehension or fear that sharing may reduce or jeopardize competitiveness
3. Low awareness of the value and benefit of knowledge sharing
4. Poor verbal/written communication and interpersonal skills
5. Lack of social network
6. Fear of taking ownership of intellectual property due to fear of not receiving just recognition and accreditation from lecturer and fellow students
7. Lack of trust in people because they may misuse knowledge or take unjust credit for it
8. Differences in national culture and ethnic background and their associated values and beliefs (including language).

Potential Organizational Barriers

One of the key issues of sharing knowledge in an organizational context is related to corporate environments and their conditions. After reviewing the relevant literature, we have outlined twelve organization-based barriers to knowledge sharing, illustrated below:

1. Missing or unclear integration of knowledge management strategy and sharing initiatives into the company's goals and strategic approach
2. Lack of leadership and managerial direction in terms of clearly communicating the benefits and values of knowledge sharing practices
3. Shortage of formal and informal spaces to share, reflect and generate (new) knowledge
4. Lack of transparent rewards and recognition systems that would motivate people to share more of their knowledge
5. Insufficient support for sharing practices by existing corporate culture
6. Hierarchical organization structure inhibits or slows down sharing practices
7. Low prioritization of knowledge retention of highly skilled and experienced staff
8. Shortage of infrastructure to support sharing practices
9. Communication and knowledge flows are restricted to a certain direction (e.g. top-down)
10. Deficiency of company resources that would provide adequate sharing opportunities
11. Physical work environment and layout of work areas restrict effective sharing practices
12. High levels of internal competitiveness within business units, functional areas and subsidiaries

Potential Technology Barriers

Knowledge sharing is as much an issue for people and organizations as it is for technology. There is little doubt that technology can encourage and support knowledge sharing processes by making knowledge sharing easier and more effective. The key issue is, however, how to choose and implement a suitable technology that provides a close fit between people and organizations.

Technology that works effectively in some organizations may fail in others. Several potential technology barriers are listed below:

1. Lack of integration of IT systems and processes
2. Lack of technical support (internal and external)
3. Unrealistic expectations of users as to what technology can and cannot do
4. Incompatibility between diverse IT systems and processes
5. Incompatibility between individuals' needs and integrated IT systems and processes
6. Lack of user training and familiarization of new IT systems and processes
7. Reluctance to use IT systems due to lack of experience with them
8. Lack of communication and demonstration of the advantages of any new systems over existing ones.

Research by Hofstede and Hofstede [3] found that while common barriers to knowledge sharing are found globally in public and private sectors, as well as in universities, cultural influences can differ. Recent research on organisational learning and knowledge creation indicates that learning, knowledge sharing, and communication are profoundly influenced by the cultural values held by individual employees.

Review of literature on knowledge sharing studies in universities confirms similar results. For example, 84 percent of students participating in a knowledge sharing study at King Fahd University of Petroleum and Minerals in Saudi Arabia indicated they would not share knowledge voluntarily while 44 percent of students from three universities in Singapore indicated they are willing to share knowledge voluntarily [4,5].

Barriers to knowledge sharing can be identified in most organizations. In the last decade, efforts have been taken to encourage, facilitate and improve knowledge sharing.

Best practices on the subject have started to gain increased attention amongst researchers and business leaders. In terms of organizational and individual learning, knowledge sharing practices and initiatives often form a key component of knowledge management programs and strategies. Research by Keyes [13] confirmed that communities of practice (COP) have a positive impact on people's willingness to share knowledge. However, there are only a few studies in the knowledge management literature that investigate the usefulness of COP for knowledge sharing among students in higher education, particularly in classes where the students are coming from multicultural and multiethnic backgrounds.

This paper describes a case study that assesses the usefulness of COP for knowledge sharing among undergraduate students working in a multicultural setting. The scope of the case study includes three successive courses of knowledge management, namely KM 2012, KM 2013 and KM 2014, for undergraduate students at Seinäjoki University of Applied Sciences (Seinäjoki UAS) in Finland. During the KM 2012 course, it was observed that students were not sharing knowledge as they should. COP was introduced and implemented during the KM 2013 course. While the introduction of COP encouraged students to share knowledge, the initial COP implementation itself was not successful. Reasons of failures are discussed in Section 5 using activity theory. Based on the lessons learnt from previous years, a design for COP based on "social object" is proposed in Sections 6. Section 7 concludes with further research.

2 Communities of Practice (COP)

Wenger [6] defines communities of practice as self-managed groups of individuals who share a common concern, a set of problems or a passion about a topic, and who deepen their knowledge and expertise in this area by interacting on an ongoing basis. According to Wenger, a community of practice is different from a community of interest or a geographical community in that it implies a shared practice. A COP defines itself along three dimensions:

Common goal (Shared Domain) – 'joint enterprise' acts as the glue that holds members together. Reasons for interacting with one another typically include personal goals and contributions toward the community's goal. The common goal is understood, shared and continually negotiated by its members.

Commitment by all members (Community) – 'mutual engagement' binds members together into a social entity.

What capability it has produced (Practice) – Over time, members develop a 'shared repertoire' of communal resources (routines, sensibilities, artefacts, vocabulary, styles, etc.)

Communities of practice also move through various stages of development characterized by different levels of interaction among the members and different kinds of activities. They develop around things that matter to people. As a result, they reflect the members' own understanding of what is important.

All organisations have COP. Because membership of the community is based on participation rather than on official status, these communities are not bound by organizational affiliations; they can span institutional structures and hierarchies. The membership involves whoever participates in and contributes to the practice. People can participate in different ways and to different degrees.

This permeable facility creates many opportunities for learning, as outsiders and newcomers study the practice in concrete terms, and core members gain new insights from less-engaged participants. A community of practice is different from a team in that the shared learning and interest of its members are what hold it together. It is defined by knowledge rather than by tasks, and exists because participation has value to its members. Indeed, a community of practice's life cycle is determined by the value it provides to its members.

COP is also different from a network in that it is not merely a set of relationships, but is actually "about" something. The community itself has an identity which in turn shapes the identities of its members. A COP exists because it produces a shared practice as members engage in a collective process of learning. According to Wenger [6], communities of practice fulfil a number of functions with respect to the creation, accumulation and diffusion of knowledge in an organization:

1. They are nodes for the exchange and interpretation of information
2. They can retain knowledge in "living" ways, unlike a database or a manual
3. They can steward competencies to keep the organization on the cutting edge
4. They provide homes for identities.

Wenger, McDermott, and Snyder [7] have derived seven principles for cultivating COPs.

1. Design for evolution
2. Open a dialogue between inside and outside perspectives
3. Invite different levels of participation
4. Develop both public and private community spaces
5. Focus on value
6. Combine familiarity and excitement
7. Create a rhythm for the community.

We agree with Wenger et al. [7]; because communities of practice are voluntary, what makes them successful is their ability to generate enough excitement, relevance and value to attract and engage members. In order to inspire a community over time, it is therefore necessary to design for organic growth and aliveness. Because communities are built on existing networks and evolve beyond any particular design, the purpose of a design is therefore not to impose a structure but to help the community develop. The design of a COP must deliver value to the teams on which community members serve, to the community members themselves, and to the organisation. Communities need to create events, activities and relationships that help their potential value emerge and enable them to discover new ways to harvest it.

Communities of practice structure an organization's learning potential in two ways: through the knowledge they develop at their core and through interactions at their boundaries. To develop the capacity to create and retain knowledge, organizations must understand the processes by which these learning communities evolve and interact. We need to build organizational and technological infrastructures that do not dismiss or impede these processes, but rather recognize, support, and leverage them. Communities of practice may arise naturally, but this does not mean that organisations can't do anything to influence their development. It is important to carefully seed and nurture COP.

3 Activity Theory (AT)

According to Kuutti [8], activity theory is a philosophical and cross-disciplinary framework for the study of different forms of human practices as development progresses, with both individual and social levels simultaneously interlinked. In activity theory, a minimal meaningful context for individual activities must be included as the basic unit of analysis. This entity is called an activity. An activity is undertaken by a subject (individual or subgroup) using tools to achieve an object (objective), thus transforming objects into outcomes, as illustrated in Figure 1. Kuutti [8] argues that transforming the object into an outcome motivates the existence of an activity.[1]

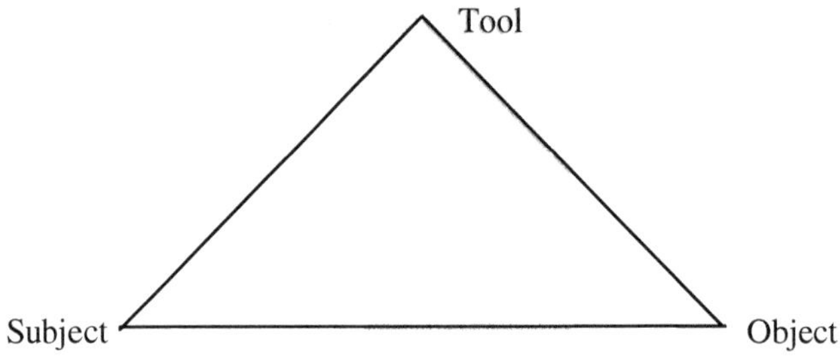

Fig. 1. Mediated Relationship at the Individual Level

An object can be material thing, but it can also be less tangible, such as a plan, or totally intangible, such as a common idea, as long as it can be shared for manipulation and transformation by the participants of the activity. It is possible that the object and motive themselves will undergo changes during the process of an activity. The relationship between the subject and the object of an activity is mediated by a tool. An activity always contains various artefacts (e.g. instruments, signs, procedures, machines, methods, laws, and forms of work organisation). Activities are realised as individual and cooperative actions, and networks of such actions are related to each other by the same overall object and motive. Participants in an activity perform conscious actions with defined goals. An activity may be realised using different actions, depending on the situation. One and the same action can belong to different activities, in which case the different motives for the activities will cause the action to have a different personal sense for the subject in the context of each activity.

Activity systems can be summarised with the help of five principles outlined by Engeström [9]. The first principle is that a collective, artefact-mediated and object-oriented activity system, seen in its network relation to other activity systems, is taken as the prime unit of analysis. Goal-directed individual and group actions, as well as automatic operations, are relatively independent but subordinate units of analysis, eventually understandable only when interpreted against the background of entire activity systems. Activity systems realise and reproduce themselves by generating actions and operations.

The second principle is the multi-voicedness of activity systems. An activity system is always a community of multiple points of view, traditions and interests. Different positions for the participants are created by the division of labour in an activity. The participants carry their own diverse histories, and the activity system itself carries multiple layers and strands of history engraved in its artefacts, rules and conventions. This multi-voicedness is multiplied further in networks of interacting activity systems. It is a source of trouble and innovation, demanding actions of translation and negotiation.

The third principle is historicity. Activity systems take shape and are transformed over lengthy periods of time. Their problems and potentials can only be understood against their own history. Both the local history of the activity and its objects, and the history of the theoretical ideas and tools that have shaped the activity, must be studied.

The fourth principle is the central role of contradictions as a source of change and development. Contradictions are not the same as problems or conflicts. They historically accumulate structural tensions within and between activity systems. Activities are open systems. When an activity system adopts a new element from the outside (e.g. a new technology, or a new object), it often leads to an aggravated secondary contradiction, where some old element (rules or division of labour) collides with the new one. Such contradictions create disturbances and conflicts, but also generate innovative attempts to change the activity.

The fifth principle is the possibility of expansive transformations in activity systems. Activity systems move through relatively long cycles of qualitative transformations. As the contradictions of an activity system are aggravated, some individual participants begin to question and deviate from its established norms. In some cases this escalates into collaborative envisioning which in turn effects a deliberate collective change. An expansive transformation is accomplished when the object and motive of the activity are re-conceptualised to embrace a radically wider horizon of possibilities than the previous mode of the activity.

Why Activity Theory?

In activity theory, an individual's relation to the surrounding world is not immediate, but it is always mediated by culturally created artefacts [10]. Thus, an individual's actions are always situated in a culturally determined context and are impossible to understand outside of that context. According to Kuutti and Molin-Juustila [10] the context in which individual actions occur is a historically developed activity system, which is the smallest possible unit of analysis that still preserves its distinctively human quality.

According to Vygotsky [11], activity theory looks at collective activity directed towards some outcome. It focuses on an activity rather than individual actions. It allows us to analyse relationships between practical activity and organisational contexts. An activity cannot be separated from the (socio-technical, cultural) environment/context in which it takes place. It encompasses mediating mechanisms, e.g. tools, methods, rules, etc. There are opportunities for learning within activity systems over time. Activities evolve. There are always conflicts, inconsistencies and dilemmas in activity.

The concept of contradiction is important in activity theory. It can provide a simple analytical tool for analysing a Knowledge Management System (KMS). Engeström analyses how contradictions, both internally in a considered central activity and between the central activity and related activities, are the driving forces in development. According to Engeström [12], any activity system has four levels of contradictions that must be attended to in the analysis of a working situation. The primary contradiction is the contradiction found within a single node of an activity. This contradiction emerges from tension between use value and exchange value. It permeates every single corner of the triangle and is the basic source of instability and development. Secondary contradictions are those that occur between the constituent nodes. Tertiary contradictions arise between an existing activity and what is described as a more advanced form of that activity. This may be found when an activity is remodelled to take new motives or ways of working into account. Quaternary contradictions are those that occur between the central activity and the neighbouring activities, e.g. instrument-producing, subject- producing and rule-producing activities.

4 Case Study

This case study was carried out in Seinäjoki University of Applied Sciences (Seinäjoki UAS), a multidisciplinary institution of higher education and a key player in education and research, development and innovation (RDI) in the region of South Ostrobothnia in West Finland.

The knowledge management course is one of the courses offered by Seinäjoki UAS. The course is going into its third year, with a stable attendance of forty to fifty students from various countries each year. Taught in English, the course program consists of theoretical lectures in knowledge management and a case study where students are divided into multi-national teams. The classroom sessions consist of the following topics:

1. Introduction to knowledge and knowledge management, including knowledge sharing and communities of practice
2. Knowledge management models and processes
3. Knowledge management strategies
4. Development of knowledge management

For the case study, the students are requested to form a team. Each team is tasked to plan and develop a project about knowledge management for a real or virtual company. The grade is based on the quality of project, team presentation and individual examination. At the end of the course the students are requested to complete questionnaires that are then used to assess the quality of the course as well as the quality of teaching. The scope of this case study includes three successive knowledge management courses for bachelor students, namely KM 2012, KM 2013 and KM 2014.

KM 2012

KM 2012 focused on teaching as a traditional one-way flow of information from lecturer to students and was concerned mainly with existing knowledge. KM 2012 was attended by fifty-three students from different countries. Observations by the lecturer and comments from students have identified that some students, for various reasons, were not keen to share knowledge.

KM 2013

KM 2013 focused on learning as a collaboration and was concerned with new knowledge creation ("innovation"). KM 2013 was attended by twenty-six students from twelve different countries. Taking the KM 2012 experience into account, a plan was developed to improve team work and knowledge sharing among the students. Based on research by Keyes [13] which, as stated earlier, confirmed that communities of practice have a positive impact on people's willingness to share knowledge. Communities of Practice was introduced in KM 2013 using a practical model developed by Wenger et al. [7] based on three fundamental elements:

1. Domain of knowledge, which defines a set of issues
2. Communities of people who care about this domain
3. Shared practice developed by communities in order to be effective in this domain.

The researcher participated in the case study as an observer during the first two sessions of the course. Despite the response from the students that COP encouraged them to share knowledge, there was little knowledge sharing among students working in the same group, and no interaction or knowledge sharing between the different groups.

The next section of this work (Section 5) uses activity theory as a lens to understand why the students did not share knowledge. Based on the evaluation of and lessons learnt from KM 2012 and KM 2013, an improved design for COP is proposed in Section 6, to be implemented in KM 2014.

5 Evaluation of COP Using Activity Theory

Using the activity system, the COP implementation in KM 2013 is shown in Figure 2.

A short evaluation carried out after the course identified several problems with COP implementation. It is therefore important to analyse the issues identified based on sound theoretical perspectives. These issues are analysed below using activity theory.

Firstly, creating and implementing an effective, working COP within the short time span of eight weeks was a big challenge. Presentation and introduction sessions alone proved to be insufficient to create and implement COP effectively. Activities in activity theory are not static or rigid entities. They are under contiguous change and development. This development is not linear or straightforward, but uneven and discontinuous. This means that each activity has a history of its own. Parts of older phases of activities often stay embedded within them as they develop, and historical analysis of the development is often needed in order to better understand the current situation. Kaptelinin and Nardi [14, 15] define activity theory as a philosophical and cross-disciplinary framework for studying different forms of human practices as historically developed cultural systems that inter-link individuals and society. It requires that human interaction with reality be analysed in the context of development. Boer et. al [16] argue that in activity theory, all practices are seen as continually being reformed and are shaped by historical development. In other words, an activity system is always situated in time.

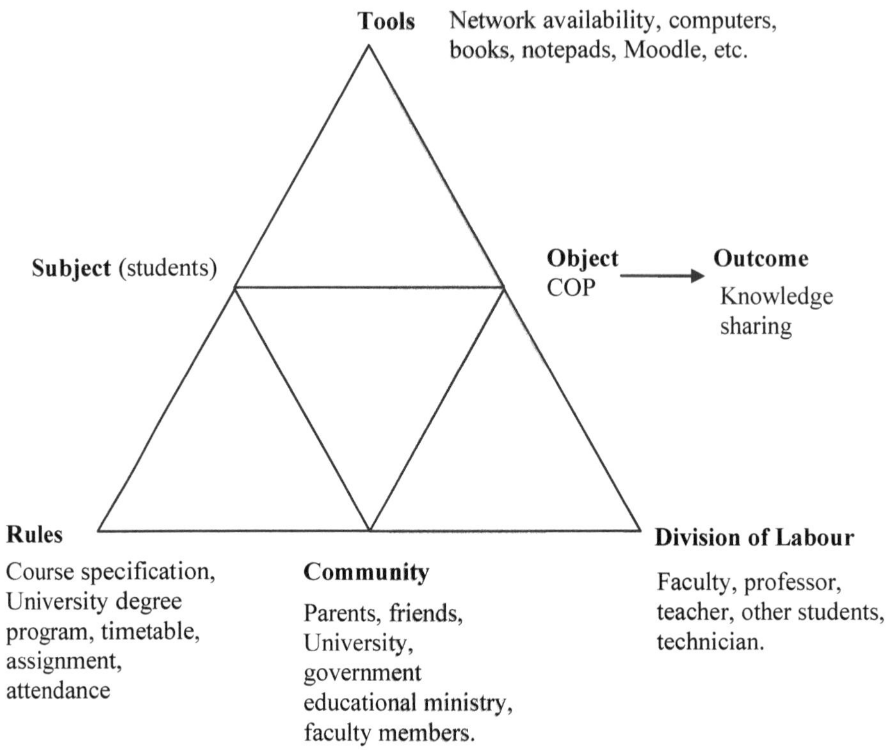

Fig. 2. COP Evaluation using Activity Theory

Secondly, there were different levels of motivation among students. Although each of the students shared the same object, that is COP, each had their own motive in the project. Activity theory recognizes that there is no need for each participant to know the details of the entire activity, but only the context of their own actions in relation to the whole activity. Because a participant is motivated by the objective of an activity, only an understanding of how the goal of their own actions contributes to this overall objective, and the freedom to seek efficiencies and/or variety in achieving that goal is required. This explains why the different groups of students pursuing different goals did not see the benefits of sharing knowledge.

Thirdly, there was little understanding of COP among students. According to the object- orientedness principle of activity theory, it is important to clarify the purpose of the activity. In activity theory, learning and doing are inseparable, and they are initiated by an intention. According to Jonassen and Rohrer-Murphy [17], intentions are directed at objects of activity. It is important to clarify the motives and goals of the activity system in order to understand the context within which an activity occurs. The reasons are to understand the context within which activities occurred in order to reach a thorough understanding of the motivation for the activity being modelled and any interpretations of perceived contradictions.

Fourthly, roles and responsibilities of COP members were not clear to students. Moreover, COP implementation without an active COP facilitator and knowledge broker is not feasible. All work practices carried out by humans are typically collective activities involving cooperation and mutual dependence between participants. According to Bardram [18], in activity theory there is strict division of labour, enabling participants to specialise in certain actions and design certain artefacts that encapsulate actions in an efficient way.

Fifthly, cultural differences among students were difficult to overcome. According to Engeström [12], how people achieve their objectives in their organisations is mediated by several cultural factors, including the following:

- The tools they have as their resources, such as computer equipment and electronic whiteboards, as well as languages
- The ways their work and tasks are organised within teams or hierarchies
- The rules governing the ways they work, both formal and informal
- Their relationships with other business units, their customers, suppliers, subcontractors and so on.

Finally, students preferred to use own social network software. This is a secondary contradiction as identified in activity theory. According to Engeström et. al. [19], by identifying the tensions and interactions between the elements of an activity system, it is possible to reconstruct the system in its concrete diversity and richness, and therefore explain and foresee its development.

Having evaluated and learned from the case study in KM 2013, we propose, in the following section, a design for COP based on social objects that shall be implemented during KM 2014.

6 A Design for COP Using Social Object

According to Lave and Wenger [20], the development of a community can be viewed as an ongoing performance: an improvisation that is enacted and re-enacted by the members of the community as they go about their daily activities. Thus the learning that takes place in Communities of Practice is not just situated learning but "generative social practice" that can change lives. The emphasis is on ways to manage the community and the role it can play within an organisation. A company wishing to introduce communities of practice as a best practice sharing mechanism needs to know where to start and how to start.

A community of practice defines itself along three dimensions:

1. **What it is about:** its joint enterprise as understood and continually renegotiated by its members
2. **How it functions:** its mutual engagement that binds members together into a social entity
3. **What capability it has produced:** members develop a shared repertoire of communal resources (routines, sensibilities, artefacts, vocabulary, styles, etc.) over time.

A community of practice moves through various stages of development characterised by different levels of interaction among the members and different kinds of activities. Communities of practice develop around things that matter to people.

According to Weller [22], a social object is "something (it can be real or virtual) that facilitates conversation, and thus social interaction". According to Demsey [23], the linking theme is that people connect and share themselves through "social objects", i.e. pictures, books, or other shared interests. Thus successful social networks are those which form around such social objects. According to McLeod [24] the interesting thing about social objects is not the objects themselves, but the conversations that happen around them.

J. Engeström [21] uses the term "social objects" and the related phrase "object-centered sociality" to address the distinct role of objects in online social networks. Engeström [21] argues that discrete objects, not general content or interpersonal relationships, form the basis for the most successful social networks. Social objects are the things that people like to share, "like" and comment on within their networks. A social object can be an announcement, a piece of music, a picture, a compelling video, an idea, a question. "Literally everything can be a social object as long as it triggers interaction. Social objects should have the ability to spark conversation."

Engeström [21] also argues that the term "social networking" makes little sense if we leave out the objects that mediate the ties between people. He argues that objects are the reason why people affiliate with specific individuals and not just anyone. Social networks are not just made up of people.

They consist of people who are connected by a shared object. Social networks require a shared object; in other words, they need a theme. It is important to ask what is it that binds a social network together if we are building something electronic to facilitate a social network. For example, in Flickr, the social object is photographs. Just as a library connects people via books instead of reading, Flickr connects people via photos instead of art-making. People do not socialize generally about photography or pictures. Instead, they socialize around specific shared images, discussing discrete photographic objects. Each photo is a node in the social network that triangulates the users who create, critique and consume it.

In view of the above, we believe that social objects can conceptually be used to design for a knowledge sharing COP at Seinäjoki University of Applied Sciences.

7 Conclusion

Promoting knowledge sharing among students is not easy, especially when those students come from diverse cultural backgrounds. Communities of practice provide a platform for students to share knowledge with one another. However, developing and implementing an effective COP can be difficult, particularly when there are time constraints. The evaluation of the implementation of COP in KM 2013 provided us with invaluable knowledge and experience for the implementation of COP in KM 2014. We also learned that implementing an effective COP requires a longer timeframe and more efforts than what we had invested in our case study in KM 2013. We also concur with Wenger et al.[7] that COP must be managed and cultivated actively and systematically. Building on these premises, the following critical success factors will be implemented in KM 2014:

1. Duration of KM 2014 has been extended to allow more time for COP awareness, understanding, acceptance and proper implementation
2. The design for COP using social objects will be promoted
3. COP will be implemented using a practical model developed by Wenger et al. [7] which is based on three fundamental elements:
    a. a domain of knowledge which defines a set of issues,
    b. communities of people who care about this domain
    c. shared practices that they develop in order to be effective in their domain.
4. A COP facilitator and knowledge broker will be nominated and will play an active role during KM 2014
5. "Team space" for each team will be created as a platform for knowledge sharing among COP members, but they are free to use their preferred social media, e.g. Facebook
6. "Open space" in Moodle (Seinäjoki UAS Online Media for teaching) will be created for inter-team/COP discussions and knowledge sharing
7. Physical spaces will be available for face-to-face team/COP meetings.
8. After completion of KM 2014, a number of students will be interviewed to find out if the new COP design and implementation had a positive impact on knowledge sharing among the students. The findings will be shared in the 8th International KMO Conference that will take place on 2–5 September 2014 in Santiago, Chile.

References

[1] Sun, P.Y., Scott, J.L.: An investigation of barriers of knowledge transfer. Journal of Knowledge Management 9(2), 75–90 (2005)
[2] Riege, A.: Three-dozen knowledge-sharing barriers managers must consider. Journal of Knowledge Management 9(3), 8–35 (2005)
[3] Hofstede, G., Hofstede, G.J.: Culture and Organization. McGraw-Hill, New York (2005)
[4] Eid, M., Nuhu, N.A.: The impact of learning culture and information technology use on knowledge sharing on Saudi students. Knowledge Management Research & Practice 9, 48–57 (2011)
[5] Shaheen, M., Ting, J.Y.: Information and Knowledge Sharing by Undergraduate Students in Singapore. In: Khosrow-Pour, M. (ed.) Emerging Trends and Challenges in Information Technology Management, vols. 1 and 2. Idea Group Publishing, Hershey (2006)
[6] Wenger, E.: Communities of Practice: Learning, Meaning, and Identity. Cambridge University Press, Cambridge (1988, 2008)

[7] Wenger, E., McDermott, R., Snyder, W.M.: Cultivating Communities of Practice. Harvard Business School Press, Cambridge (2002)
[8] Kuutti, K.: Context and Consciousness: Activity Theory and Human-Computer. MIT Press, Cambridge (1995)
[9] Engeström, Y.: Expansive Learning at work. Journal of Education and Work 14(1), 133–156 (2001)
[10] Kuutti, K., Molin-Juustila, T.: Information system support for "loose" coordination in a network organization: An activity-theory perspective. In: Hasan, H., Gould, E., Hyland, P. (eds.) Information Systems and Activity Theory: Tools in Context, pp. 73–92. University of Wollongong Press, Wollongong (1998)
[11] Vygotsky, L.S.: Mind in Society: The Development of Higher Psychological Processes. Harvard University Press, Cambridge (1978)
[12] Engeström, Y.: Learning by Expanding: an activity-theoretical approach to developmental research. Orienta-Konsultit Oy, Helsinki (1987)
[13] Keyes, J.: Identifying the Barriers to Knowledge sharing in Knowledge Intensive Organizations (2008), http://www.newarttech.com/KnowledgeSharing.pdf
[14] Kaptelinin, V., Nardi, B.A.: Acting with Technology: Activity Theory and Interaction Design. MIT Press, Cambridge (2006)
[15] Kaptelinin, V., Nardi, B.A., Macaulay, C.: Methods & Tools: The activity checklist: a tool for representing the "space" of context. Magazine Interactions 6(4), 27–39 (1999)
[16] Boer, N.I., van Baalen, P.J., Kumar, K.: An Activity Approach for Studying the Situatedness of Knowledge Sharing. In: Proceeding of the 35th Annual Hawaii International Conference on System Sciences, Erasmus University, Rotterdam, The Netherlands. Department of Information and Decision Management (2002), Retrieved from IEEE Xplore Digital Library, http://www.ieeexplore.ieee.org
[17] Jonassen, D.H., Rohrer-Murphy, L.: Activity Theory as a Framework for Designing Constructivist Learning Environments. Educational Technology Research and Development 47(1), 61–79 (1999)
[18] Bardram, J.E.: I love the system: I just don't use it. In: Proceeding of the International ACM SIGGROUP Conference on Supporting Group Work: The Integration Challenge, New York, pp. 251–260 (1997)
[19] Engeström, Y.: Innovative learning in work teams: Analyzing cycles of knowledge creation in practice. In: Engeström, Y., Miettinen, R., Punamaiki, R.L. (eds.) Perspectives on Activity Theory, pp. 377–404. Cambridge University Press, Cambridge (1999)
[20] Lave, J., Wenger, E.: Situated Learning: Legitimate Peripheral Participation. University of Cambridge Press, Cambridge (1991)
[21] Engeström, J.: Why some social network services work and others don't – Or: the case for object centered sociality (2005), http://www.zengestrom.com (retrieved)
[22] Weller, M.:: Social objects in education (2008), Retreived from 'The Ed Techie', http://www.nogoodreason.typepad.co.uk
[23] Demsey, L.: Some thoughts about egos, objects and social networks (2008), http://www.orweblog.oclc.org (retrieved)
[24] McLeod, H.: Social Objects for beginners (2007), http://www.gapingvoid.com (retrieved)

The Learning of Metacognitive Skills through Task Management Structures (TKS) – A New Opportunity for Dental Student Education

John H. Hamilton

Department of Oral Diagnostic and Surgical Sciences,
School of Dentistry, University of Otago, Dunedin, New Zealand
john.hamilton@otago.ac.nz

Abstract. Today, we are preparing students to learn throughout their lives. Dental students must have problem solving, critical thinking and independent learning skills to meet the challenges of becoming effective clinicians. Dental students, however, find diagnostic and treatment planning challenges difficult to manage as many do not have the cognitive framework to solve them. The practice of dentistry is experiential. It contains a large body of tacit knowledge. To help students to become effective learners and acquire lifelong learning skills, they need to be taught to problem solve, think critically, and to communicate and learn independently. Most of the continuous professional development (CPD), post graduation, is independently assimilated and delivered in a didactic style; so these new learning skills will also equip the new graduate with the critical thinking and problem solving tools they will need to self review, to reflect upon and to process new insights throughout their professional careers.

Problem-Based Learning (PBL) is an instructional method that challenges students to 'learn to learn', through working co-operatively in groups to seek solutions to real world problems. It prepares students to think critically and analytically, and to find and use appropriate learning resources. However, the implementation of PBL is both time consuming and resource intensive. It is our belief that the learning of metacognitive skills can also be facilitated through task knowledge structures (TKS). This paper argues how the use of TKSs can help dental students to learn the metacognitive skills that they should have in order to prepare them for lifelong learning.

1 Introduction

A report on education in USA concluded that society's future depends on a citizenry that can think and reason creatively and deliberately. It also suggests that they will need to develop sound judgments of information, understand and contend effectively with rapid and constant change [1]. Students today will continue learning throughout their professional lives to meet the rapid changes of technological innovation and keep abreast with the latest knowledge and skills in their respective careers. This requires the learning of problem-solving, critical thinking, metacognitive and

L. Uden et al. (Eds.): LTEC 2014, CCIS 446, pp. 149–154, 2014.

self-directed learning skills, rather than specific skills and knowledge. This has important implications for the teaching and learning of our dental students.

The author has being concerned about the frustration faced by students in their learning. Many students have experienced that learning is difficult, especially when it comes to problem solving and critical thinking, around diagnosis and treatment planning. They have no idea where to begin to integrate information, despite their familiarity with subject content. These students can memorise facts and procedures, but are unable to explain observed phenomena, to solve real-world problems, or to analyse problems and to think critically. Many of these students may pass examinations, but be unable to *apply* the same knowledge to solve new problems. They have difficulty in utilising the knowledge and skills acquired via formal learning. It is clear from contemporary thought in the field of education that lecture style methods of teaching are not effective. We must change the way we teach and help students learn to solve problems and think independently [2] that is to develop strategies that teach content in ways that also teach thinking and problem-solving skills.

The practice of dentistry is by its nature experiential; it contains a large body of tacit knowledge. This tacit knowledge is understood to be subjective, informal and for the most part, internalised; it is related to our social and physical experiences, our cognitive abilities, somatic skills and mental and physical perceptions. It is therefore more personal, experiential, context specific and consequently hard to formalise [3,4]. It has been argued [5] that tacit knowledge is impossible to pass on due to its extreme stickiness, however most tacit knowledge is transferable [6,7].

Tacit knowledge is fundamentally different from explicit or propositional knowledge. Explicit knowledge is knowledge, which is general, conventional and easy to express in commonly comprehensible language. It is possible to share explicit knowledge, codify and convert it as principles, formulae, data, processes and information [8,6]. Explicit knowledge is easy to access and transfer, often being referred to as "knowing about", subjective or declarative knowledge [9].

Tacit knowledge, according to Harry Collins [7], can be divided into three distinct sub types. Relational Tacit Knowledge comprises knowledge that is tacit because some of its attributes are subjected to interpersonal interaction or attention. These include knowledge such as trade secrets, knowledge kept hidden deliberately and unrecognised as knowledge.

Somatic tacit knowledge consists of knowledge that is tacit due to our body's inherent physical limitation and abilities. Most of us, for example, know perfectly well how to ride a bicycle yet would find it impossible to put into words how we do so [10]. Collective tacit knowledge consists of knowledge that is ingrained in society and depends largely on how the society works. An example of collective tacit knowledge is the implicit clue of an anecdote that only people with shared culture might understand.

Nonaka and Konno [11] have described two dimensions to tacit knowledge: the technical dimension, i.e. the "know-how", and the cognitive dimension, i.e. beliefs, ideals, values, mental models, and schemata. The Technical dimension of tacit knowledge relates to the task familiarity, the mastery of experience. The cognitive dimension of tacit knowledge shapes the way we perceive the world [11]. This cognitive dimension of tacit knowledge has also been described as "mental models" by Senge [12]. These models shape people's actions and are, vice versa, shaped by them. Since knowing the way a person thinks about the world helps to understand that person's actions, focusing on the cognitive dimension allows us to specify the process of externalisation, as the mechanism that enables the flow of knowledge between communities.

The externalisation process enables people with different backgrounds to share tacit knowledge. According to Nonaka and Takeuchi [6], metaphors, analogies, and dialogue are methods used for externalisation.

In order to help students to acquire these important skills, it is important that we opt for problem-based learning for dental students. Although problem based learning (PBL) is an effective approach to help students to develop metacognitive skills, it is time consuming and labour intensive to implement. To overcome this, it is our belief that the use of task knowledge structures (TKSs) can be used. This paper proposes the use of TKSs to help dental students to develop metacognitive skills needed by dental students. The paper begins with a brief review of PBL, followed by a review of TKS. A TKS model is proposed as an approach to teach the learning of metacognitive skills for dental students

2 Problem Based Learning

Problems in life are complex and few are presented with all the information needed to understand them well enough to make valid decisions about their cause and resolution. More information is generally required. The needed information can be obtained by investigating the problem, making observations, testing and probing. To do this requires reflection, thought and deliberation. Barrows [14] calls these activities metacognition; they regulate how we go about learning [15].

According to Barrows [14], metacognitive skills are thinking about thinking. These are the skills that provide the key to the positive, active role of the tutor. Metacognitive skills are used when one is confronted with a difficult, unexpected, or puzzling problem or situation. Because metacognition plays such an important role for students in learning, students must acquire, through practice, well-developed metacognitive skills to monitor, critique and direct the development of their reasoning skills as they work with life's ill-defined problems; to critique the adequacy of their knowledge and to direct their own continued learning [14].

PBL is a type of constructivist learning. In constructivism, meaning is created by ourselves, rather than existing in the world independent of us. There are many ways to structure the world and there are many meanings or perspectives for any given event or concept. Meaning, in the constructivist view, is indexed by experience [16]. Constructivism is concerned with how we construct knowledge. The construction of knowledge is a function of the prior experience, mental structures and beliefs that one uses to interpret objects and events.

The constructivist assumptions of learning can be described as follows [17]:

1. All knowledge is constructed (albeit socially) and not transmitted.
2. Knowledge and meanings result from activity and are embedded in activity systems.
3. Knowledge is distributed in persons, tools and other cultural artifacts.

4. Meaning arises out of interpretation and thus multiple perspectives are recognised.
5. Meaning construction is prompted by problems, questions, issues and authentic tasks.

Problem-based learning (PBL), according to Barrows [14] is," ... *the learning which results from the process of working towards the understanding of, or resolution of, a problem.*" Barrows describes the main educational goals as to firstly develop students' thinking or reasoning skills (problem solving, meta-cognition, critical thinking) and then secondly to help the students become independent, self-directed learners (learning to learn, learning management).

The purpose of PBL is therefore to produce students who will:

1. Engage a challenge (problem, complex task, and situation) with initiative and enthusiasm;
2. Reason effectively, accurately, and creatively from an integrated, flexible, usable knowledge base;
3. Monitor and assess their own adequacy to achieve a desirable outcome given a challenge;
4. Address their own perceived inadequacies in knowledge and skills effectively and efficiently;
5. Collaborate effectively as a member of a team working to achieve a common goal.

According to Elder and Paul [18], critical thinking is best understood as the ability of thinkers to take charge of their own thinking. Critical thinking skills are now recognised as important for those who will enter the twenty-first century workforce, where the information age requires individuals who are flexible, dynamic and resilient. Teaching students to become effective thinkers is increasingly being recognised as the main aim of today's education. If students are to function effectively in a rapidly changing and highly technical society, they must be equipped with lifelong learning and thinking skills necessary to acquire and process information in an ever-changing world [19].

Task Knowledge Structures

According to Johnson and Johnson [20], task knowledge is represented in a person's memory and can be described by a Task Knowledge Structure (TKS). TKSs are assumed to be acquired through learning and reflecting on previous task performances, and are dynamically represented in memory. This is akin to the theoretical position taken by Schank [21] in assuming that the knowledge of frequently occurring events is structured into meaningful units in memory. The assumption is that all the knowledge a person possesses about a task is contained within the TKS and that the TKS is activated in association with and during the performance of a given task.

If we assume the existence of these task knowledge structures, people use to structure their knowledge in a particular way, it then follows that this task knowledge can be analysed, modeled and predicted [20]. This has important implications for learning. It suggests that by understanding a knowledge structure, recall and processing could be optimised to give quick and efficient task performance by appropriate training techniques and interface design. According to Johnson and Johnson [20], people acquire knowledge about tasks and subsequently transfer this knowledge to new or different tasks. Therefore usability and learnability are directly related to the amount of knowledge that the person is able to transfer from one task to another. The benefits to be gained from enhancing this transfer come in the form of reduced time and the achievement of a higher level of task performance in a shorter length of time.

A TKS is related to other TKS by a number of different relationships, which include temporal or experimental relationships [20]. TKS theory provides a method for the analysis and modeling of the tasks in terms of goals, procedures, actions and objects. In addition, TKS theory also identifies the representitiveness (typicality) and centrality (importance) of a particular aspect of task knowledge. Within each TKS, different types of knowledge can be represented. There are four components to a complete TKS model. These are as follows:

1. A goal-oriented substructure.
2. Task procedures.
3. A taxonomic substructure comprising the generic task actions and objects.
4. A summary task knowledge structure.

3 Conclusion

Critical thinking and metacognitive skills are vital for today's students as they prepare themselves for the rapidly changing world they will meet once they graduate. Problem Based Learning does offer students a pathway to learn these skills. However, the implementation of Problem-Based Learning is both time consuming and resource intensive.

Task Knowledge Structures have been used successfully to assist in the design process and the subsequent testing of User Interfaces in the computer industry. By using task knowledge structures it is also possible to help dental students to develop important diagnostic skills such as problem solving, critical thinking and metacognition. Whilst experience builds mental models, we want our students to have these models earlier in their learning. These experientially developed mental models or frameworks, structure the information received by the clinician. Teaching the information without the framework diminishes the potential value of the existing knowledge to the student. It is clear from contemporary thought in the field of education that lecture style methods of teaching are not effective. By using TKSs we can enable students to build more useful mental models, earlier in their training to facilitate a more rapid assimilation of tacit knowledge prior to graduation. We are currently working on the development of TKSs, informed by experienced clinicians, to better shape the teaching of diagnostic skills for our dental students. We believe that by developing a better understanding of the existing knowledge structures, we can use problem based learning methodologies more effectively to enable students to learn the cognitive skills they need in today's dynamic world.

References

1. Tennyson, K., Bruer, M.: Complex-Dynamic Simulations to improve Higher-order Thinking Strategies. Journal Struct. Learn. 11(1), 27–37 (1991)
2. Bransford, J.D., et al.: Anchored instruction: Why we need it and how technology can help. In: Nix, D., Sprio, R. (eds.) Cognition, Education and Multimedia. Erlbaum Associates, Hillsdale (1990)
3. Saviotti, P.: On the Dynamics of Appropriability of Tacit and of Codified Knowledge. Elsevier Journal Research 26(7-8), 843–856 (1998)
4. Leonard, D., Sensiper, S.: The Role of Tacit Knowledge in Group Innovation. California Management Review 40, 112–132 (1998)
5. Szulanski, G.: Exploring Internal Stickiness: Impediments to the Transfer of Best Practice Within the Firm. Strategic Management Journal 17, 27–43 (1996)
6. Nonaka, I., Takeuchi, H.: The Knowledge-Creating Company: How Japanese Companies Create the Dynamics of Innovation. Oxford University Press, London (1995)
7. Collins, H.: Tacit and Explicit Knowledge. University of Chicago Press, US (2010)
8. Polanyi, M.: The Tacit Dimension, 108 + xi pages. Anchor Books, New York (1967)
9. Kogut, B., Zander, U.: Knowledge of the Firm, Combinative Capabilities, and the Replication of Technology. Organization Science 3(3), 383 (1992)
10. Mackenzie, D., Spinardi, G.: Tacit knowledge, weapons design, and the uninvention of nuclear weapons. The American Journal of Sociology (AJS) 101, 44–99 (1995)
11. Nonaka, I., Konno, N.: The concept of "ba": Building a foundation for knowledge creation. California Management Review 40, 40–54 (1998)
12. Senge, P.M.: Die fünfte Disziplin. Kunst und Praxis der lernenden Organisation. Klett-Cotta, Stuttgart (1996)
13. Barrows, H.S.: The tutorial process. Southern Illinois University School of Medicine, Springfield, Il (1992)
14. Barrows, H.S.: The tutorial process. Southern Illinois University, School of Medicine, Springfield IL (1988)
15. Blakey, E., Spence, S.: Developing Metacognition. ERIC Digest. ERIC Clearing House on Information Resource, Syracuse (1990)
16. Brown, J.S., Collins, A., Duguid, P.: Situated Cognition and the Culture of Learning. Educational Researcher 18, 32–42 (1989)
17. Uden, L.: Editorial. International Journal of Learning Technology 1(1), 1–15 (2004)
18. Elder, L., Paul, R.: Critical thinking: Why we must transform our teaching. Journal of Developmental Education 18(1), 34–35 (1994)
19. Robinson, I.S.: A program to incorporate higher-order thinking skills into teaching and learning for grades K-3, p. 16. Nova University (ED284689), Fort Lauderdale (1987)
20. Johnson, P., Johnson, H.: Human Computer Interaction: psychiatry, task analysis and software engineering. McGraw-Hill (1992)
21. Schank, R.C.: Dynamic Memory: A theory of reminding and learning in computers and people. Cambridge University Press (1982)
22. Nonaka, I., Von Krogh, G.: Tacit Knowledge and Knowledge Conversion: Controversy and Advancement in Organizational Knowledge Creation Theory. Organizational Science 20(3), 635–652 (2009)

KM Tools and Techniques from the Cloud Based on GNU Can Be Applied in Educational Organizations

Roberto Ferro, Rubén González, and Sandro Bolaños

Universidad Distrital Francisco José de Caldas Bogotá Colombia
Universidad Internacional de la Rioja Madrid España
{rferro,sbolanos}@udistrital.edu.co1, ruben.gonzalez@unir.net

Abstract. This paper presents some applications based on free software that allow some steps related to knowledge management, these can be implemented in organizations own servers or new hosting services in the cloud as a Nixiweb for creating various scrip free and without advertising becoming an excellent starting point for communities that wish to implement practical inexpensive tools and great popular acceptance. For each KM activity some GNU free tools are discussed while additional ones are referred to in the existing manuals. At several points views in this paper links with other contributions from the Asian Productivity Organization APO, as is also done the other way round. It is concluded that there is already a comprehensive set of tools available on the web, but for some peculiar aspects of knowledge assets there are not still development yet.

Keywords: Knowledge Management, free GNU tool, Drupal, Jcow, Moodle, Asian Productivity Organizations.

1 Introduction

Today many organizations are aware and create policies to implement knowledge management models to improve all processes, but unfortunately they do not have large economic resources to purchase software from vendors such as SharePoint to Microsoft [1] and other solutions, which is why the teams should implement in their network servers based on free software that if applied properly can potentiate staff resources solutions that integrates the educational organization.

To verify this we chose several free tools there between Joomla [2], Moodle [3], Jcow [4] and Drupal [5] initially testing Joomla were made but it was not possible to use this tool on the stage of intelligent search of refined information due to the limitations it has in the modules that form, then tests were conducted in Moodle but the same approach to the educational part is making the application more emphasis on student testing and presentation of a very specific educational format and like Joomla not have a search unit of intelligent information , to perform a more detailed search tool free Drupal was found.

L. Uden et al. (Eds.): LTEC 2014, CCIS 446, pp. 155–162, 2014.

Drupal is a Content Management System (CMS), is a free and open-source content management framework written in PHP and distributed under the GNU General Public License, Drupal is highly configurable and modular multipurpose used to publish, images, articles and other things or other files and added services like forums, surveys , polls , blogs and user management and permissions. It is a dynamic system because instead of storing its contents in static files on the server file system permanently, the textual content of pages and other settings are stored in MySQL [6], PostgreSQL, or SQLite [7] database and edited using a Web environment.

Now in the specified time to create a complete system of knowledge management is important to consider recommendations relating to this aspect, to achieve compliance with related earlier, perform and retrieve important bibliographical sources for information on which elements should be taken to implement a model of knowledge management, according to the above we find the book of the Asian Productivity Organizations APO [8] this companies can establish that there are methods and non-IT and IT tools that support proper management of knowledge, hence the need for a system based on ICT to enable any organization to create its own educational system with an intranet and an extranet that meet each of the schemes from purchase to properly implement all processes.

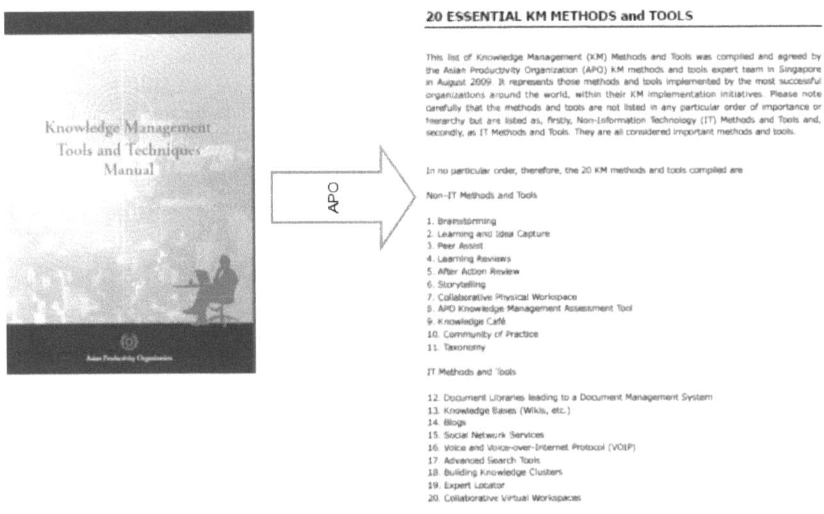

Fig. 1. 20 Essential KM methods IT and not IT tools from APO book [8]

2 Essential Elements in KM Process

In 1993 Peter F. Drucker [9] proposes that knowledge management models become more competitive to businesses or companies, some of these as Chevron [10], HP [11], British Petroleum BP [12], Ford [13] and others have developed their own models in order to preserve the most important which is the prevailing intellectual capital on the completion of extensive manual with information that will eventually be archived without generating more knowledge regarding the purchase. Currently, knowledge management models are being implemented in small and medium-sized Asian companies belonging to the APO.

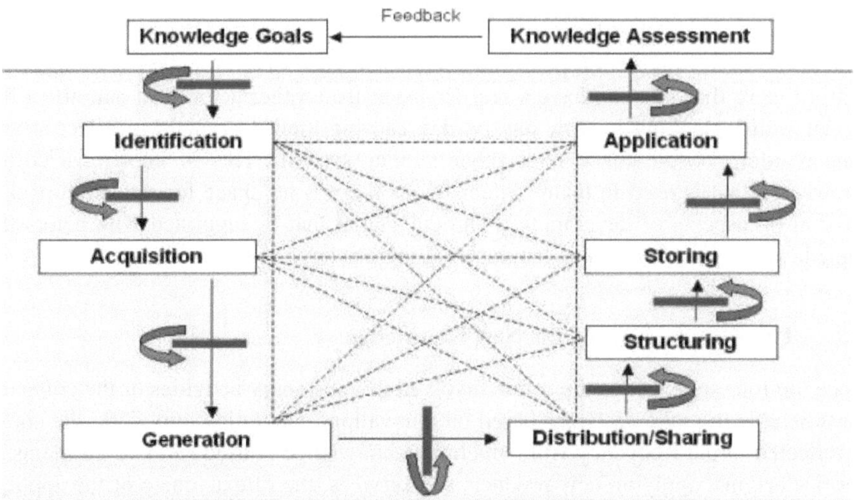

Fig. 2. Essential elements for creating a knowledge management model based in systems classification according to Brandt/Hartmann [14]

2.1 Acquire and Identification of Knowledge

It involves identifying the knowledge about the subsystems have been implemented at the organization, its current status, type of information performed and the state of the art with respect to new developments. Use brainstorming with all team members to have a clear understanding of the aspects in question. The use of the Joomla and Drupal it is a good possibility for make this stage.

2.2 Creation of Knowledge

All data collection, information or subsequent elements of the subsystems should be created and must sit in some way different from the traditional which was based on a culture of writing on paper, the classification is required of it by taxonomy or by an ontology in more elaborate cases you can get to build thesaurus; for this stage we can use a Drupal because has a special module searches that allow more efficient search of information and thus can refine it if the organization requires.

2.3 Storage and Structured the Knowledge

At this stage you must perform a data sheet preferably on an intranet to save the most important aspects of each of the subsystems to track optimal and efficient in every aspect related to these you can use a database MySQL or a similar software for capturing and storing them in a digital repository or data mining capabilities of Artificial Intelligence.

2.4 Share and Distribution the Knowledge

One of the most important aspects must be to share and distribute the knowledge as it is from there that you can have a real feedback from other actors that can affect the model well in making it grow day by day causing them to remain in effect at any time avoiding obsolescence over other similar systems. This is known as coffee knowledge that is used in many organizations there is no space for reflection or discussion on aspects of developing a particular goal that is suggested with actors the same level preferably in other geographical regions have a similar mission.

2.5 The Ability to Apply the New Knowledge

Once the four steps above the actors involved in missionary activities of the company must be able to make decisions based on innovation, integration into work, the above is reflected in the frequency with which new knowledge is used to solve problems of various origins, applying new products and services, the effectiveness of the application of knowledge is seen as an improvement in efficiency.

According to the above topics are organizations worldwide that use this tool is licensed for Microsoft SharePoint having all modules that can be applied to a system of knowledge management.

Fig. 3. Microsoft SharePoint software for knowledge management in enterprise companies [1]

3 Proposed Tools for Technological Upgrading

Once verified all requirements for KMS to meet and verify the different modules that are systems licensed software, we are proposing the use of the portal Nixiweb [15] which offers cloud services and can use hosting and free domains such as "uni.me" , also has more than 100 open source applications and it is best to not have any commercial messages or advertisements; for our particular case we can install Drupal , Moodle and Jcow without using local servers or acquire a public IP , if necessary here also have an option for a hosting with annually payments.

Fig. 4. View the Nixiweb hosting offers free web hosting. Supports PHP , MySQL , Joomla , phpBB , WordPress [15]

3.1 Acquire and Identification of Knowledge

To this point we recommend checking the documentation related subsystems:

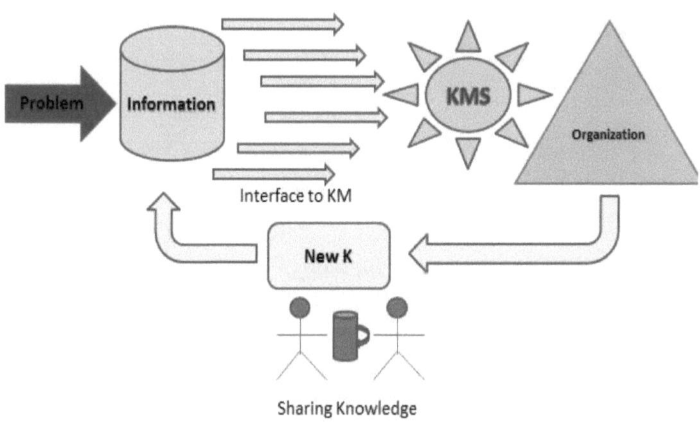

Fig. 5. Knowledge Management Model proposed for the IT tools in educational organizations

3.2 Creation of Knowledge

Once all the subsystems are needed for a detailed description of these effects is how the respective taxonomy where each sort key elements that make up the building and need to be detailed for sub-sequent operations within the model of knowledge management.

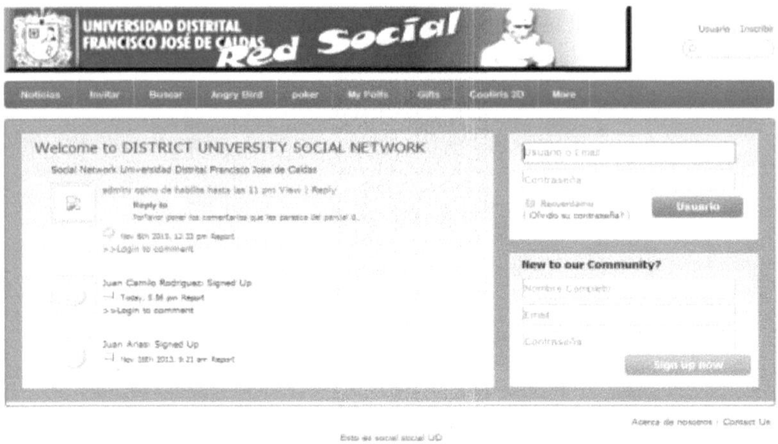

Fig. 6. Educational website created with the tool in an educational organization Jcow from the Distric University [16]

3.3 Storage and Structured of Knowledge

To store the knowledge we use Drupal which has an intelligent database to support SQL and it uses PHP Data Objects to abstract the physical database. Drupal core also

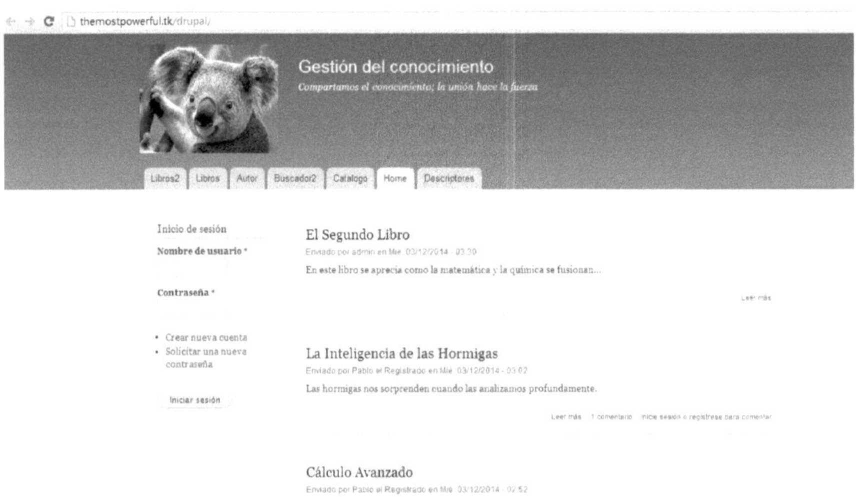

Fig. 7. Academic design web in the cloud with Drupal in the Nixiweb free hosting [16]

includes a hierarchical taxonomy system, which allows content to be categorized or tagged with key words for easier access; this core also includes a hierarchical taxonomy system, which allows content to be categorized or tagged with key words for easier access and also store and share important information.

For our particular case we installed Drupal and created different categories for indexing information from books, catalogs and specialty items.

3.4 Share and Distribution the Knowledge

To share the knowledge you can use you can use the free tool and use a Drupal based on Taxonomy module; where you can share knowledge among these is the community for the development of intellectual capital and knowledge management. "It's a good tool for aimed at improving communication between people who know. You can go there to see what is happening with people and skills to know, learn and do ".

3.5 The Ability to Apply the New Knowledge

Taxonomy is the science of classification and Drupal is used to catalog the contents based on different vocabularies. A vocabulary is a set of terms that allow us to label one or more types of content or information from tacit knowledge. In Drupal we can create as many vocabularies as we need to have options based on terms, hierarchy, catalogs and descriptors.

Once implemented the Drupal modules can make intelligent search of correct information from specific people and at the key moment, in this way it is possible to use Taxonomies have the information in a timely manner and thus create new searches having a quick alternative robust and based on this tool free to use.

4 Conclusion

Thanks to free portals we have been able to install and test the effectiveness of some GNU tools to be used to create complete systems of knowledge management, Moodle creates all work related to the development of an educational platform environment Jcow creates communities of experts around an academic and research and Drupal social network creates all documentary functionality through the use of taxonomies and detailed information refined search, that turns any website into a major organizational development that provide a competitive advantage over graduates as SharePoint development of Microsoft.

References

1. Microsoft Corporation, http://office.microsoft.com/en-us/sharepoint/
2. Joomla official web site, http://www.joomla.org/
3. Moodle official web site, https://moodle.org/
4. Jcow, Social networking Software, http://www.jcow.net/

5. Drupal CMS, https://drupal.org
6. MySQL is the world's most popular open source database, http://www.mysql.com/products/
7. Postgresgl, The PostgreSQL Global Development Group, http://www.postgresql.org/
8. Young, R.: Knowledge Managemen Tools and Techniques Manual, Tokio, Asian Productivity Organization (APO), http://www.apo-tokyo.org, ISBN: 92-833-7093-7
9. Drucker, P.T.: Above and Beyond KM, http://aboveandbeyondkm.com/tag/peter-drucker
10. Grant, R.M.: The Development of Knowledge management in the oil and Gas Industry, Chevron Texaco Corporation. The Chevron Texaco Way, San Francisco (2002), http://ubr.universia.net/pdfs_revistas/articulo_352_1381330772384.pdf
11. HP.: HP Service Manager Knowledge Management module empowers your staff and end users by enabling and leveraging organizational wisdom, http://static.ziftsolutions.com/files/8a7c9fef21c24ec60121c712cf1016e3
12. Prezi.: Best practices of KM at British Petroleum company, http://prezi.com/zh1xlmlpc6us/best-practices-of-knowledge-management-at-british-petroleum/
13. Ford company, Knowledge management in Ford motors, http://www.ukessays.com/essays/management/knowledge-management-in-ford-motors.php
14. Brandt, D., Hartmann, E.: Editorial: Research Topics and Strategies in Socio-technical Systems. Human Factors and Ergonomics in Manufacturing 9(3), 241–243 (1999), http://sic.ici.ro/sic2002_1/art01.htm
15. Nixiweb, free cloud hosting in the web, http://www.nixiweb.com
16. Universidad Distrital Francisco José de Caldas. Bogotá Colombia, http://www.udistrital.edu.co

Two Decades of e-learning in Distance Teaching – From Web 1.0 to Web 2.0 at the University of Hagen

Birgit Feldmann

University of Hagen

Technology changed the way of learning and teaching during the last twenty years to today a great deal. The change started in the 70's with the increasing use of technology in education and spread out at the beginning of the 90's with the upcoming Internet, was followed by the development of Learning Management Systems and nowadays the new and easy to use possibilities of Web 2.0. All these technologies could lead to new forms of learning, teaching, information gathering and managing, communicating, collaborating, and networking. It seems natural to adapt the new technologies to higher education, especially to distance education, as there a many known problems: E. g. in Germany no study fees are allowed. How to finance highly interactive, small classes? Another problem are the professional restrictions of distance students, their time budget is limited. The consequence is that normally students have very limited contact to their peers and their tutors until the final examinations. The drop-out rates are extremely high (more than 80%) and a lot of students study more than six years to reach a degree.

The deployment of virtual teaching improved the situation substantially, but not enough. Web 2.0 could open up new possibilities to improve this situation.

In Germany a nation-wide study examined the impact of Web 2.0 on the studying process. Unfortunately, only on-campus students were included in this survey. However, research and experience in the field of e-learning clearly show that technology based learning is especially interesting and useful for distance students. The University of Hagen, the only public distance teaching university in the German speaking countries with about 80.000 students, is the perfect test-bed for new forms of technology-supported learning. Therefore we did a research survey about the effect of Web 2.0, especially community usage, on distance students to find out the students' current preferences and needs. The results of this study revealed important insights into the use of new technology and particularly into the wishes and needs of distance students. These insights lead to a new understanding of essential aspects of e-learning not only in distance education. An interesting example is the low value students attribute to traditional learning management systems. This paper will give a short review from the beginning to today and then compare the outcome of the two studies in relevant areas and gives suggestions for Web 2.0 usage in e-learning environments.

Keywords: e-learning, Web 1.0, Web 2.0 distance education, learning management systems.

L. Uden et al. (Eds.): LTEC 2014, CCIS 446, pp. 163–172, 2014.

1 Introduction

At the University of Hagen (FernUniversitaet in Hagen), the only public distance teaching university in German speaking countries, e-learning has been practiced since more than 15 years using various teaching methods such as online courses, virtual seminars and practical trainings. Experience has shown that teaching methods with a high rate of group activities, using electronic communication possibilities, have the quality to break down the students' isolation, to enable long-lasting learning communities with completely new communication qualities that are fundamentally different from traditional ways of distance teaching and learning [1, 2]. Also some of the groups students took part in during a learning event lived much longer than the event itself. In some cases the relationship between the group members stayed active long after their studies were finished. [1, 2]. Related research results approve these findings, i.e. Kerres [4] and Glowalla [5] describe similar results. Others, i.e. Leh [6], Palloff and Pratt [7] also state the importance of communication and cooperation. Since the early days a lot changed in the meantime. Nowadays e-learning and e-teaching are widespread in all areas of education. Even though the general idea that the new possibilities of Web2.0 offer many advantages for distance teaching students is obvious, specifics are not available so far: which needs should be fulfilled, which functions are used for which purpose, and so on. The existing research about Web2.0 and teaching/learning is focused on campus students, not on distance students. Therefore, we started a survey and evaluation within the 80.000 student population of the University of Hagen. A lot can be learned from the results, part of which are rather surprising and suggest a new understanding of e-learning. The paper is structured in the following parts: Part One will give a short overview over the last beginning of e-learning in Hagen and the current situation. It then describes the HISBUS study with on-campus students, followed by the survey of the University of Hagen. Part four compares relevant outcomes of both studies. Part Five discusses the findings and derives suggestions for future use of Web 2.0 in e-learning environments.

2 The View Back

Especially for a distance university, like the University of Hagen, it seemed to be a natural decision to use the Internet. Hagen has an experience and a tradition of distance education with using modern media for teaching and learning since more than 35 years. Therefore, it was a logical consequence to use the Internet for learning and teaching purposes. The benefits of distance education, time- and location independence and the advantages of the Internet (fast information, easy communication and co-operation possibilities) were combined in the project virtual university, Germany's first complete virtual university, a typical example for a modern education system. The project was experimenting with and evaluating different forms of teaching and learning. As for that time and for our purposes no suitable commercial platform was available, we were forced to create a new one, using Internet technologies combined with a commercial database system. It is a virtual university system that integrates all functions of a university into a complete, homogeneous, extensible and cost-effective system with an easy to use and intuitive student-centered user-interface. We started with only a few courses of electrical engineering and computer science. The system is since the beginning open for all departments of the university, in the first year after the start; more than the half of all courses were social sciences and economics course. This demonstrates that the development of the platform was not only useful for the technical oriented departments (as expected) but also for all other departments. Actually more than 80.000 students are using e-learning at the University of Hagen. In contrast to the beginning of e-learning, as the idea was to build up everything in one platform, the University now implemented a set of software to allow all kinds of teaching events for the students.

Table 1. E-learning software at the University of Hagen

Learning-management-systems	Group-ware	Assign-ments	Conferen-cing	Communi-cation / Information	Student Support
Moodle Lerraum Virutelle Universität (LVU)	CURE BSCW	Lotse WebAssign	Adobe Connect IRC	Email Newsgroup Blogs	Self-manage-ment-tool (SMT)

3 The HISBUS Study: Studying in Web 2.0

HISBUS is an online portal for students funded by the German government and carried out by a cooperation of HIS and the Multimedia Kontor Hamburg[1]. The goal of this project is to analyze the students' needs in order to improve the governmental support of higher education. The HISBUS Panel is designed as a virtual community whose members function as representatives for the average on-campus students [8]. The study itself was conducted as an online-survey inside the HISBUS Panel in the summer term 2008 (September, 8 to October, 8) with 4.400 responses, a rate of return of about 40 %, which is quite high, but explainable as the participants are all from a specially chosen student community.

[1] HISBUS is an abbreviation consisting of HIS: Higher Education Information Systems and BUS as a synonym for different thematic areas. HIS supports German institutions of higher education (universities and universities of applied sciences) and their administrations as well as higher education policy-makers in their efforts to fulfill their tasks effectively [http://www.his.de/english/organization]. The Multmedia-Kontor is an enterprise funded by different universities in the city of Hamburg to provide IT-based services for the universities.

3.1 HISBUS Findings

The results of the study can be divided into five main areas: Internet usage in general, social communities, knowledge and information platforms, e-learning and study-related offers on the Internet. We do not discuss the category of questions which deals with the use and rating of different e-learning offers as this is not of interest for the subject of this paper.

Web 2.0 Usages in General

The first question for the participants was about the duration of his/her active every-day Internet usage. Not surprisingly, it turned out that the Internet is the most important communication medium in the students' everyday life. Almost three quarters of the students spend 1 to 3 hours daily on the Internet and a quarter even 4 to 6 hours. For what purpose do students use the Internet? Which Internet offers do the students access particularly often? The information given for these topics show that the online encyclopedia Wikipedia is the most popular source. About 60% of the students indicated to access Wikipedia often or very often, closely followed by social communities (StudiVZ, Facebook, XING etc.) which were accessed with a frequently by 51%. About 35% of the students use chat rooms and instant messaging offers. This demonstrates that communication and knowledge platforms are particularly popular and intensively used.

Knowledge Platforms and Platforms of Information

Knowledge and information platforms like Wikipedia are – as explained above– used particularly often. To examine this fact, the kind of the usage of Wikipedia or similar online encyclopedias was investigated with two questions. It turned out that the reading of articles (80%) is the most common action. The possibilities of revising an article, to take part in discussions or to write new articles, are very rarely used. Though it does not come as a big surprise, this confirms that the majority of the students are only interested in using the already available information, while only a small minority is involved actively in the development of the online encyclopedia. With regard to the reliability of the information on Wikipedia 52% of the interviewees consider the information to be very dependable or at least reasonably dependable. Concerning other online encyclopedias the students agree by majority that they are not able judge the reliability. The simple reason for this is the fact that these platforms are less well known among students.

Social Communities

As described, half of all students use social communities. The main reason is the communication with friends with 72% or finding old friends with 52%. At least 34% of the questioned students assert that they communicate via communities about study-related topics. Less important is the possibility to get new contacts (10%) or to observe the behavior of other community members (20%).

Another question examined how students use communities for study-related matters. The aspect of contact care with fellow students was the most important reason for community usage (66%), closely followed by subjects like self-study (59%), exam preparation (55%) or exchange of documents (49%). The fact that social communities are regularly used by the students actively and have become an essential part of students' communication behavior in addition to the classical campus communication is of special importance for further developments in the field of e-learning.

Study-Related Web 2.0 Offers of the University

Usually students could use learning and teaching oriented web-based offers provided by the university itself, e.g. study information, organizational offers (for example enrollment, lecture and exam registrations, feedback etc.), evaluation, student communities and learning management systems. Due to this fact, the participants were asked about the value of these services on a 5-figure scale from "very useful" to "completely useless". Study information and organizational offers were classified as "very useful" to "useful" by more than 80-percent of the interviewees. The value of these services is high because of the fact that the individual study planning is getting more and more complicated. Also student online communities in the department or in the university are rated highly useful by the majority of the students. Surprisingly, only 43% rated learning management systems like Moodle or Illias (very popular in German universities) as "useful" to "very useful". This indicates that learning management systems only provide marginal added value for on-campus students. Even more striking is the fact that only 19 % use the offered e-learning courses. Wikis have topmost popularity as valuable tools for studying. Not surprisingly, at the end of the scale of study-related Internet offers are chat or discussion forums with 38% as on-campus students usually use social networking platforms for contact care (see Social Communities above) and also as these types of communication methods are meanwhile outdated. In the study not only the usefulness of the offers was investigated, but also the frequency of usage. As one would expect, it turned out that the frequency of usage depends on the perceived value of the offers. The higher students' rates an offer the more often will this offer be used.

4 The Hagen Study: Community-Usage in Distance Education

At the University of Hagen (FernUniversität in Hagen) students benefit from a modern distance education system which combines pedagogically well prepared study units with individual support, net-based co-operation in seminars and working groups, online communication offers and face-to-face sessions. Contact and contact persons for the students are available on the main campus at Hagen as well as at various study centers in Germany, Austria, Switzerland and Central and Eastern Europe. Four faculties (humanities, mathematics and computer science, business administration and law) offer an alternative to on-campus studies with high-quality final degrees (Bachelor, Master and Doctorate) and a wide variety of continuous education. Currently, about 81,000 students are enrolled [http://www.fernuni-hagen.de/english/profile/index.shtml]. The central goal of the online survey documented in the following was to find out how distance students use Web 2.0 tools. Of special interest was the question which tools are well-known and how are these used. The survey 'Community Usage by Distance Students at the University of Hagen' was carried out by the Department of Information Systems and Databases [http://isdb.fernuni-hagen.de/index.php/en.html] as a standardized online survey using LimeSurvey. The field phase lasted four weeks in the summer term 2010. 18.700

randomly chosen students from all faculties (studying a minimum of five semesters to eliminate the early beginners) were invited via email to take part in the survey 2.326 complete feedbacks could be included in the investigation which is a very good return rate for distance students (12%). The data were evaluated with the statistics program SPSS Statistics 18 versions 18.0.0.

The questionnaire contained 12 questions which were divided into two subject complexes. In the first group demographic data as for example age and gender were asked for. The second group with eight questions was about the usage behavior of the students, organized as multiple choice questionnaires via URL in the e-mail invitation. Of course, a set of questions had to be open (for example, in the form "What tools do you wish for your study and why?") and had to allow free text; these are described in part four of this paper. The evaluation is descriptive. Results are given in full percent figures and refer to the total of participants (N = 2.326), thus results do not always add up to exactly 100%.

4.1 Hagen Results

Which Web 2.0 applications do students know and use in the distance university? Which use do they make of the Web 2.0 features offered by the university Hagen? What are the wishes and the needs of distance students concerning web-supported learning possibilities, social networks and learning management portals? In the following an overview about particularly important and interesting results of the survey will be given. First the demographic data are briefly described and second the usage of Web 2.0 in general. Then the study related Web 2.0 offers of the university will be examined.

Demographic Data

Demographic data like gender, age, student's status and faculty were asked for, but there was no requirement to provide them in the questionnaire. For the evaluation of the surveys' second part, Web2.0 usage, this information was not considered on an individual level for data privacy reasons. About 45% of the returns came from female students, 55 % from male students. The distribution of the participants as to faculty, study type (e.g. bachelor, master etc.), gender and age is almost equivalent to the totality of all students and therefore statistically representative. Most of the participants were studying to achieve a bachelor degree, 45% were between 26 and 35 years old, 30% between 35 and 45 years.

Web 2.0 Usages in General

The fact that the Internet is an extremely important medium for distance students is indisputable. But which of the many offers of social software are known and how are these used? These questions were evaluated in the questions 5 "do you know the following Internet offers?" and 6 “do you use the following Internet offers?". The results are as follows: Offers like e-mail (100%) and online encyclopedias are not only well-known (100%), but also highly used (>98%). These forms of information exchange on the Internet have been completely assimilated by the students. Also communities and social networks like XING or Facebook are well known (91%) and are used frequently (59%), but not as regularly as e-mail and online encyclopedias. Also chat, instant messaging or Skype are well known (88%), 59% are using these tools regularly. An even bigger discrepancy between knowing and using occurs with services like RSS Feeds, Twitter, Podcasts and weblogs. Although more than two thirds of the interviewees know about these tools, only an average of 25% uses these actively and regularly. An explanation seems to be the average age of the distance students: they are older than campus students, and user statistics show that the services mentioned, in particular Twitter, are much more intensively used by younger people. Social Bookmarking pages are less well known (35%) and only a few students use them (6%).

Study-Related Web 2.0 Offers at the University

The University of Hagen offers a variety of different modern Internet based services like email, newsgroup and mailing lists, learning management systems, wikis, chat, blogs, groupware tools, RSS-Feeds and also Twitter. How well-known are the single services and are these services of value for the students? These issues are examined in the questions 7 "do you know the following offers of the University of Hagen?" and 8 "do you use the following offers of the University of Hagen?".

At the top of the awareness level and the usage scale are the communication services e-mail (96% / 82%), newsgroups (77% / 51%) and mailing lists (68% / 31%) followed closely by learning management systems. The most popular learning management system is the Virtual University, an in-house development of Hagen (92% / 84%). The second system, Moodle, is known to 61% of the interviewees, used by 47%. Due to the fact that only three out of four faculties offer content on this platform these numbers are not surprising, the important fact is that if there are offers, students do use these tool. Surprisingly, the groupware tools BSCW and CURE are not very well known and even less used. Only 15% know BSCW, 6% CURE, and a very low number of only 8% respectively 3% make use of these tools. Blogs (4%), RSS Feeds (4%) and Twitter (1%) have similarly low numbers of users. Another important subject is what the motivations are for students to use certain services.

It became clear that beside the exchange of information (91%) the offered services are used mainly for preparing examinations (84%) and to become answers to study-related questions (83%). Astonishingly, the exchange about private matters or for purposes of human relations is relatively low with 7% and 23%. The comments show that most of our students use public communication and networking tools for these purposes. More than half of the students (56%) use the learning management systems for exchange and production of documents. Finally, the participants were asked about the value of the offered services. For this purpose, students could choose on a 5-degree scale (very useful to completely useless). If the service was not known, a suitable choice could be made (unknown). Information presentation and delivery has the highest ranking (69%), followed by study portals with organizational functionalities like enrollment, examination results, planning tools etc. (52%). The expectations of students regarding the teaching and learning environment have changed over the last years. In the study we found that about 43% of our students want more Web 2.0 functionality integrated in the university learning environment. This includes communities, blogs, wikis and especially social networking. Related research is consistent with these findings, e. g., Glowalla [5] and Kerres [16].

5 Similarities and Differences

Both studies examined the usage of Web 2.0 services by students. The HISBUS survey questioned German students at universities and universities of applied sciences, while the study of Hagen focused on the distance students of the University of Hagen. It is interesting to see where the two evaluations show similarities and differences. Concerning study-related Web 2.0 offers like Wikis, social network services and chats no differences could be found. Distance students as well as on-campus students rate these services as the most valuable. An interesting fact is that almost all distance students (98%) use online encyclopedias in comparison to only 60% of the on-campus students. This is presumably because of the availability of physical information resources as they are provided in an on-campus library. About the use of blogs, RSS feeds and podcasts an interesting difference can be found: Only 6% of on-campus students use these services but 19% of the distance students. These rather new services are a lot more accepted by the distance students. As to study-related Web 2.0 offers at the university, there are again some remarkable differences:

Distance students use the Web 2.0 social network platforms only rarely for the exchange of private subjects (7%) and personal relations (23%). In contrast, on-campus students use these mainly for personal relations (66%) and communication with friends (72%). Analysis of the free text answers showed that for distance students data privacy is of high importance; they do not trust the open social networks and therefore demand the integrations of social networking functionalities in the university portal. Finally, both types of students value functionalities like online study information and online organizational services, e.g., enrolment. Both studies stated very clearly, that the students' society estimates the usefulness of online information and student's information portals as very high. HISBUS examined the intensity of utilization more closely and found that more than 50% of the students use these services often to very often. Both studies questioned the students about the value of using communities, social networking and related platforms, it came out that the two student groups value the usefulness of these services quite differently. Whereas more than 50% of the on-campus students rate these applications as valuable, only about 25 % of the distance students consider them valuable. As stated before, this fact could be explained by the privacy issues of these services. An evident difference is also the use of learning management systems. These systems are rated as highly valuable by the distance students whereas only 44% of the on-campus students rate them as valuable. The use of traditional communication systems like chats or newsgroups is not highly rated in both studies: with 33% rating by the distance students and 38% by campus students these are at the end of the scale.

To sum up, both types of students have a very similar behavior in some areas of using Web 2.0 for studying. The clearest difference between the requirements of the two groups is that distance students need more integrated communication functionalities. They also explicitly demand an integrated learning management system with all necessary services to support their special needs.

6 Conclusion

The results have shown that a new system for learning and teaching is necessary, with a strong focus on communication and collaboration functionalities in preferably one easy to use environment. The need of students, regardless if on-campus or distance students, for an integrated study environment centered on social support by comprehensive communication and interaction instruments is clearly given. The evaluation of students leaving the university without a degree verified these findings: the main reason mentioned by the participants, is the missing contact to other students and to the teachers [see 17]. The integration of available social web applications in the existing portal has to be accompanied with integrated interface design and professional information and knowledge management. Also messaging, networking, blogs, social bookmarks etc. should be realized. Planning instruments like study planner, appointment planner, a learning diary are also essential as seen in both studies. Another and very important aspect is to guarantee a very high privacy standard. New developments like e.g. MOOCs – with all the typical problems like in distance education – [see 18] in education also demand new forms of student support to help the learners to have success with their studies. Tutoring and tutoring services could also be a business model for big teaching events. Students, teachers and management should form a virtual Community to:

- Organize content and communication and interaction processes,
- to archive, discuss and publish content,
- to discuss specific problems and to solve them together and
- to create temporary and long-term social networks.

Pedagogy, learning and curriculum and even assessment are more important than the technology and should be focused first before developing new systems.

The detailed model of such a system is the subject of the author's doctoral thesis.

References

1. Feldmann, B., Schlageter, G.: Five Years Virtual University – Review and Preview. In: Proc. of the WebNet 2001, Orlando. AACE (2001)
2. Becking, D., Betermieux, S., Schlageter, G.: Virtualising Online Seminars Entirely - A Variation of the Variables. In: Proc. HCI 2005, Las Vegas (2005)
3. Fritsch, H.: Aktiv und Online (Active and Online, German publication), ZIFF-Papers, University of Hagen, p. 10ff (2004)
4. Kerres, M.: Multimediale und telemediale Lernumgebungen (Multimedia and Telemedia Learning Environments – German publication), Munich (2001)
5. Glowalla, U., Glowalla, G., Kohnert, A.: Studierverhalten in Online-Bildungsangeboten (Study Behaviour in Online Education Environments – German publication). In: Issing, L.H., Klimsa, P. (eds.) Information und Lernen mit Multimedia und Internet (Information and Learning with Multimedia and Internet – German Publication), Weinheim, pp. 359–372 (2001)

6. Leh, A.S.C.: Computer-Mediated Communication and Social Presence in a Distance Learning Environment. International Journal of Educational Telecommunication 7(2), 109–128 (2001)
7. Palloff, M., Pratt, K.: The Virtual student. A Profile and Guide to Working with Online Learners. Jossey-Bass (2003)
8. Kleimann, B., Özkilic, M., Göcks, M.: Studieren im Web 2.0 (Studying in the Web 2.0 – German publication), HIS Projektbericht (2008), `https://hisbus.his.de/hisbus/docs/hisbus21.pdf`.
9. Kreijns, C.J., Kirschner, P.A., Jochems, W.M.G.: The sociability of computer-supported collaborative learning environments. Journal of Educational Technology & Society 5(1), 8–22 (2002)
10. Haake, J., Schwabe, G., Wessner, M.: CSCL-Kompenium. Oldenbourg (2004)
11. Strijbos, J.W., Kirschner, P.A., Martens, R.L.: What We Know About CSCL. Kluwer Academic Press (2004)
12. Andriessen, J.H.E.: Working With Groupware. Understanding and Evaluating Collaboration Technology. Springer (2004)
13. Tajfel, H., Turner, J.C.: The social identity theory of intergroup behavior. In: Worchel, S., Austin, W.G. (eds.) Psychology of Intergroup Relations, pp. 7–24. Nelson-Hall, Chicago (1986)
14. Rechtien, W.: Angewandte Gruppendynamik (Applied Group Dynamics – German publication), Beltz (1999)
15. Granovetter, M.: The Strength of Weak Ties. American Journal of Sociology 78, 1360–1380 (1973)
16. Kerres, M., Nübel, I.: The Status of E-learning at German Higher Education Institutions. In: Dittler, U., Kahler, H., Kindt, M., Schwarz, C. (eds.) E-learning in Europe – Learning Europe. How have new media contributed to the development of higher education?, vol. 36, pp. 29–50. Waxmann, Münster (2005)
17. Stössel, K., Ihme, T.A., Barbarino, M.-L., Fisseler, B., Stürmer, S.: Diversity and Distance Education: Who Drops Out from Academic Programs and Why? Research in Higher Education (2013) (under review)
18. Boyatt, R., Joy, M., Rocks, C., Sinclair, J.: What (Use) is a MOOC? In: The 2nd International Workshop on Learning Technology for Education in Cloud. Springer Proceedings in Complexity, pp. 133–145 (2014)

Needs of Learners in Campus Development – Blended Learning

Marja Naaranoja

University of Vaasa, P.O. Box 700, 65100 Vaasa, Finland
marja.naaranoja@uva.fi

Abstract. This paper focuses on the needed physical space for group or individual learners when using blended learning. Virtual environment designers and Campus developers need to understand the role of the physical space in learning. The study shows that the students often prefer to study at the university even when there is possibility to study at home. In the case universities there are not enough spaces for self-study or group work at the university. In addition, the learners have difficulties to recognize the possibilities to use spaces like lobbies and restaurants for learning. The campus developers want to increase the efficient use of spaces by creating possibilities to use a space for different purposes.

Keywords: Blended Learning, Learning at Home, Group-work, Space for Learning.

1 Introduction

Students are encouraged to take responsibility of their learning in order to develop thinking skills such as analysis, synthesis and evaluation. Most students learn best if they can choose their pace, time, and place of learning. The blended learning offers possibility to this. According to Lonka [14] blended learning environments contain physical, virtual, social, mobile and mental spaces of learning.

Informal, social learning may happen virtually but also physical space have role in it. The informal collaboration and informal learning happens in so called third places. According to Oldenburg and Brisset [19] a third place is a public setting accessible to its inhabitants and appropriated by them as their own, it is taken-for-granted part of their social existence. The third places at Universities can be for example, cafés, bookstores, guild houses, squares as large entry halls with people crossing by and "hanging out", together with sports halls and so on [20, 21].

In this paper we will focus on what is the role of physical space when the previously mentioned skills are learned. The design of physical learning spaces focuses normally on designing classrooms not how the physical spaces can help learning outside classrooms [13, 15, 18, 24, 3, 7, 8, 22]. The aim of this paper is to find out the role of physical space when the students take the responsibility to learn in groups or alone outside the classrooms.

L. Uden et al. (Eds.): LTEC 2014, CCIS 446, pp. 173–182, 2014.

Dondi and Delrio [6] pointed out among other things that first generation e-learning did not consider the isolated position of learners and lack of collaboration and campus social context. Still only a little focus is given to where the learners are situated when they use e-learning material. SBDU [23] 'Schools for the Future: Exemplar Designs', identifies emerging themes for schools of the future. These are flexibility, adaptability, indoor courtyards, outdoor classrooms, comfort and sustainability.

The following chapters describe first the perspective of a learner in campus development and the needs of learners based on two case studies. The campus development is understood as development of physical buildings and especially what the students need in order to learn in blended learning environment when most of the course assignments are planned to be done outside classrooms.

2 Learners Perspective in Campus Development Project

The aim of a campus is to educate professionals for society needs. The new learning technology like game environments require new kind of places for groups and individuals to study. Areas were the games can be used is one of the design tasks. Sometimes the student dormitory builders and campus developers do not sufficiently think about how a student or student groups use the spaces when they are doing their course works. Figure 1 describes the blended learning environment outside classroom. It is commonly understood that we need technology and contents, assessment systems and good quality material but we often forget that also the physical space matters.

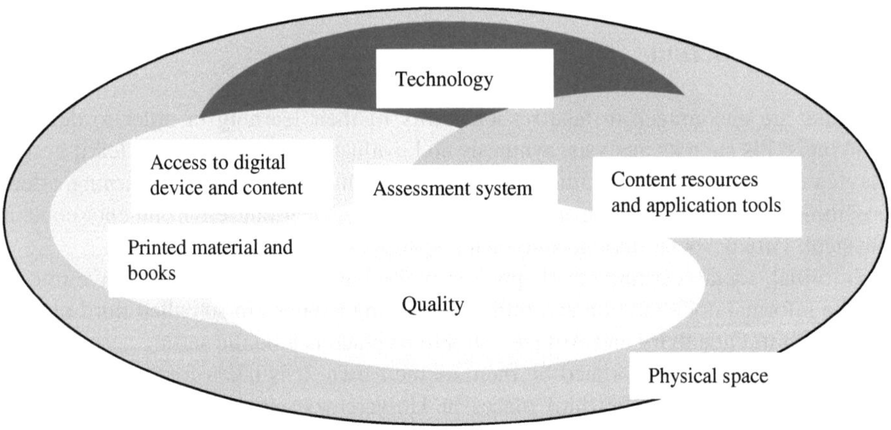

Fig. 1. Environment for student-centred active learning outside classroom

We tend to focus in the classroom behaviour. The libraries are planned for self study. Bryant [2] found out when observing students in the library that even mathematic studying can be a team work. According to her observation strangers can help each other with problems when they are physically next to each other. She found out that in the library variety of different kind of spaces are needed. Her observation showed that the library study area was used both for studying and socializing.

Conventional planning focuses on planning the spaces not planning the learning landscape [5]. The planning should focus on to enable that the learners to get skills of future workers like ability to be creative, to think critically, to solve problems, to make decisions, to communicate, to collaborate, to use information and communications technology, and to create a sustainable lifestyle [2]. In the changed viewpoint it is important to understand the needs of learners and plan a learning landscape that is for example, context aware, supports the learning process (Figure 2).

Learning Landscape Model

Conventional Campus Planning	Learning Landscape Planning
Campus **focused**	Learning Landscape **context-aware**
Looks backward: planning standards	**Forecasts** changing needs of users
Linear process: analysis, conception, implementation	Nonlinear process, emphasising co-creation of concepts with users
Implement a **"plan"**	**Strategies** and concepts: refined, tested
Needs assessment by school and dept	Engages hybrid groups to complement needs assessment
Spaces drive planning process	**Activities** drive the planning process
Prioritises formal instructional spaces	Focuses on informal as well as formal learning environments
Focuses on **classroom** experience	Plans **networks** of physical and virtual learning spaces
Single-use space types	Mix of specialised & flexible, multi-purpose spaces
Single-owner model	**Layered ownership** model, from public to invited to private space

Fig. 2. Learning landscape model [5]

Learning is often a messy, nonlinear, unpredictable process that involves both individual and collaborative effort. The best learning processes are exciting and activate a learner's natural curiosity and contribute the motivation for self-direction and reaching the desired skills. Learning space should allow learners to be co-creators of the learning process, and support the ability to focus on learning even without the lecturers.

3 Needs of Learners

Learning takes place everywhere were learners are situated—on city sidewalks, in trains, in restaurants, in bookstores, and on playgrounds. Human beings—wherever they are—have the capacity to learn through their experiences and reflections. Institutions of higher education are charged with fostering specific kinds of learning, for example higher-order thinking abilities, communication skills, and knowledge of the ways of disciplinary experts. Campus developers create structures that support this learning. Space can have a powerful impact on learning; we cannot overlook space in our attempts to accomplish our goals.

Learning theories impact on the ways in which learning most likely takes place. The role of the learner has impact on how the learner wants to use the place. The importance of prior experience, the fitting of knowledge into existing schema or the establishment of new schema, and the active processing of information are all components of this model that emphasize high learner involvement. Environments that provide experience, stimulate the senses, encourage the exchange of information, and offer opportunities for rehearsal, feedback, application, and transfer are most likely to support learning.

Learning depends on the individual way of processing information [1], whether the learner wants to watch or do and at the same time think or feel. This determines the individual learning style and it is assessed by ranking preferences for feeling, thinking, acting and reflecting [10]. Each learning style is ideally supported differently.

Learning environment is all the factors affecting learning process. Common factors that are present in a learning environment are the open space (place), content (information), methods and social factors (other people) [17]. Internal learning environment is the mind of the learner. In learning, especially subjective attitudes, beliefs and emotions may enhance or hinder learning [11, 17]. External learning environment include physical and social factors that guide the learning. Intelligent activity is basically situation dependent, which means that developing professionalism means working in authentic cases or in challenging projects. The modern technology gives possibilities to take learning also into virtual learning environment [11, 12, 16]. Social factors such as other students, teams and working groups, coaches, faculty, business people are important in the learning process [9] (figure 3).

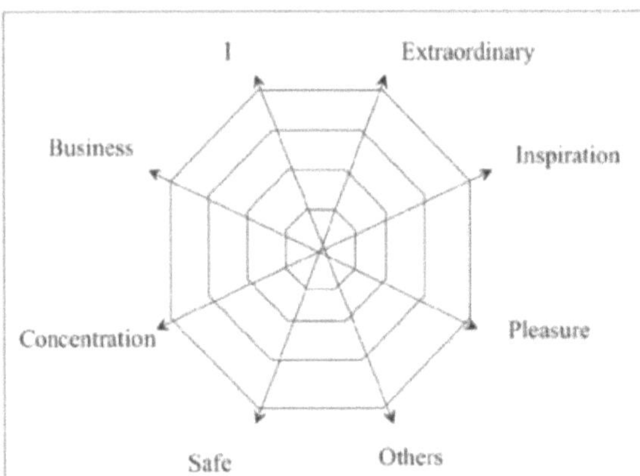

Fig. 3. Safety network of learning [9]

The inspiration to study is important – one example of such an inspiration is when one is inspired to study in the library when he/she is able to observe other students who are studying. There needs to be right balance between focusing on the subject (business) and having fun (pleasure). Students may be afraid to fail in front of other students therefor it is important that the teacher can support in making safe learning environment. The learning environment as a whole should support learning by building an environment where the students feel safe and motivated to engage in trial and error processes that are needed in creative problem-solving processes.

The physical learning environment affects how we learn. The typical classroom environment enhances habitual classroom behaviour. It is suggested that in order to break formal ways of thinking and acting, the teacher may use different learning environments to stimulate new ways of learning. For example, visiting the actual site of the case organization may help to find new ways of thinking. [9]

Understanding the safety network is especially important when the learners are left to study in a group or alone. The material presented has a role but also where the location plays a role. Lonka [14] points out that we should not forget the importance of human contact even when we us technology to support learning.

4 Method

The research method is case study. The data was gathered by using two case studies. These case studies are called 'Learning at home at home' and 'third learning spaces'. The used data gathering and analysis method is described under.

Case study 1: Learning at home (bachelor level students)

- A group of students were asked to describe how they learn at home or at the university when preparing their course assignments. The task was given to a group of 32 students and all of them described their own way of working at home and whether they preferred to do their assignments at the university.
- The task was a study assignment and the students learned at the same time how the end user requirements are gathered and analysed. Each student had to describe in which location they studied at home and how much time they used weekly at home for studying and what they exactly did at home when studying. They were also asked whether they would prefer to do the group or individual assignments at home or at university. The teaching materials are in Moodle and the amount of contact hours was about 27 % of the planned learning time, in addition some of the students do not take part in the lessons all the time. The course assignments were mostly planned to be done in distance mode at home.
- The material was studied and the learning styles and used methods were found out. Also the preferred way of working at the university or at home was found out.

Case study 2: Third learning spaces

- An internet survey with open ended question was sent to university staff and students. In the campus area there are several restaurants that are used by personnel and students. About 400 persons use daily the restaurant. The questions were formulated in the way that the respondents were not lead to think the restaurant and lobby area as a learning space. The questionnaire was sent to the potential users of the space. The sample size was about 5 400 persons. There were 103 respondents, response rate ~2%. If we compare the number of respondents to the amount of users of restaurant the response rate is 27 %.
- The data was analysed by first dividing the answers into themes question per question. Since the author wanted to analyse how the learners and teachers perceive the lobby and restaurant space as a learning environment special focus was in learning issues.

5 Case Studies

This chapter presents the results of the two case studies.

5.1 Study at Home

Twenty five students out of 32 had motivation problems when working at home and in discussion they told that it would be better to study at the university since it is more motivating to see other students working and they can easily support each other. At the university there was earlier a large place for self study. The students told that this place was very useful and they used it especially when they did their group works. Now when there is no such a place and the library has too little space for all students they were forced to work after the lessons in the classrooms but it did not succeed always since the classrooms were locked after teaching. Six students documented that there is no peaceful place to study at home. Five students documented that their children disturbed the concentration. The students worked either in the kitchen or sofa only four students used a separate table or even a working room that was used for studying. The reason to study in kitchen was the large table and since there were no disturbing issues like TV. The reason for using kitchen was the large table. They needed to calculate and have a lot of material on the table. Example of one answer is described in figure 4. The students had very different kind of answers to all the question. The most often mentioned disturbing issues are beside motivation: disturbing partners or children, noise level, coldness or heat.

Self recorded weekly study time at home varied from 2 to 10 hours. According to the curriculum learning time outside classroom should be around 29 hours. The time used in studying at home was in average divided into 30% in Internet, 30 % in reading course material, 30 % in calculating, 30 % in writing the assignments and 10% for group works. The group works were mainly done at the university during brakes if there was no time to concentrate during the lessons. The little time used in studying outside contact hours are reason to the poor study results.

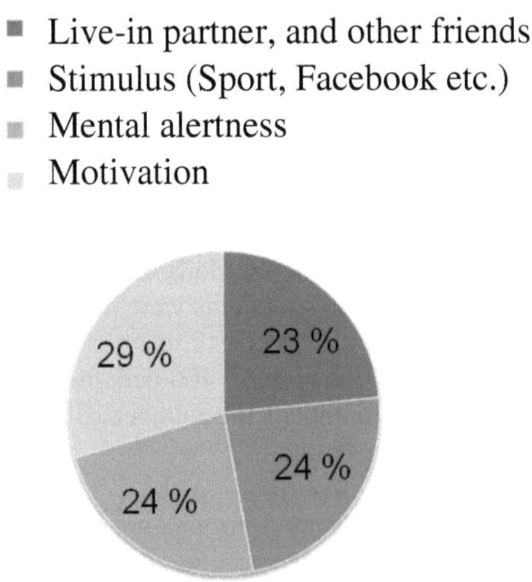

Fig. 4. Factors preventing the study at home (example)

5.2 Third Learning Spaces

The aim was to find out how the respondents perceive the use of campus restaurant and its lobby area for study purposes and which kind of needs the respondents had in further developing the restaurant and the lobby area. There were 103 persons responded to the questionnaire. Majority of the respondents were students but there were 8 staff members also. The survey consisted of five open question. In the following the answers to the questions are explained:

1) Which kind of space is needed in the area?
   The response focused on creating a lounge for students and other visitors to wait and hang around and maybe study (N55). Some people wanted to have a coffee automat or other automats that would give a possibility to eat though the restaurant would be closed (N9) and ten people wanted to make the restaurant larger so that the entrance area would be used partly for it.
   Many respondents (N10) pointed out that better lights and the colorful walls or furniture would make a big difference.
2) Do you need more spaces for self or group study in this university building?
   According to 48 respondents there are not enough spaces to either have quite place for self-study or studying in groups. Some wanted possibility to have virtual meeting possibilities (N4). Many of the respondents (N10) did not know there are places for self-study or group work in the building
3) What is now functioning well in the restaurant?
   Respondents (N76) focused on the food or service saying food is enough good or telling that the service personnel is nice. None of the respondents found the restaurant serve as a learning space.
4) What are the main development areas in the restaurant?
   Respondents complaint about lack of tables (N46), noise level and/or that the space is too cold (N45), logistics system of food serving and buying (44), the food (N20), and that the restaurant closes too early (N7). Eight respondents pointed out that in the campus area there is a cafeteria that serves as a meeting point and there should be more this kind of area.
5) How should it be in the restaurant in order to relax and be inspired to study?
   Respondents defined the characteristics of relaxing and inspiring environment in the following way: cosy atmosphere, silent, a meeting place, maybe a lounge outside the restaurant area to drink coffee and talk, private places, newspapers, colours, lounge type. However, there were 5 persons who thought the question was odd or even ridiculous. One wrote that if the space would be cosy the rush hour would just last longer. Some respondents proposed dividing the space to different types for relaxing and some for just eating.

5.3 Analysis of the Case Studies

The respondents perceived the restaurant as an area where you should eat fast and you need to go away [compare 11, 17]. The use of restaurants and lobbies for study purpose was a surprising idea for some of the respondents. According to respondents at least the space should be divided for different purposes in order to make it clear which space belongs to restaurant and which can be used for learning. Interestingly when students are at home they use most often kitchen for studying. At home they feel free to use the spaces as they wish. The feeling of owning the space seems to be the one of the differences of the restaurant and the kitchen. The students told that there is big difference since at home they can leave the study things there as long as is needed but in the restaurant they have only 2 hours to do the work before they have to clean the desk for others to eat. However, the restaurant could be ideal for group work.

The respondents complained the noisy echoing restaurant. The same problem prevented the learning also at home. The learners lost motivation also at home especially due to the noise of neighbours or children. So, the physical environment can prevent the motivation. However, when the motivation to study is lacking the respondents did not even think about studying they thought about resting and they started to watch TV. According to the respondents the motivation to study is got by looking at others studying – this is not possible at home unless they can observe the classmates working at the virtual arena even if they don't open the virtual environment.

The students wished to enjoy in the restaurant or coffee area: they wish to have pleasure so that they can relax and continue to study after that. These viewpoints show that concentration, inspiration and resting are important for learners [compare 9].

The safety of the environment has also a role. This role can found in the sentences like "now the space (lobby area) is too empty and large space for studying". Many respondents told that an inviting atmosphere would be better and they wanted to have couches to sit and think when doing the group work. At home the students worked also in groups – however many students preferred to do the group work at university.

There are several lessons to learn from these studies. Firstly, the third spaces at the university like restaurant and lobby area need to be made so that the students feel the space is their own. Secondly, the third space should make the collaboration possible. Thirdly, the students prefer to work at the university in order to make the collaboration easier with the other students. Also random collaboration is there possible.

Fourthly, when designing multipurpose spaces like restaurants that are used for learning and eating we have to pay attention to the fact that when it is eating time people should understand the use of such a place to be more a restaurant and this gives a possible conflict. However, the space efficiency needs are obvious universities cannot afford a space that is only a single use place.

There is a change in the education sector and we should correspondingly challenge our preconceptions of the nature and form that the campus should take in the future. Currently, university environments are not very different from what they were a hundred years ago, whilst the design of homes, the workplace, retail spaces, hospitals, transport and communications have changed.

6 Conclusion

The physical space has a role in the blended learning or distance learning. Students feel motivated if they can work in group setting. Social environment encourages students to study when they can see other students working. Also the students need to find a space where he/she is not disturbed. The university campus development takes into account the group or individual leaning needs but at the same time they need to save in the facility costs. This results designing multiuse spaces like restaurants and lobbies for self-study or group work and at the same time they have the original use as providing space for eating and/or hanging around.

The challenge is how to motivate the students to get extraordinary results and take risks. Can the space support by creating a social learning environment? The learning space needs to take into account the physical space since it can either prevent or support the learning. This research shows what might prevent to get the desired results – lack of motivation when studying alone and disturbance at home.

The planning of blended learning or virtual learning environments require also understanding of the physical space where the students are located when they are studying. Future research area could be to find out how the location really effects on the learners for example, by using big data.

Acknowledgements. The author would like to express gratitude to the organisations and students involved in the research effort behind this paper. Particularly I would like to mention Suomen Yliopistokiinteistöt –corporation and thank its personnel for their interest towards research based new solutions for the university campus development.

References

1. Ackerman, D.S., Hu, J.: Effect of type of curriculum on educational outcomes and motivation among marketing students with different learning styles. Journal of Marketing Education 33(3), 273–284 (2011)
2. ATC21S 21st Century Schools: Learning Environments for the Future. Building Futures (2013), http://dera.ioe.ac.uk/6568/1/2201.pdf
3. Bennett, S.: Learning Behaviors and Learning Spaces. Portal: Libraries and the Academy 11(3), 765–789 (2011)
4. Bryant, J.: What are students doing in our library? Ehnography as a method of exploring library user behavior. Library and Information Research 33(103), 3–9 (2009)
5. Chism, http://teaching.unsw.edu.au/guideline11
6. Dudgale, S.: Space strategies for the new learning landscape. Educause Review (2009)
7. Dondi, C., Delrio, C.: Technology supported lifelong learning: The need for a new vision and implementation models. In: Proceeding of the 10th World Conference on continuing Engineering Education (WCCEE) Vienna University of Technology, Austria (2006)
8. Francis, R., Raftery, J.: Blended Learning Landscapes. Brookes. eJournal of Learning and Teaching 1(3), 1–5 (2005)
9. Harrison, A., Cairns, A.: The Changing academic workplace. DEGW UK LTD (2008), http://ipddirectedstudios.files.wordpress.com/2011/01/the-changingacademic-workplace-degw-27-10-08.pdf
10. Jaskari, M.: Using Pictorial Collages in User-centred Construction and Effective Learning Environment. Asia Pacific Advances in Consumer Research 10 (2013)
11. Kolb, A.Y., Kolb, D.A.: Learning Styles and Learning Spaces: Enhancing Experiential Learning. Higher Education. Academy of Management Learning & Education 4(2), 193–212 (2005)

12. Koli, H.: Oppimisprosessin ohjaus uusissa oppimisympäristöissä. In: Kotila, H. (ed.) Ammattikorkeakoulupedagogiikka, pp. 153–169. Edita Publishing, Helsinki (2003)
13. Koli, H., Silander, P.: Verkko-opetuksen työkalupakki. Oppimisahioista oppimisprosessiin. Saarijärven Offset, Saarijärvi (2003)
14. Lievonen, M., Vesisenaho, M.: Translating user perspective into spatial design. In eLearning Papers 34 (2013), http://www.openeducationeuropa.eu/en/elearning_papers
15. Lonka, K.: Engaging Learning Environments – blending physical, virtual, social and mental spaces of learning (2011), http://www.slideshare.net/eden_online/occ2011-keynotes-kirsti-lonka
16. Mäkitalo-Siegl, K., Zottmann, J., Kaplan, F., Fischer, F. (eds.): Classroom of the Future: Orchestrating Collaborative Spaces. Technology Enhanced Learning. Sense Publishers, Rotterdam (2010)
17. Mänty, I., Nissinen, P.: Ideasta toteutukseen – verkko-opetuksen suunnittelu ja hallinta (From idea to implementation – designing and managing virtual material). Laurea-ammattikorkeakoulun julkaisusarja C-9, Vantaa (2005)
18. Nissinen, P.: Verkkovälitteinen opetus ammattikorkeakoulussa (Virtual teaching in applied science universities). In: Kotila, H. (ed.) Ammattikorkeakoulupedagogiikka, pp. 122–238. Edita Publishing, Helsinki (2003)
19. Oblinger, D.G.: Learning Spaces. Educause e-Book (2006), http://www.educause.edu/researchand-publications/books/learning-spaces
20. Oldenburg, R.: Making College a Great Place to Talk. The Best of Planning for Higher Education: An Anthology of Articles from Premier Journal in Higher Education Planning (1997), http://www.eric.ed.gov/ERICWebPortal/search/detailmini.jsp?_nfpb=true&_&ERICExtSearch_SearchValue_0=ED472314&ERICExtSearch_SearchType_0=no&accno=ED472314
21. Oldenburg, R., Brisset, D.: The Third Place. Qualitative Sociology. Human Sciences Press (1982), http://www.springerlink.com/content/m562717u421703mg/
22. Poutanen, J.: Third Places at the University Campuses and Their Potential as New Learning Environments. In: Architecture as Human Interface 2012 Conference, October 26-27 (2012)
23. Savolainen, A.: Yläkoulun oppimistilat: Muunneltavia ja funktionaalisia tilaratkaisuja oppimistiloihin (Learning spaces at secondary school: flexible and functional solutions for learning spaces). Kuopion Muotoiluakatemia, Tuotemuotoilu, Opinnäytetyö/thesis 3035/2011 (2011), http://publications.theseus.fi/handle/10024/26303
24. SBDU, Schools for the future. Exemplar Designs Concepts and Ideas (2004), http://www.scribd.com/doc/50506030/Schools-for-the-Future-Exemplar-Designs-Compendium
25. UBC Learning Space Design Guidelines: Place of Mind. Section 3: Key Principles (2012), http://www.infrastructuredevelopment.ubc.ca/facilities/learningspaces/learningspace.asp

Comparing the Differences between Taiwan and China in Business Simulation Game Learning

Yu-Hui Tao[1,*] and Kung-Chin Hung[2]

[1] Department of Information Management,
National University of Kaohsiung, Taiwan, Republic of China
ytao@nuk.edu.tw
[2] Top-BOSS International Corp
kc@top-boss.com.tw

Abstract. Business simulation game (BSG) has been widely studied worldwide. However, only a limited number of BSG studies had been conducted in Asian countries such as Taiwan. With the rapidly increasing cross-strait cultural and educational exchanges, no study that would help understand subcultural differences in using educational technologies between Taiwan and China had been reported. This investigation on sub-cultural differences is particularly important because BSG has been widely adopted in both Taiwan and China, and many students from China had become exchange students in Taiwanese classrooms in the recent years. Numerous cross-strait studies had been conducted since the 1980s, especially those related to subcultural differences. However, none has been found to be related to BSG. Hence, this study aims to understand the general status of cross-strait comparative research and BSG studies conducted in Taiwan. Two research directions have been proposed, with the collaborative effort of scholars from Taiwan and China. One immediate research goal is to initiate a collaborative examination between Taiwan and China, which has been established by the authors in the Business School of Nanjing University. Therefore, a prominent BSG cross-strait comparative research may be obtained by the conduct of this study.

Keywords: educational technology, business simulation game, subculture.

1 Introduction

Business simulation game (BSG) has been a known concept for over 50 years [1] and has been widely adopted by colleges for 15 years now [2]. Although BSG has been extensively studied, research has demonstrated mixed results [3].

In the literature, BSG studies are limited in contrast to the extensive research from the West. In Taiwan, the development of BSG started in 1973 [4], and more than 130 out of 160 colleges had purchased BSG for the acquisition of skills by playing. One logical consequence is that only a few BSG studies conducted in Taiwan are presently available in the literature, such as that of Tao, Yeh, & Hung [3].

* Corresponding author.

L. Uden et al. (Eds.): LTEC 2014, CCIS 446, pp. 183–186, 2014.

Although BSG is widely used in China, we can hardly find related studies in the literature as compared with those conducted in Taiwan across the Taiwan Strait. While cross-strait cultural and educational exchanges are rapidly increasing, no research study has been implemented to understand sub-cultural differences in using educational technologies between Taiwan and China. Although students in Taiwan and China generally share the same language and culture, significant differences exist in many aspects as a result of cross-strait political standing for over 40 years. Accordingly, many cross-strait studies had been conducted since 1980s, especially on subcultural differences.

This paper aims to discuss the potential comparative research regarding BSG between Taiwan and China. A background review is provided first in the succeeding sections before proposing possible research directions.

2 Cross-Strait Research and BSG Research in Taiwan

China is a large country where different regions and several subcultures within one nation exist, as claimed by Kwon [5]. Comparative studies in the early days involved different Chinese cultural regions such as Hong Kong and Taiwan [6]. In recent years, an increasing number of cross-strait comparative studies focusing on different concerns between Taiwan and China can be seen in literature. For example, Wang [7] compared the differences between Taiwan and China in work and family resources, work-family conflict, and consequences among full-time employed women. Given the large number of Taiwanese corporations operating in China, a number of studies had compared job-related value or subcultural issues between Taiwan and China, such as Wu [8] who examined the work value influenced by cross-strait personal profile and macro factors. Education-related cross-strait comparative studies are also seen in literature, such as the Classics-reading situation between Taiwan and China [9].

BSG research studies conducted in Taiwan became prevalent in literature in recent years after the extensive research in the West. These studies include [10] which investigated the perceived continuing usage of BSG by college students via validation of a proposed model. Tao, Cheng & Sun [11] also conducted a similar yet separate research on college teachers and compared the similarities and differences between two empirically validated models using their obtained results and practical implications. Lin and Tu [12] applied means-end chain approach to interview 70 college students for establishing their perceived attribute-consequence-value path regarding BSG.

3 Potential Subcultural Comparative Research Directions

Intuitively, the following are two possible directions of cross-strait comparative research for BSG.

The first direction is replicating the current research settings and designs in studies that have been conducted in Taiwan for China, and then proceed with a post outcome-based comparison of the results from both countries. The research approach can refer to the study of Tao, Cheng & Sun [11] as an example in conducting a comparison between two empirically validated models. With this post-outcome analysis, insightful and valuable discussions and implications can be attained. As a quick and easy way to pursue research outcomes, existing BSG literature can adopt the post-outcome analysis method for the initial research on emergent issues or important agenda.

The second direction is initiating a new research agenda using a research design that can be simultaneously implemented in Taiwan and China for the data collection, allowing the conduct of a comparison under the same research settings. All previously mentioned BSG studies in Taiwan can be used as reference for this research direction, such as Tao, Cheng & Sun [10-11], Tao, Yeh, & Hung [3], and Lin and Tu [12]. A number of BSG studies from the West can also be cross-referenced with the above citations. This second approach will consume a longer time for planning and design before the actual implementation. Therefore, this direction is suitable in handling critical and insightful BSG research questions, especially those which have not been discussed yet in existing literature.

4 Conclusions and Future Work

Based on the basic information related to the specific educational technology, BSG, we have demonstrated the importance of understanding the differences between Taiwan and China in their research and practices and presented two research directions for cross-strait BSG comparative studies. One immediate future work is to initiate a collaborative research between researchers in Taiwan and China. The authors have approached a distinguished professor in the Business School of Nanjing University, who has adopted BSGs developed in Taiwan for a long period of time. Nanjing area is the largest customer base of that major BSG provider in Taiwan and thus a sales office was established in the Nanjing area. Currently, research collaboration has been achieved to cover the two proposed directions. One goal of the collaboration is to replicate the research design of Tao, Cheng & Sun [10] in recruiting college students with Taiwanese BSG experiences in the Nanjing area. The other is to initiate a new and insightful research to understand the differences among human resource evaluation using BSG and the team dynamics between Taiwan and China. Therefore, with the collaborative efforts of scholars from Taiwan and China, this study has thus demonstrated a prominent, prospective cross-strait BSG comparative research.

Acknowledgement. This research was partially sponsored by Ministry of Science and Technology of the Republic of China under Grant numbers NSC 100-2410-H390-009-MY and MOST 103-2410-H-390-018-MY2.

References

1. Kibbee, J.M., Craft, C.J., Nanus, B.: Management Games. Reinhold, New York (1961)
2. Faria, A.J., Schumacher, M.: Business Simulation Games: Current Usage A Ten Year Update. Developments in Business Simulation & Experiential Exercises 11, 220–225 (1996)
3. Tao, Y.-H., Yeh, C.R., Hung, K.-C.: Effects of the Heterogeneity of Game Complexity and User Population in Learning Performance of Business Simulation Games. Computers & Education 59(4), 1350–1360 (2012)

4. Kung-Hwa Management Foundation: Business Operation Simulation System, http://www.mars.org.tw/products/boss.php
5. Kwon, J.-W.: Does China Have More Than One Culture? Exploring Region-al Differences of Work Values in China. Asia Pacific Journal of Manage-ment 29, 79–102 (2012)
6. Huo, Y.P., Randall, D.M.: Exploring Subcultural Differences in Hofsted's Value Survey: The Case of the Chinese. Asia Pacific Journal of Management 8(2), 159–173 (1991)
7. Wang, T.-M.: The Sub-Cultural Differences in Work-Family Resources, Conflicts, and Their Consequences among Working Women in Taiwan and Mainland China, Unpublished mater thesis, Graduate Institute of Human Resources Management, National Central University, Taiwan, R.O.C. (2008)
8. Wu, C.-F.: The Comparative Research of the Differences on the Job Value of the Across-Strait Employees, Unpublished master thesis, Graduate Institute of Human Resources Management, National Central University, Taiwan, R.O.C. (2004)
9. Tang, C.-A.: A Study of the Current Situation of Classics-reading Education in Taiwan and China. Journal of Cultural and Creative Industries Research 2(3), 243–254 (2012)
10. Tao, Y.-H., Cheng, C.J., Sun, S.Y.: What Influences College Students to Continue Using Business Simulation Games? The Taiwan experience. Computers & Education 53(3), 929–939 (2009)
11. Tao, Y.-H., Cheng, C.-J., Sun, S.-Y.: Alignment of Teacher and Student Perceptions on the Continued Use of Business Simulation Games. Educational Technology & Society 15(3), 177–189 (2012)
12. Lin, Y.-L., Tu, Y.-Z.: The Values of College Students in Business Simulation Game: A Means-end Chain Approach. Computers & Education 58(4), 1160–1170 (2012)

Student's Behavior in Free Learning Environment and Formal Education System

Vello Kukk

Department of Computer Control, Tallinn University of Technology, Ehitajate tee 5, 19086 Tallinn, Estonia
vello.kukk@dcc.ttu.ee

Abstract. The learning environment under discussion is free from deadlines or any other restriction of formal systems (no regular actions, including lectures). Instead, a student has access to a web-based learning environment where the basic element is a task which is connected to a set of low-level competences. Learning itself means activation of competences, automatically or manually, at lower or higher level and automatic processing of student's answers. It is expected that reaction from the system is instant and so the student has discussion with a partner who is smart enough to motivate the learner. Such an environment produces quite different behavior from learners and new effects and problems appear.

1 Introduction

The system considered in this paper has been developed over fifteen years through several more or less serious modifications. From 2004 it has been fully web-based, meaning that all activities are performed in the web [1]. A few lectures are delivered for courses, but only in the beginning to introduce students to the learning environment. All further contacts are almost personal, in the lab (class) where students come on the basis of pre-registration. Experiments are also guided through the web interface with instant reaction to answers. As an exception, some homework still exists, which need a teacher's assessment, but the goal is to minimize the number of such tasks.

All courses in this environment are open all the time and so, every student can start learning at any time and can also finish any time. Finishing means that student 'takes' the grade proposed by system if it is acceptable. Formal completion may happen any time after that (the grade is preserved in the system forever) provided that formal preconditions are met (e.g., declaration). What makes teachers happy is that there are very few students which 'take' the minimal grade and a remarkable number of students try to reach maximum grade.

This approach has been used for a decade and appears to be very motivating, therefore no principal modifications have been made. What has been changed several times is the accounting mechanism behind the main program. The problem has been that formal systems do not consider the amount of knowledge acquired, but uses only a 'grade' that does not represent the structure of knowledge. As all attempts to

L. Uden et al. (Eds.): LTEC 2014, CCIS 446, pp. 187–194, 2014.

introduce variable count of credit units into a formal system have failed, a modified grading algorithm was introduced in 2013, which will be described below.

Student behavior has been monitored for years and some characteristics do not seem to change. Unfortunately, this means they cannot be changed by force and thus used to control the learning process. The ratio 15-40-15 was observed, meaning that about 15% are starting early, 15% at the very end, and 40% are in the middle. Nothing has influenced this, but much smoother learning has been achieved in the competence-based environment. Students appeared to have 2 distinctive behaviors in class tests. One is solving a huge amount of tasks (30-50) and the other is minimal (less than 10). It seems that students in those groups have some built-in behavior which cannot be changed. Students' preferences when needing help are similar: first friends, teachers, internet, and lastly the textbook. Minimum activity appears at 5 a.m. Weekly minimum activity has been detected for the period from 6 p.m. on Saturday to 6 p.m. on Sunday, which is why some service work has been planned just for those periods.

2 Competences and Grades

As mentioned above, the environment is based on (micro-)competences which are very low level concepts, like multiplication of integers or complex numbers, Ohm's law as V=RI, relations between measurement units etc. Learning means that a student's actions are reflected on states. A state related to competence consists of an ability level (integer 0...127), and two forgetting parameters (reference date and decay value). Power law [2,3,4] is used to model forgetting and it has worked well for 5 years (exponential law was used for couple of years with much less success). The model is similar to, but simpler than that described in [5,6]. Analyis for one year periods is presented in [7].

In addition, for formal grading, a concept of level confirmation is used. If the learning process is free (whenever and anywhere) then to obtain a formal grade, one has to go through special part of learning, called class test. This means that a student comes to certain place where he/she is given problems that are based on competences in which the student has achieved threshold level (7). Successful solution related competences are marked as 'confirmed'. Of course, confirmation may be witheld if the result is not positive enough.

To calculate grade, all competences related to the course have some weight – number of mCU (milli Credit Units) which represents 'volume' of competence for particular courses (values assigned by course teacher). So, a competence has different weights for different courses. All confirmed competence credits and weighted sum of levels are represented in plane with grade strips as shown on Fig 1. A student can see this figure and if his/her grade is positive the question is given: "Do you want to take it or not?" So, answering "YES" will fix the grade and the course closes in the system and the grade will be transferred to the formal database when possible. Note that grade as a function of course and related abilities is always available, before and after official grading.

This approach appears to be very motivating as most of students do not take the first available grade (i.e. 1 or F), but decide to continue for better result. The most frequent reason for taking the lowest grade is time – when a formal grade has to be fixed then students take the grade available. Note that continuation is not safe: as the result represents knowledge with some uncertainty then it is possible that the grade may not only decrease, but also may reach the state *failed.*

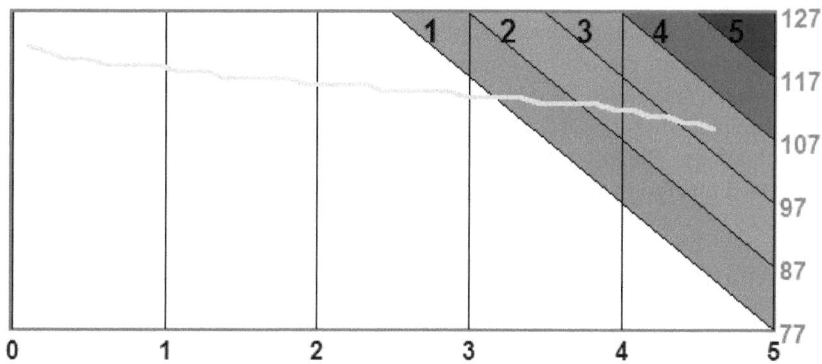

Fig. 1. Grading: horizontal axis – CU, vertical axis – weighted ability levels. The grade proposed is 3 (C in the scale A-F).

3 Tasks and Competences

Implementation of learning as modification of a learner's state (model) is based on a set of tasks. Formally, we start just from tasks and determine knowledge elements needed to solve the tasks. A task is a fixed element, meaning that it will not change and solutions produced are saved infinitely. However, relations to competencies may change (and they are changing) because smarter, more up-to-date processing and understanding of knowledge behind the task is progressing. Practice has also shown that processing must be sometimes radically changed because of changes in real life and a better understanding of the knowledge behind problem-solving. The average number of competences is 2.6 per task (total number of tasks was more then 38,300 in March 2014).

Task difficulty is one of key parameters used when selecting a task for the learner (competence is selected first and then a task is searched). A 3dB measurement is used: the success factor should be near -3dB or probability 0.7 to keep the student happy, as 7 from 10 solutions bring positive emotions. This level has proved to be both psychologically acceptable and formally solid (few corrections per year needed) for 10 years.

Tasks by nature are 1) 'theoretical' ones which can be solved without leaving the screen where the task is presented, 2) labs in which some experiment must be done, and 3) where teacher's assessment is needed (e.g. summary, review, program).

On the set of competences an equivalence is defined which generates partition of the set into classes (groups). Titles from that level are used to synthesize descriptions of learner's knowledge in the understandable language. Competences in this model are very low-level ones if compared to many other approaches [8, 9].

Groups determine which tasks are 'proper' ones i.e. belonging to particular group with all competences attached. Other tasks are related to more groups and determine connections between groups which can be applied for learning control: moving from a group with high ability to neighbors based on competences from both groups. The average number of competences in group is 5.5. As competences are considered rather expanding and the old ones may be set passive, groups are less stable and are modified more frequently because of new tasks appearing and dissection of concepts. Some examples of groups are: Oscilloscope, Diode, Hashing, Resonance, Paging, and Nanotechnology. The last one is example of developing concept, very huge in fact but existing as a one group at the moment when content is under development.

4 Analysis of Processes

4.1 Time to Grading

We consider time from beginning of semester to accepting the grade. Fig 2 shows number of students completed the course vs. time from the beginning of semester in semi-logarithmic scale. The course is *Circuits, Signals and Systems* (ISC0011) and semester is *fall 2013*. Linear approximation obtained minimizing square error is also shown.

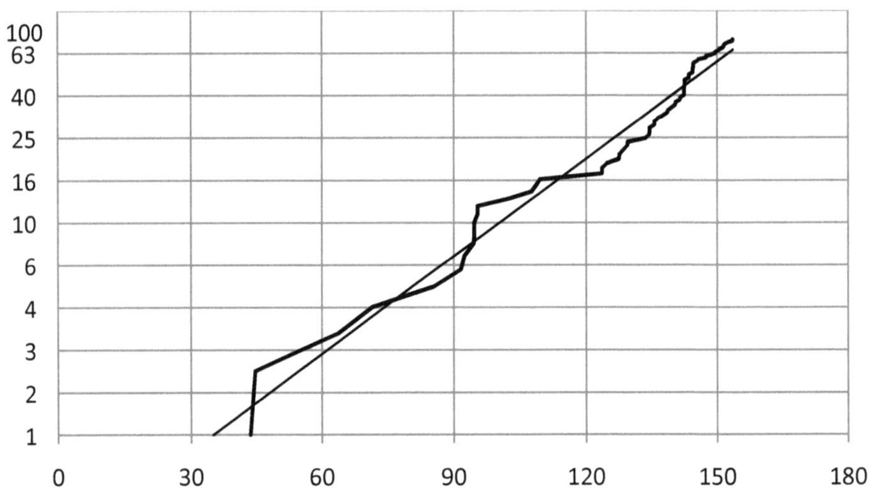

Fig. 2. Number of students completing the course vs. days from beginning of semester (ISC0011)

Comparison of the results over several years is shown in Table 1 where Day1 is the day when the first grade was issued and τ1 is time constant.

Table 1. Parameters of approximation for course completion time (ISC0011)

	ISC0011		
	2011	**2012**	**2013**
Day 1	39	51	35
τ1 [day]	26	23	28

So, in the fall semester of 2013 completion of the course can be described by the following function:

$$N(t) = e^{\frac{t-35}{28}}, \text{ for } 35<t<153 \tag{1}$$

Of course, this is very rough, but a rather small variation of time constant in Table 1 is remarkable and allows making certain predictions. Such predictions (when and which grade could be achieved) had been available for students but we cannot confirm that such information had been motivating.

There is another course (Operating Systems) where the same relationship is different as shown in Fig 3. In this case approximation (in linear scale) contains three regions: high rates in the first and third regions, and lower rate in second region.

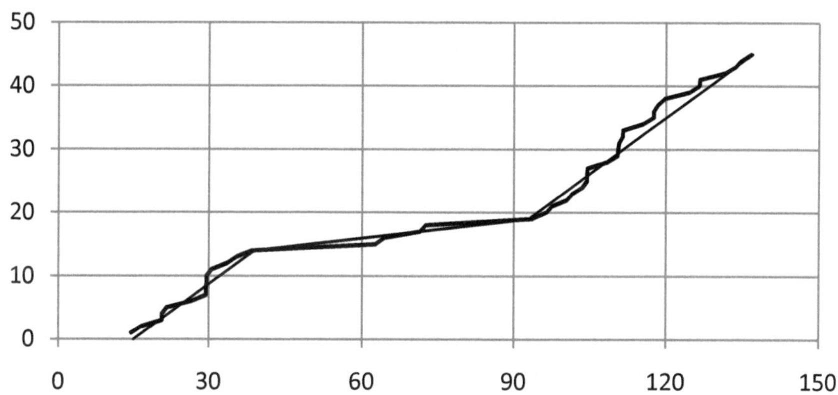

Fig. 3. Number of students completing the course vs. days from beginning of semester (ISC0030)

In Table 2 we show a comparison of approximations from several semesters. Slopes in sections are k1, k2, k3 and T1, T2, T3 are lengths of sections (in days). One can see, that in 2011 the behavior was different – the middle section is short and with higher slope, as in 2012 and 2013 the behaviors are similar - with long middle section and low slope. There is no clear reason to explain such differences. For 2014, only the first section is available and having similar characteristics as in previous years.

Table 2. Parameters of piece-wise linear approximation for course Operating Systems

	2011	2012	2013	2014
k1	0.46	0.73	0.58	0.63
k2	1.27	0.11	0.09	
k3	0.67	0.64	0.59	
T1	48	15	24	19
T2	25	65	54	
T3	33	42	44	

4.2 Grades

We calculate correlation coefficients between final (formal) grades (from 1 to 5) and several parameters describing learning parameters for course ISC0011. Results are shown in Table 3. In the table, Start Time means the date of first action, Elapsed time is from start to taking grade.

Table 3. Correlation coefficients berween grades learning parameters

	2011	2012	2013
Start time	-14%	4%	-14%
Elapsed time	0%	-20%	**-41%**
Number of solutions Q	**26%**	**42%**	4%
Number of solutions L	8%	1%	17%
Date of grading	**-10%**	**-21%**	**-55%**

One can see that correlation is positive for amount of work (Q- theoretical tasks, L – lab experiments) but is varying remarkably and therefore our recommendation for students is simply to do more work to achieve better final grade. However, as a student has his/her state visible at all times, such recommendation is not needed.

It is interesting that shorter elapsed time has become important factor for better overall result – correlation coefficient has reached -41%. The same concerns completion date – it is directly connected to elapsed time. So, for a good final grade, it is useful to start early and work with high intensity.

A number of certain interests for students during learning is the number of visits to class tests (confirmation of abilities). This number is rather stable: for example average and standard deviations for years 2012 and 2013 have been (8.1, 2.4) and (9.8, 3.3). At the same time correlation between the number of visits and final grade is between 0% and 40% - very unpredictable.

Changes in some coefficients may be related to the fact that several students have started in previous semester, but elapsed time in our analysis starts from the beginning of the current semester.

We do not show correlation coefficients in detail but confirm that all time characteristics have become relevant. For example, correlation between grading date and grade has increased almost to -60% and start and elapsed time correlations has also more significant (-30 ... -40 %).

5 Discussion and Conclusions

The first principle considered when developing the system was that the most important in learning is what a student does. The second one was that learning is not collecting points, but making progress in competences. It follows that the result of learning should include prediction of abilities not simply fixing status which very soon becomes history.

There are many factors influencing students' learning activities and performance. Some external factors may be very important, like formal conditions (when and how much to pay, deadlines, working, quality of previous studies etc.). However, some indicators do not change much, or changes are not correlated with effects expected.

Some conclusions can be made from comments by students, for example the question asked several times: have you any more such courses? It seems that such interactive environment motivates students to work and quite frequently they want to stay overtime in the lab. There is nothing done to make the system like a game, with visual effects etc. Some comments we have received even asked to remove items not having direct relation to the task to be solved.

The courses have some overlapping which presents precisely defined prerequisites. So, instead declaring other courses to be passed as conditions we can use real data representing student's abilities. Learning starts from that state which is formed from previously acquired (and forgotten) knowledge.

The formal education system causes some real problems that are very difficult to solve inside that system if we want to preserve exactness of our model representing student's knowledge. A variety of students taking the same course with very different backgrounds is increasing. Their choice may be determined by curricula which appears to be rather fixed and complex without any adaptation to real students.

In our model, it is possible to evaluate learner's abilities at any time and convert those data into another format, for example grade, which is very poor characteristic. Unfortunately, the formal system (at least so far) is not ready to accept such information that student N has achieved U credit units in course C with the grade G. Instead, this student is considered having learned nothing. Of course, we can also transfer full data concerning the model and this could be used by student, other teachers, and employers.

With regard to lectures and other scheduled activities, it seems that their role will drop further. From our experience, after few weeks from the beginning of the course, it is very difficult to find topics that are useful for all. Lectures as a real theater will remain, but as only few, open, and of very high quality. Adapting to real learners, their changing goals and abilities makes learning much more efficient. Nowadays, formal education is very inefficient: people are wasting too many hours 'participating' in events which do not contribute to the learner's knowledge.

We hope that what we have seen – students sitting in the lab only solving problems and performing 80% of actions at home - will help them to use their time profitably.

The main conclusion is that free learning is possible in the strict formal system because the data that has to be presented to system are always available. However, the formal system should be updated to make learning more efficient and personal.

Acknowledgment. This work was partly supported by Estonian Science Foundation Project 9463.

References

1. Kukk, V.: Analysis of Experience: Fully Web Based Introductory Course in Electrical Engineering. In: Proceedings of the 1st International Workshop on e-learning and Virtual and Remote Laboratories, Setubal, Portugal, August 24-25, pp. 111–118 (2004)
2. Wixted, J.T., Carpenter, S.K.: The Wickelgren Power Law and the Ebbinghaus Savings Function. Psychological Science 18(2), 133–134
3. Kukk, V., Jaanus, M.: Student Forgetting Model: Practical Experience. In: 19th EAEEIE Annual Conference, Tallinn, Estonia, June 29-July 2, pp. 112–117 (2008)
4. Kukk, V., Jaanus, M., Umbleja, K., Shvets, O.: Developing Integrated Learning Environment – Analysis. In: International Conference on Engineering Education, ICEE 2010, Poland, Gliwice, July 18-22 (2010)
5. Hoffmann, M.H.W.: Fairly Certifying Competences, Objectively Assessing Creativity. In: 2011 EDUCON, Amman, Jordan, April 4-6, pp. 270–277 (2011)
6. Hoffmann, M.H.W.: Learning as a feedback – control process. In: ICEE 2005, Gliwice, Poland, July 25-29 (2005)
7. Kukk, V., Umbleja, K.: Analysis of forgetting in a learning environment. In: 13th Biennial Baltic Electronics Conference, Tallinn, Estonia, October 3-5, pp. 335–338 (2012)
8. Vaca, J.M., Agudo, J.E., Rico, M.: Adaptive Competence-Based System in an E-learning Platform: Adapting Support Tasks to Students. In: IEEE 12th International Conference on Advanced Learning Technologies, pp. 720–721 (2012)
9. Hertlein, M., Smolnik, S.: How Can Knowledge Management Support Competence-Based Learning? Towards a Research Agenda. In: 45th Hawaii International Conference on System Science (HICSS), Mayi, HI, USA, pp. 3661–3668 (2012)

Using the Technology Acceptance Model to Explore the Behavioral Intentions toward Blended Learning

Li-Yang Hsieh[1], Ying-Jui Lu[1], and Yao-Hsien Lee[2]

[1] Dept. of Tourism and Leisure Management, China University of Technology, No 530, Sec. 3 Jhong-Shan Rd., Hukou, Hsinchu, Taiwan, R.O.C.
hsieh.liyang05@gmail.com
[2] Chung Hua University, 707, Sec. 2, WuFu Rd., Hsinchu, Taiwan, R.O.C.
hsien@chu.edu.tw

Abstract. The aim of this study was to explore the relationship between blended learning courses (i.e., food and beverage preparation) and Behavioral Intentions (BIs) by using the Technology Acceptance Model. The participants were students enrolled in food and beverage preparation courses that were elective at China University of Technology. Comprehensive investigations were conducted. Statistical Product and Service Solutions software was employed for item analysis, reliability analysis, Pearson correlation analysis, and regression analysis. The study results indicated that the ease of use and usefulness of blended learning were positively correlated; the ease of use and attitude of blended learning were positively correlated; the usefulness of blended learning and learning attitude were positively correlated; the usefulness of blended learning and BIs were positively correlated; and the attitudes and BIs toward blended learning were positively correlated.

1 Introduction

A survey conducted by [1] revealed that tourists were most impressed by Taiwanese cuisine. Accordingly, aside from being a necessity for local people, Taiwanese cuisine is also an essential factor that attracts foreign tourists. In the past, Taiwanese food and beverage preparation staff were not required to have a high level of education. The ability to raise the capital and hire personnel was sufficient. Today, higher education has been popularized, and the number of students majoring in tourism and culinary arts is increasing; therefore, the education levels of culinary arts talents in Taiwan are also increasing. These phenomena facilitate the qualitative changes in culinary arts talents. The personnel turnover in Taiwan's food and beverage service industry is frequent, rendering sharing work knowledge and maintaining service quality difficult. Consequently, the amount of customer complaints is substantial. Hence, how to cultivate well-trained and specialized culinary arts talents in limited conditions is a crucial research topic[2,3,4].

In this era of knowledge economies that is also under the influence of rapidly changing information technology (IT), Internet technologies have enabled the acceleration of people's learning. Several establishments have been confronted with intensifying changes to business operations. Additionally, the learning and living habits of individuals are also gradually changing to keep pace with the trends in the digital age.

L. Uden et al. (Eds.): LTEC 2014, CCIS 446, pp. 195–203, 2014.

One recent emphasis adopted by enterprises is the integration of IT into the food and beverage service industry to develop and establish blended learning education and experience systems for food and beverage preparation. However, regarding factors such as the number of relevant opportunities available, time and space flexibility, and cost and resource management, the traditional professional education and measurement approaches employed at schools and enterprises cannot satisfy students' and enterprise employees' demands on the quantity, speed, timing, availability, interaction, and community of learning as well as the diversity of knowledge.

Briefly, blended learning refers to the process of using technologies to convey course materials to learners in classrooms, synchronous, or asynchronous online classes. The most commonly used blended learning method is supplementing classroom teaching with online classes [5]. This study aimed to implement lean services in the preparation services by students and enterprise employees through employing blended learning environments. Hence, schools and enterprises must use the advantages of modern IT to fortify the encouragements on students' and enterprise employees' learning. Subsequently, they can be fully equipped with the necessary information and adaptabilities and eventually become the main forces. [6] developed the Technology Acceptance Model (TAM) as an instrument for evaluating or predicting users' levels of acceptance of new IT systems. [7] also proposed perceived usefulness (PU) and perceived ease-of-use (PEOU), both of which were positively and significantly correlated with system usage. [8] stated that PU and PEOU can be applied to predict the behavioral intentions (BIs) of users. [9] asserted that implementing both TAM and theory of planned behavior (TPB) can predict online learning adoption intentions, but that TAM was more efficient than TPB because usefulness, ease of use, and attitudes were significant predictors in TAM.

In recent years, using technology as education and learning tools has become a common phenomenon in Taiwan. Information and communication technologies are commonly used in blended learning to establish teaching environments, which require substantial amounts of resource investment. Hence, numerous relevant studies have been conducted. For example, [10] discovered that teachers' information literacy had significantly positive influences on the PU, PEOU, and usage intentions of wireless network teaching. [11] conducted a study on the external variable interface characteristics of the TAM. The study results indicated that the interface characteristics had positive influences on PEOU and thus indirectly affected users' usage intentions. [12] conducted a questionnaire survey on users of the information system, and TAM was employed to conduct statistical analyses. That study aimed to explore the continuous behaviors of system users and the findings were used by the Ministry of Education for the establishment and promotion of efficient reading and library management programs. [13] declared that an increased number of enterprises and software have adopted the TAM to improve their efficiency and competitiveness regarding the development and application of software. [14] advocated that the execution of green production management systems for food and beverage preparation was a vital task for the development of Taiwan's tourism and food and beverage service industry.

Blended learning addresses both the learning styles addressed in traditional face-to-face teaching and online teaching. In other words, a curriculum is designed to be partially taught in a traditional classroom setting. For the rest of the time, teaching activities are conducted through channels such as the Internet, emails, television, and broadcasting, thus reducing the time spent in classrooms, improving learners' learning efficiencies, and reducing drop-out rates [15]. [16] argued that the blended learning model can increase students' aggression toward learning in multimedia courses. [17] conducted a survey after the execution of blended learning courses, and the survey results indicated that the actual outcome was superior than expected regarding teaching methods, student satisfaction, and academic achievements. [18]conducted a comparative study on college students' acceptance toward blended learning courses. The results regarding blended learning course acceptance were significant. In this study, the TAM was employed to explore the relationship between blended learning courses (i.e., food and beverage preparation) and students' BI. This study mainly aimed to examine the PU and PEOU of blended learning environments as well as propose the benefits of blended learning environments in education and the value of applying blended learning in enterprises.

2 Methods

The questionnaire survey method was employed in this study. The study scope was the food and beverage Preparation course classrooms equipped with blended learning environments at China University of Technology. The questionnaires were distributed to students taking food and beverage preparation-related blended learning courses. A comprehensive investigation was implemented, and 122 valid questionnaires were collected. In this study, the primary relationships explored were those between the PEOU and PU of blended learning, between the PEOU of blended learning and learning attitudes, between the PU of blended learning and learning attitudes, as well as between the PU of blended learning and BIs. The study structure is shown in Fig. 1.

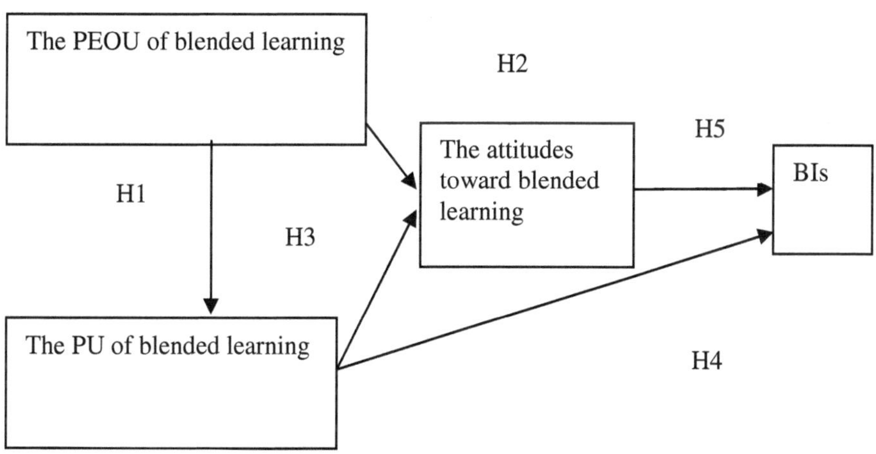

Fig. 1. The Structure of the Study

Based on the TAM structure and relevant literature, the following hypotheses (Hs) are proposed:

H1: The PEOU and PU of blended learning are positively correlated.
H2: The PEOU of blended learning and learning attitudes are positively correlated.
H3: The PU of blended learning and attitudes to blended learning are positively correlated.
H4: The PU of blended learning and BIs are positively correlated.
H5: The attitudes and BIs toward blended learning are positively correlated.

The variables observed in this study were the PU and PEOU of blended learning, and the learning attitudes and BIs toward blended learning. Based on the literature review, this study used the TAM to explore the BIs in food and beverage preparation blended learning courses. Therefore, this study obtained students' actual feelings of acceptance regarding blended learning. Additionally, this study implemented the four dimensions (i.e., PU, PEOU, attitude, and BI) of the TAM scale proposed by [19]. The questionnaire was developed based on the aforementioned variables and measurement dimensions. The five-point Likert scale was adopted as a measurement instrument. The study participants were college students enrolled in elective courses. Therefore, the personal attributes of the participants did not substantially differ and were excluded from analysis. Statistical Product and Service Solutions (SPSS) software was used for data analysis. The analysis methods implemented were item analysis, reliability analysis, Pearson correlation analysis, and regression analysis.

3 Methodology and Major Findings

3.1 Item Analysis

The means and standard deviations (SDs) are analyzed in this section (Table 1). Regarding mean analysis, the PEOU analysis results indicated that the students reported that logging onto the course material section in the student information system was the easiest; therefore, this item was scored the highest (4.32). The students stated that the teaching materials that the teachers uploaded to the course material section were the most difficult to use; therefore, this item was scored the lowest (4.03). These results indicated that the college information system platform was easy to use, but that the materials that the teachers uploaded to the course material section were hard to use for previewing and reviewing the lessons. The PU analysis results indicated that the students can find appropriate content in blended learning courses; therefore, this item was scored as the most useful (4.03). The students claimed that blended learning courses were the least useful in enhancing their learning efficiencies (3.97). In other words, although blended learning materials were easy to obtain, they were not positively correlated with the students' examination scores. The attitude analysis results indicated that the students highly accepted blended learning courses (4.03), but that blended learning courses were less likely to enhance the students' willingness toward learning (3.87). These results indicated that the students' willingness to learn did not increase for courses they were not interested in, even in blended learning environments. The BI analysis results indicated that the students liked using the Internet to engage in e-learning activities (4.00). The effectiveness of blended learning in motivating the students to submit assignments on time was low (3.75). These results indicated that although the students liked using the Internet, blended learning courses did not affect whether they submit their assignments on time.

Table 1. Item Analysis Table

Latent variables	Items	Mean	SD
PEOU	1. I think logging onto the student information system at my college is easy.	4.31	.75970
	2. I think finding the course material sections in my student information system is easy.	4.32	.68726
	3. I think the teaching materials that the teachers have uploaded to the course material sections are easy to use.	4.03	.80459
PU	1. I think blended learning courses should continue to be offered.	4.02	.77645
	2. Attending blended learning courses has improved my learning efficiency.	3.97	.78797
	3. I can find appropriate content in blended learning courses.	4.03	.83751
Attitudes	1. Blended learning motivates me to learn more.	3.87	.88149
	2. I enjoy blended learning elective courses.	4.03	.83751
	3. Blended learning is a good teaching method.	4.00	.81650
BIs	1. I like using the Internet to engage in e-learning activities.	4.00	.79972
	2. I like engaging in discussions with my classmates using the information platforms provided by the college.	3.76	.91022
	3. I like using blended learning for motivating myself to submit assignments on time.	3.75	.84363

Regarding the SD analysis, the PEOU SD analysis results indicated that the item that yielded small differences in student perceptions was "I think finding the course material section in my student information system is easy." The item that yielded comparatively large differences in student perception was "I think the teaching materials that the teachers have uploaded to the course material section are easy to use." The PU SD analysis results indicated that the item with small differences in student perceptions was "I think blended learning courses should continue to be offered." The item with comparatively large differences in student perceptions was "I can find appropriate content in blended learning courses." The attitude SD analysis results indicated that the item with comparatively small differences in student perceptions was "Blended learning is a good teaching method." The item with large differences in student perception was "Blended learning motivates me to learn more." The BI SD analysis results indicated that the item with comparatively smaller differences in student perceptions was "I like using the Internet to engage in e-learning activities." The item with large differences in student perception was "I like engaging in discussions with my cohorts using the information platforms (e.g., e-mail) provided by the college."

3.2 Reliability Analysis

Based on Table 2, the Cronbach's alpha value was 0.740 for the PEOU items, 0.832 for the PU items, 0.801 for the attitude items, and 0.700 for the BI items. In addition, the overall Cronbach's alpha value was 0.894. Accordingly, the reliability coefficients of this study ranged from 0.70 to 0.90, which was acceptable.

Table 2. The Reliability Analysis Table

Dimension	Cronbach's alpha	Overall Cronbach's alpha value
PEOU	.074	
PU	.832	
Attitude	.801	
BI	.700	.894

3.3 Pearson Correlation Analysis

The Pearson correlation analysis table (Table 3) shows that the Pearson correlation coefficient between PEOU and PU was 0.505. The double-tailed test result was 0.000, indicating a significant correlation between the two variables. The Pearson correlation coefficient between PEOU and attitude was 0.476. The double-tailed test result was 0.000, indicating a significant correlation between them. The Pearson correlation coefficient between PEOU and BI was 0.357. The double-tailed test result was 0.000, indicating a significant correlation between them. The Pearson correlation coefficient between PU and attitude was 0.794. The double-tailed test result was 0.000, indicating a significant correlation between them. The Pearson correlation coefficient between PU and BI was 0.603. The double-tailed test result was 0.000, indicating a significant correlation between them. The Pearson correlation coefficient between

Table 3. The Pearson Correlation Analysis Table

		PEOU	PU	Attitude	BI
PEOU	Pearson correlation	1			
	Significance (double-tailed)				
PU	Pearson correlation	.505(**)	1		
	Significance (double-tailed)	.000			
Attitude	Pearson correlation	.476(**)	.794(**)	1	.
	Significance (double-tailed)	.000	.000		
BI	Pearson correlation	.357(**)	.603(**)	.578(**)	1
	Significance (double-tailed)	.000	.000	.000	

** When the significance level was 0.01 (double-tailed), the correlation was significant.

attitude and BI was 0.578. The double-tailed test result was 0.000, indicating a significant correlation between them.

3.4 Regression Analysis

The hypotheses in this study were about the relationships between single dimensions. Hence, unary regression analyses were conducted. The unary regression analysis table (Table 4) shows that the explained variance of PEOU for PU was 50.5%. The standard regression coefficients (β) of the predictive variables were all positive. Therefore, PEOU positively influenced PU. The explained variance of PEOU for attitude was 47.6%. The standard regression coefficients (β) of the predictive variables were all positive. Therefore, ease of use positively influenced attitude. The explained variance of PU for attitude was 79.4%. The standard regression coefficients (β) of the predictive variables were all positive. Therefore, PU positively influenced attitude. The explained variance for PU on BI was 60.3%. The standard regression coefficients (β) of the predictive variables were all positive. Therefore, PU positively influenced BI. The explained variance of attitude for BI was 57.8%. The standard regression coefficients (β) of the predictive variables were all positive. Therefore, attitude positively influenced BI. The significance and influence levels of standard coefficients increased with their values.

Table 4. The Unary Regression Analysis Table

Item	Unary correlation coefficient	Coefficient of determination R^2	t-value	Net value of F (ΔF)	B	Significant	Verification result
PEOU - PU	.505	.255	6.140	37.703	.505	.000	Supported
PEOU - attitude	.476	.226	5.674	32.197	.476	.000	Supported
PU - attitude	.794	.631	13.72	188.032	.794	.000	Supported
PU - BI	.603	.363	7.924	62.786	.603	.000	Supported
Attitude - BI	.578	.334	7.426	55.146	.578	.000	Supported

4 Conclusion

Based on the data analysis results and discussion, the verification results and findings of this study are presented in the following. The analysis and regression analysis results as well as research hypothesis verification results are presented in Table 5.

Table 5. The Hypothesis Verification Table

Research hypothesis		Hypothesis verification
H1	The PEOU and PU of blended learning are positively correlated.	Supported
H2	The PEOU of blended learning and learning attitudes are positively correlated.	Supported
H3	The PU of blended learning and attitudes to blended learning are positively correlated.	Supported
H4	The PU of blended learning and BIs are positively correlated.	Supported
H5	The attitudes and BIs toward blended learning are positively correlated.	Supported

Regarding item analysis, the students reported that logging onto the course material section in the student information system was the easiest and that blended learning did not motivate them to submit assignments on time. Accordingly, the blended learning environments established at the college were highly easy to use and useful. Although blended learning environments enhanced the convenience of learning, because course content of blended learning courses was difficult, the students did not think that these courses encouraged them to submit their assignments on time. Regarding the students' cognitions on the variables, the students had the highest cognitive consistency on the perspective that logging onto the course material section in the student information system was easy. Comparatively, the students' cognitions varied considerably on the perspective that they did not like using the information platforms provided by the college to engage in discussions with their classmates. This phenomenon revealed that young students preferred using Line or Facebook to discuss with peers. Regarding the Pearson correlation analysis, the TAM was used to analyze the students' course election attitudes and BIs toward blended learning environments. The analysis results indicated that the correlations between PEOU, PU, attitude, and BI were all significant. The regression analysis results indicated that the correlations between PEOU, PU, attitude, and BI were positive. These results support the hypotheses proposed in this study.

References

1. Tourism Bureau, M.O.T.C. Republic of China. Tourism Market Survey Summary (2013), `http://admin.taiwan.net.tw/statistics/market.aspx?no=133` (retrieved May 2013)
2. Lin, H.-S., Hsieh, L.-Y.: Information Operational System Design In Response To Globalized Logistics Talent Training. In: International Conference on Computer Science and Logistics Engineering (ICCSLE 2011), Zhengzhou, China (2011)
3. Luo, S.-J., Chao, D.-P., Hsieh, S.-T.L.L.-Y.: Introducing Lean Service to the Blended Learning Educational Environment Structure for Food and Beverage Preparation. Journal of Applied Sciences 13(17), 3475–3482 (2013)

4. Hsieh, L.-Y., Lu, Y.-J., Lin, H.-S., Lee, Y.-H.: With Blended Learning Information Operational System Design In Response To Globalized Logistics Talent Training. In: The 2nd International Workshop on Learning Technology for Education in Cloud–e-Learning and e-Learning Model (2nd LTEC), pp. 61–72. Springer, Heidelberg (2013)
5. Oliver, M., Trigwell, K.: Can blended learning be redeemed? E-learning 2(1), 17–26 (2005)
6. Davis, F.D.: A Technology Acceptance Model for empirically testing new end-user information system: Theory and results. Ph.D. Dissertation, MIT Sloan School of Management, Cambridge, MA (1986)
7. Davis, F.D.: Perceived usefulness, perceived ease of use, and user acceptance of information technology. MIS Quarterly 13(3), 319–340 (1989)
8. Lederer, A.L., Maupin, D.J., Sena, P.M., Zhuang, Y.: The Technology Acceptance Model and the World Wide Web. Decision Support System 29(3), 269–282 (2000)
9. Ndubisi, N.O.: Factors of online learning adoption: A comparative juxtaposition of the theory of planned behavior and the Technology Acceptance Model. International Journal on E-learning 5(4), 571–591 (2006)
10. Chen, M.Y.: Effect of internet environment and information literacy on teaching will with wireless network: an example of humanities and art education of junior-high schools in Kaohsiung city. Master's thesis, Institute of Communications Management, National Sun Yat-sen University, Taiwan (2009)
11. Hung, C.P.: A Study on the Influence of Application Interface of AJAX Framework Development Based on Technology Acceptance Model - with Course Guidance Management System as a Case Study. Master's thesis, Department of Information Management, National Yunlin University of Science and Technology, Taiwan (2010)
12. Huang, C.H.: To Explore the Behavioral Intention of Using Library Management System by TAM–the case study of Chia-Yi elementary schools. Master's thesis, Department of Information Management, Nanhua University, Taiwan (2012)
13. Wang, Y.H.: Applying TAM Model Enhance Website Performance Based on Uexciting University Website Research. Master's thesis, Department of Information Management, National Taipei University of education, Taiwan (2013)
14. Yang, C.C., Wang, Y.F., Chiu, W.P., Su, Y.H., Ping, L.Y.: A Study of Development of Green Productivity Management System on Food Preparation. National Science Council, NSC98-2511-S328-006 (2013)
15. Dziuban, C.D., Hartman, J.H., Moskal, P.D.: Blending learning. EDUCAUSE Center for Applied Research Bulletin 7, 1–12 (2004)
16. Terashima, K.R., Ikai, Y., Yoshida, M., Kamei, Kubota, K.: Blended learning model for multimedia production course. Paper presented at the Meeting of World Conference on Educational Multimedia, Hypermedia & Telecommunications, Lugarno, Switzerland (2004)
17. Hoic-Bozic, N.: A Blended Learning Approach to Course Design and Implementation. IEEE Transactions on Education 52(1), 19–30 (2009)
18. Tselios, N., Daskalakis, S., Papadopoulou, M.: Assessing the Acceptance of a Blended Learning University Course. Educational Technology & Society 14(2), 224–235 (2011)
19. Lin, H.C., Tang, K.W., Lai, H.C.: Analyzing User Intention and Effect with TAM on Producing Digital Materials by JoinNet. International Journal on Digital Learning Technology 2(1), 60–78 (2010)

Author Index

MIX
Papier aus verantwortungsvollen Quellen
Paper from responsible sources
FSC® C105338

If you have any concerns about our products,
you can contact us on
ProductSafety@springernature.com

In case Publisher is established outside the EU,
the EU authorized representative is:
Springer Nature Customer Service Center GmbH
Europaplatz 3, 69115 Heidelberg, Germany

Printed by Libri Plureos GmbH
in Hamburg, Germany